CREATED BY **JOSS WHEDON**

JEREMY **LAMBERT** MARIANA **IGNAZZI** RAÚL **ANGULO** MATTIA **IACONO**

Buffy the Vampire Slayer™

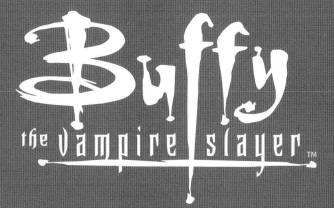

VOLUME NINE

FORGET ME NOT

Published by
BOOM! STUDIOS

Series Designer
Madison Goyette

Collection Designer
Marie Krupina

Assistant Editor
Gavin Gronenthal

Editor
Elizabeth Brei

Special Thanks to **Sierra Hahn**, **Jonathan Manning**, **Becca J. Sadowsky**, & **Nicole Spiegel**.

BUFFY THE VAMPIRE SLAYER Volume Nine, April 2022. Published by BOOM! Studios, a division of Boom Entertainment, Inc. © 2022 20th Television. Originally published in single magazine form as BUFFY THE VAMPIRE SLAYER No. 29-32. © 2021 20th Television. BOOM! Studios™ and the BOOM! Studios logo are trademarks of Boom Entertainment, Inc., registered in various countries and categories. All characters, events, and institutions depicted herein are fictional. Any similarity between any of the names, characters, persons, events, and/or institutions in this publication to actual names, characters, and persons, whether living or dead, events, and/or institutions is unintended and purely coincidental. BOOM! Studios does not read or accept unsolicited submissions of ideas, stories, or artwork.

BOOM! Studios, 5670 Wilshire Boulevard, Suite 400, Los Angeles, CA 90036-5679. Printed in China. First Printing.

ISBN: 978-1-68415-821-8, eISBN: 978-1-64668-454-0

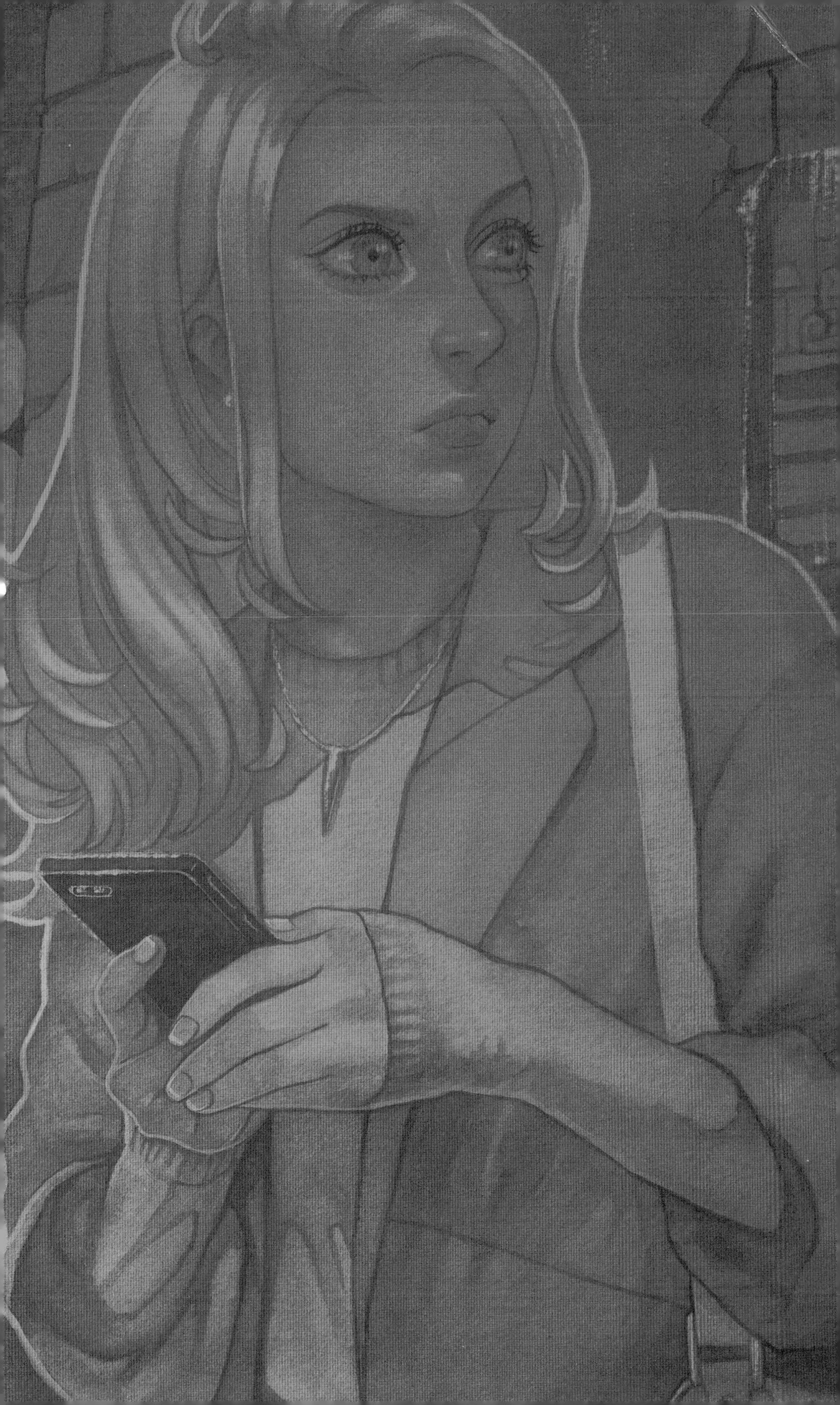

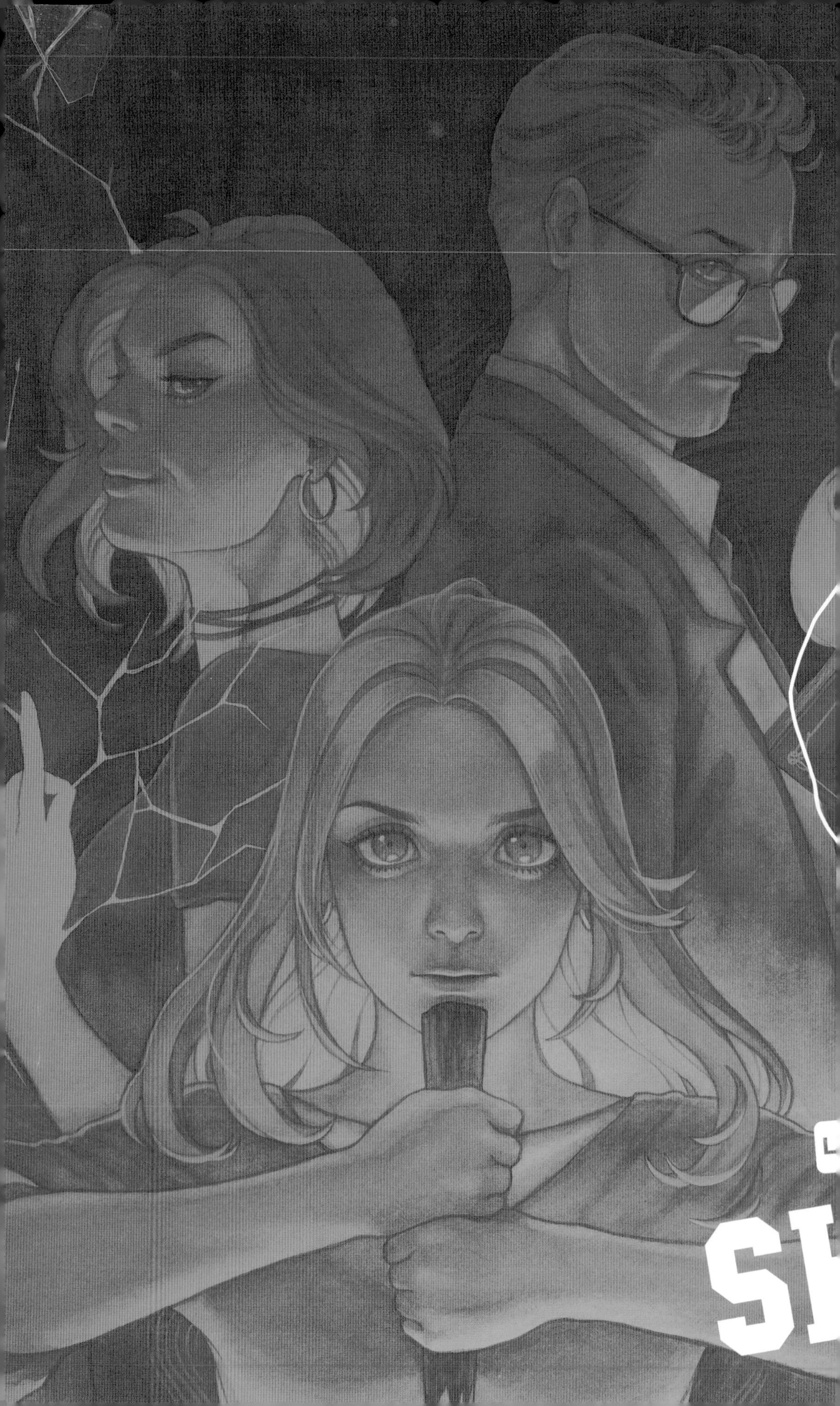

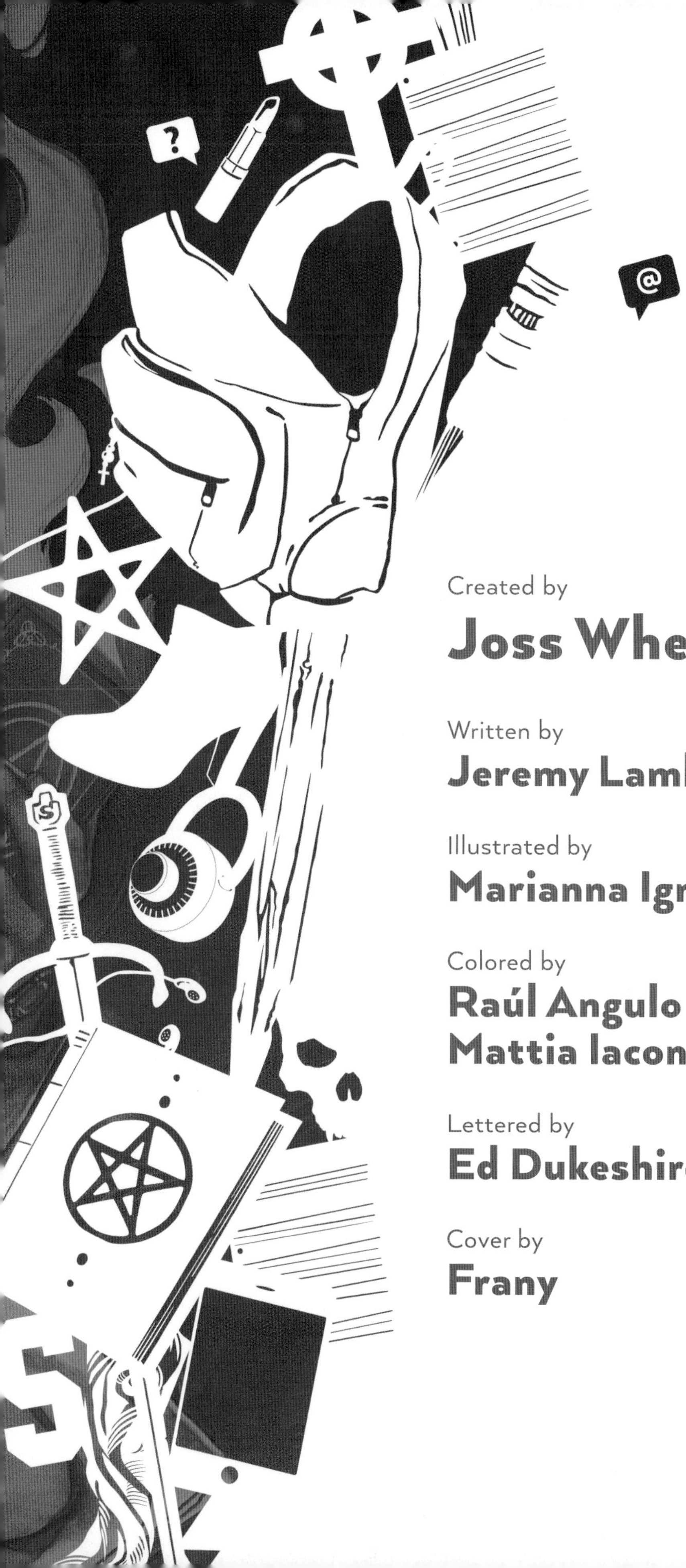

Created by
Joss Whedon

Written by
Jeremy Lambert

Illustrated by
Marianna Ignazzi

Colored by
Raúl Angulo
Mattia Iacono (Chapter 29)

Lettered by
Ed Dukeshire

Cover by
Frany

CHAPTER TWENTY-NINE

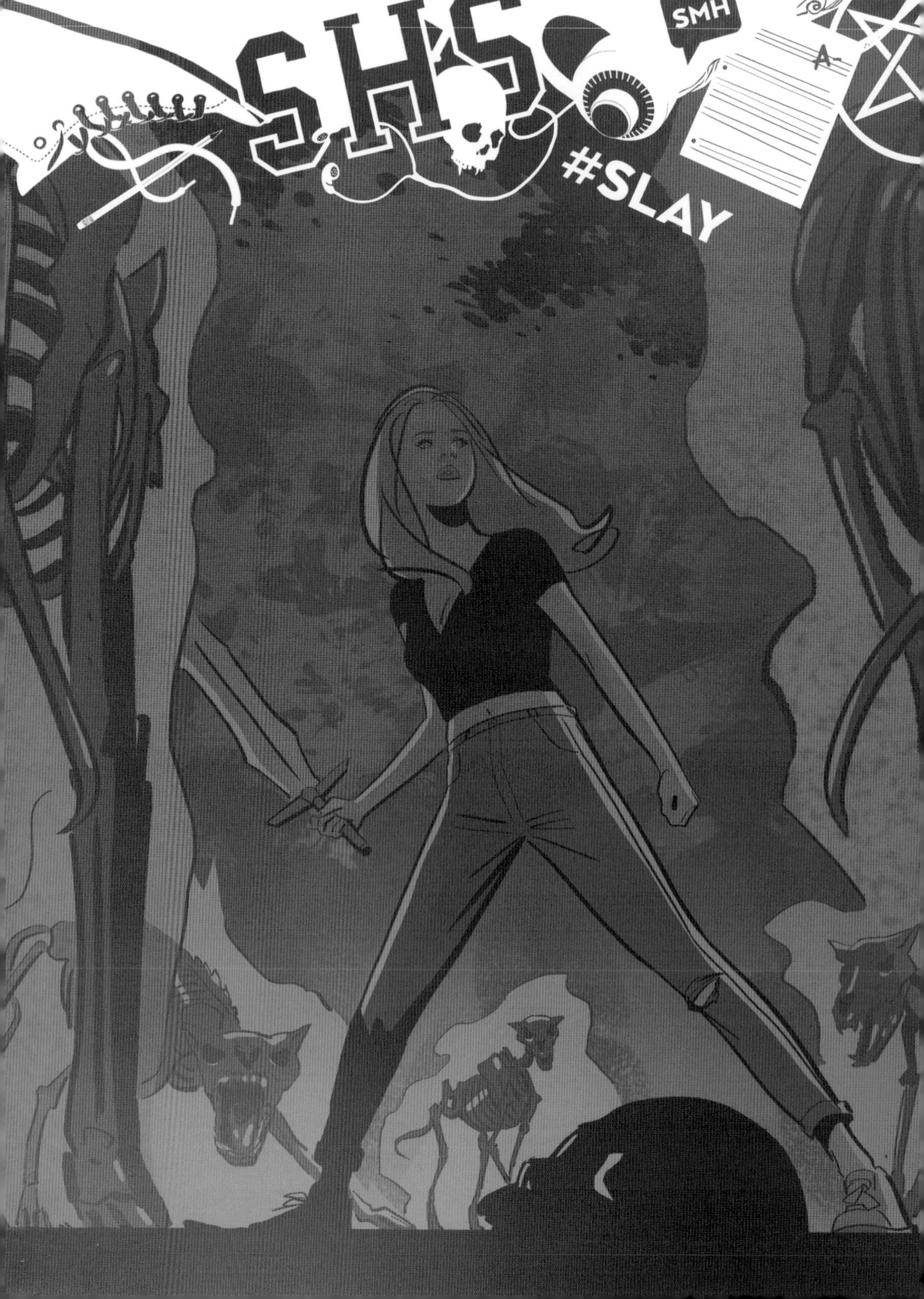
S.H.S.
SMH
A-
#SLAY

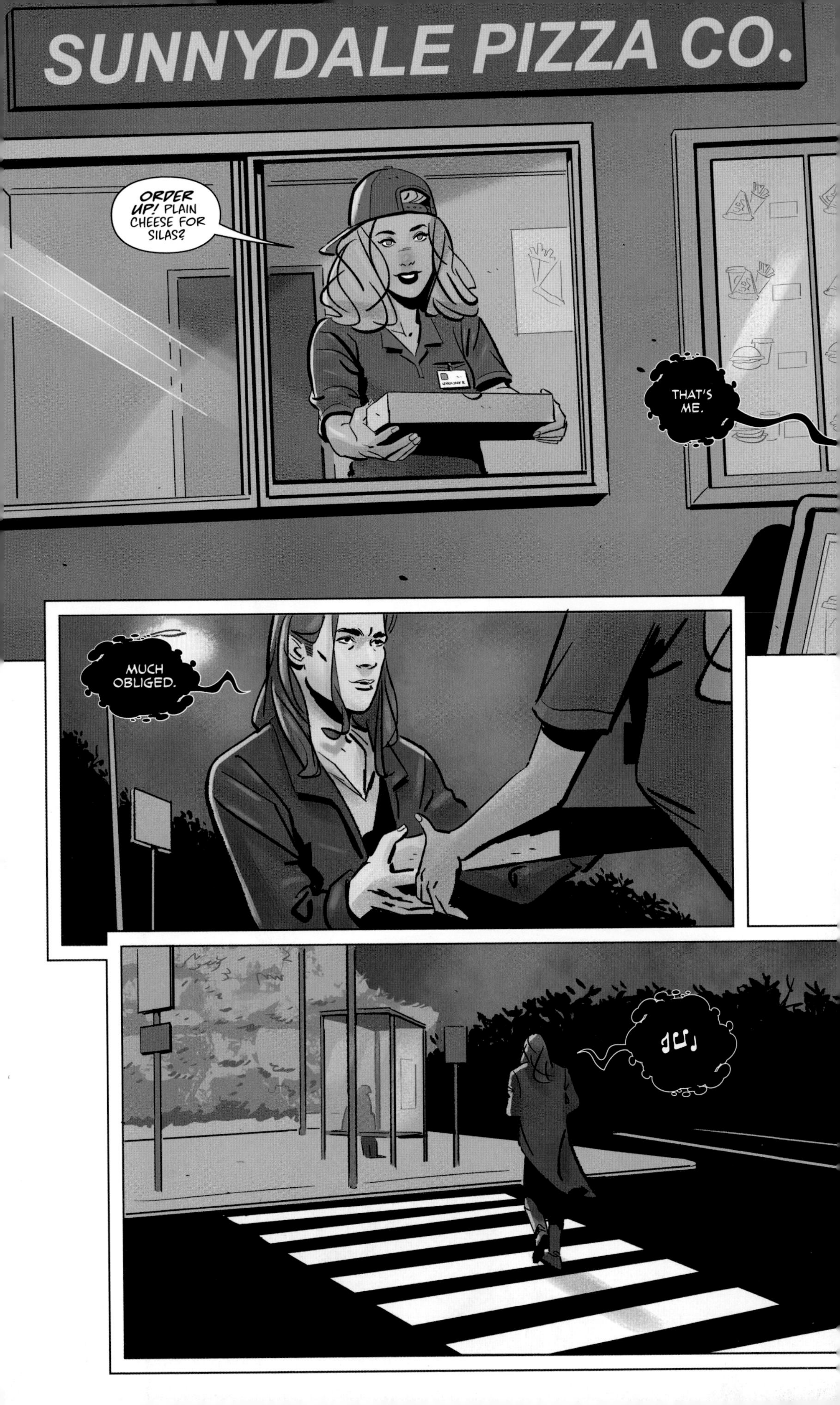
SUNNYDALE PIZZA CO.
ORDER UP! PLAIN CHEESE FOR SILAS?
THAT'S ME.
MUCH OBLIGED.

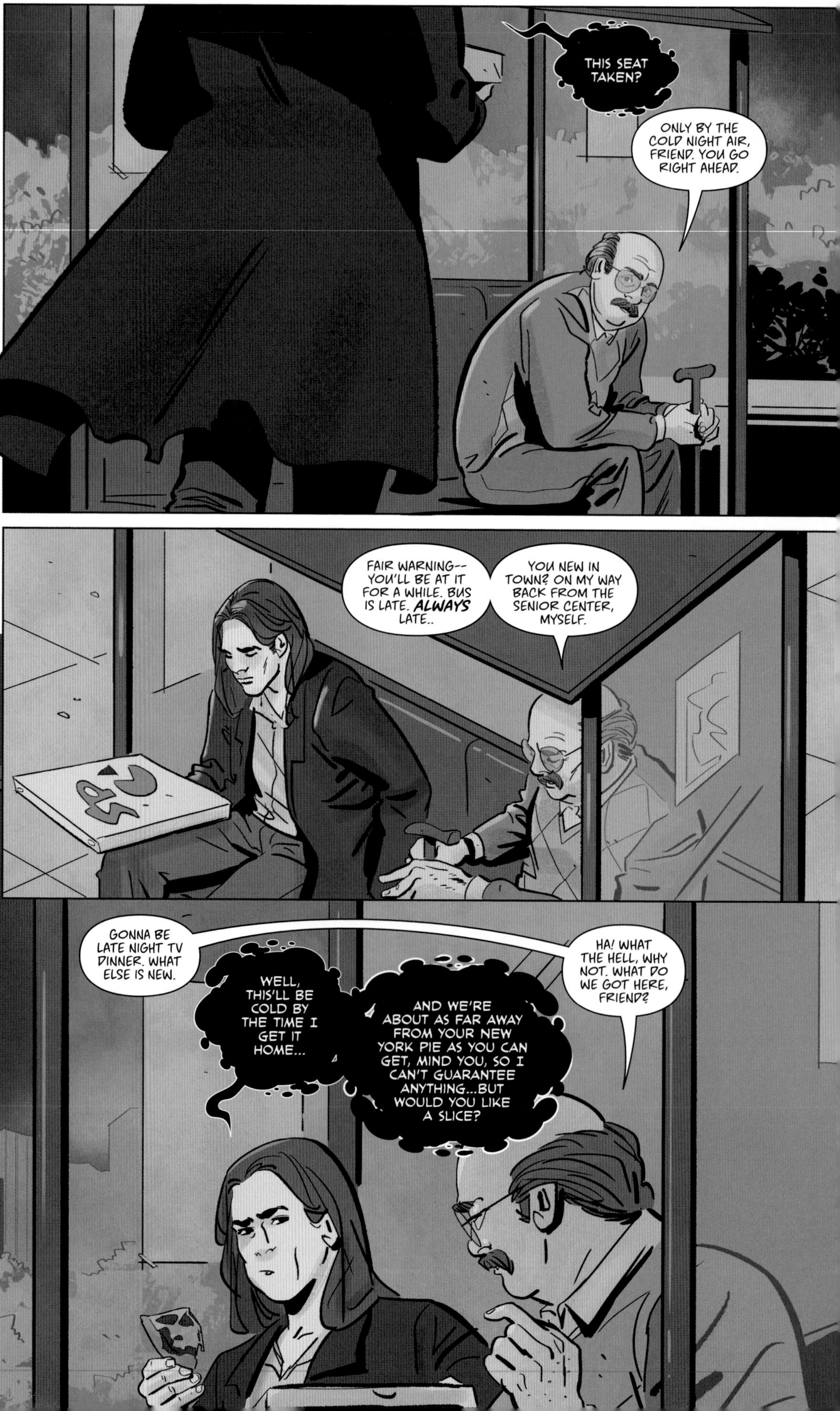
THIS SEAT TAKEN?
ONLY BY THE COLD NIGHT AIR, FRIEND. YOU GO RIGHT AHEAD.
FAIR WARNING-- YOU'LL BE AT IT FOR A WHILE. BUS IS LATE. **ALWAYS** LATE..
YOU NEW IN TOWN? ON MY WAY BACK FROM THE SENIOR CENTER, MYSELF.
GONNA BE LATE NIGHT TV DINNER. WHAT ELSE IS NEW.
HA! WHAT THE HELL, WHY NOT. WHAT DO WE GOT HERE, FRIEND?
WELL, THIS'LL BE COLD BY THE TIME I GET IT HOME...
AND WE'RE ABOUT AS FAR AWAY FROM YOUR NEW YORK PIE AS YOU CAN GET, MIND YOU, SO I CAN'T GUARANTEE ANYTHING...BUT WOULD YOU LIKE A SLICE?

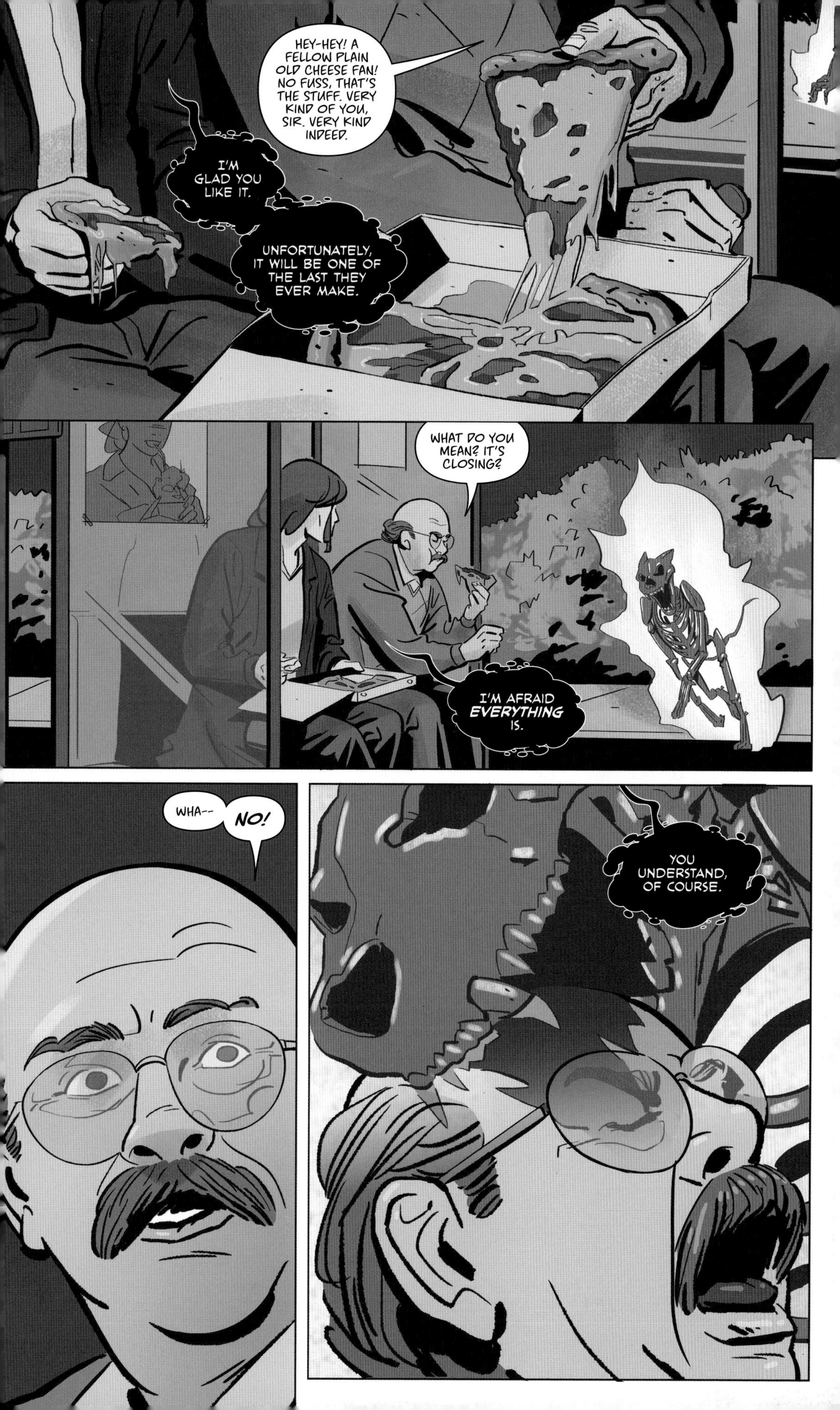
HEY-HEY! A FELLOW PLAIN OLD CHEESE FAN! NO FUSS, THAT'S THE STUFF. VERY KIND OF YOU, SIR. VERY KIND INDEED.
I'M GLAD YOU LIKE IT.
UNFORTUNATELY, IT WILL BE ONE OF THE LAST THEY EVER MAKE.
WHAT DO YOU MEAN? IT'S CLOSING?
I'M AFRAID *EVERYTHING* IS.
WHA--
NO!
YOU UNDERSTAND, OF COURSE.

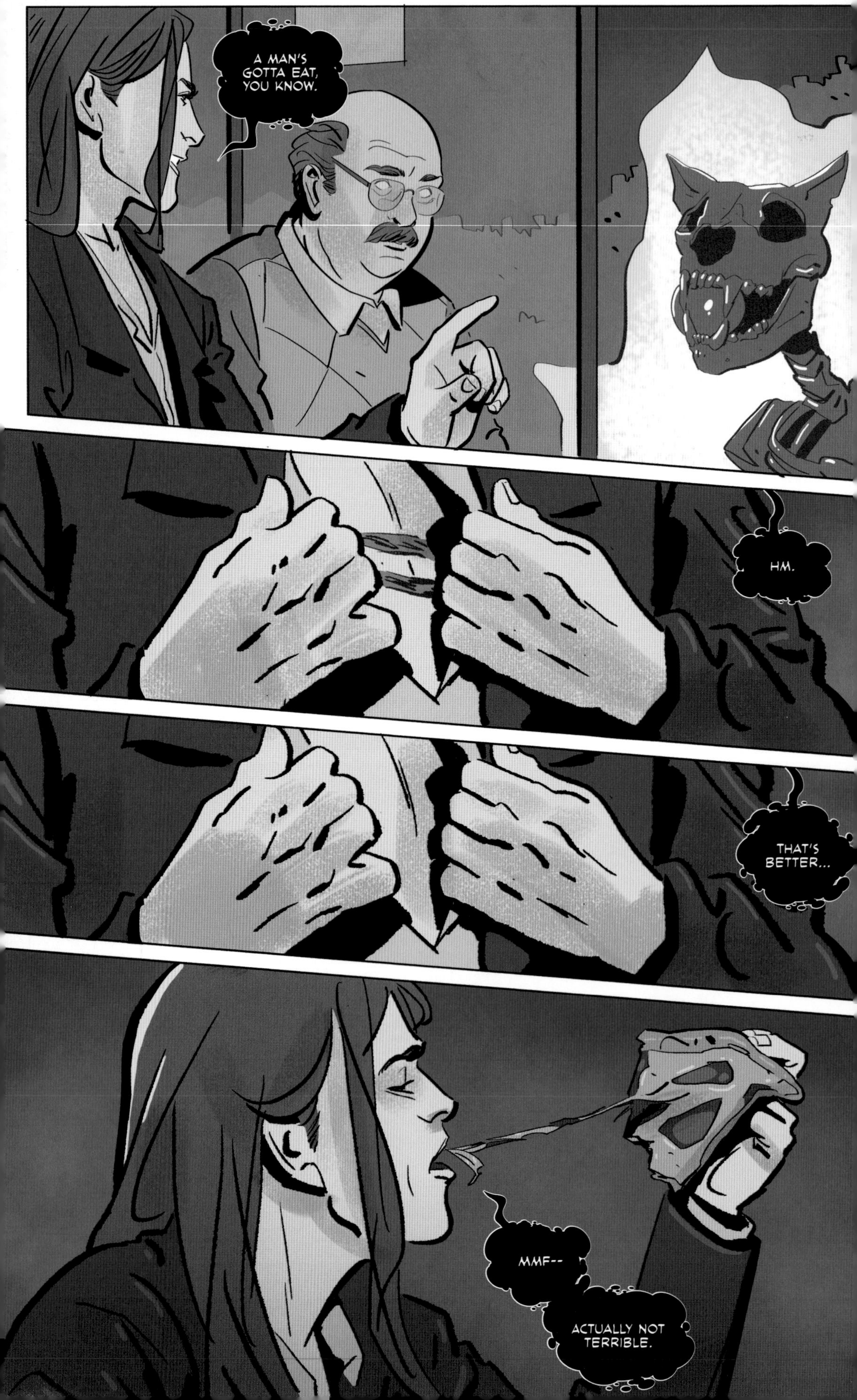

A MAN'S GOTTA EAT, YOU KNOW.
HM.
THAT'S BETTER...
MMF--
ACTUALLY NOT TERRIBLE.

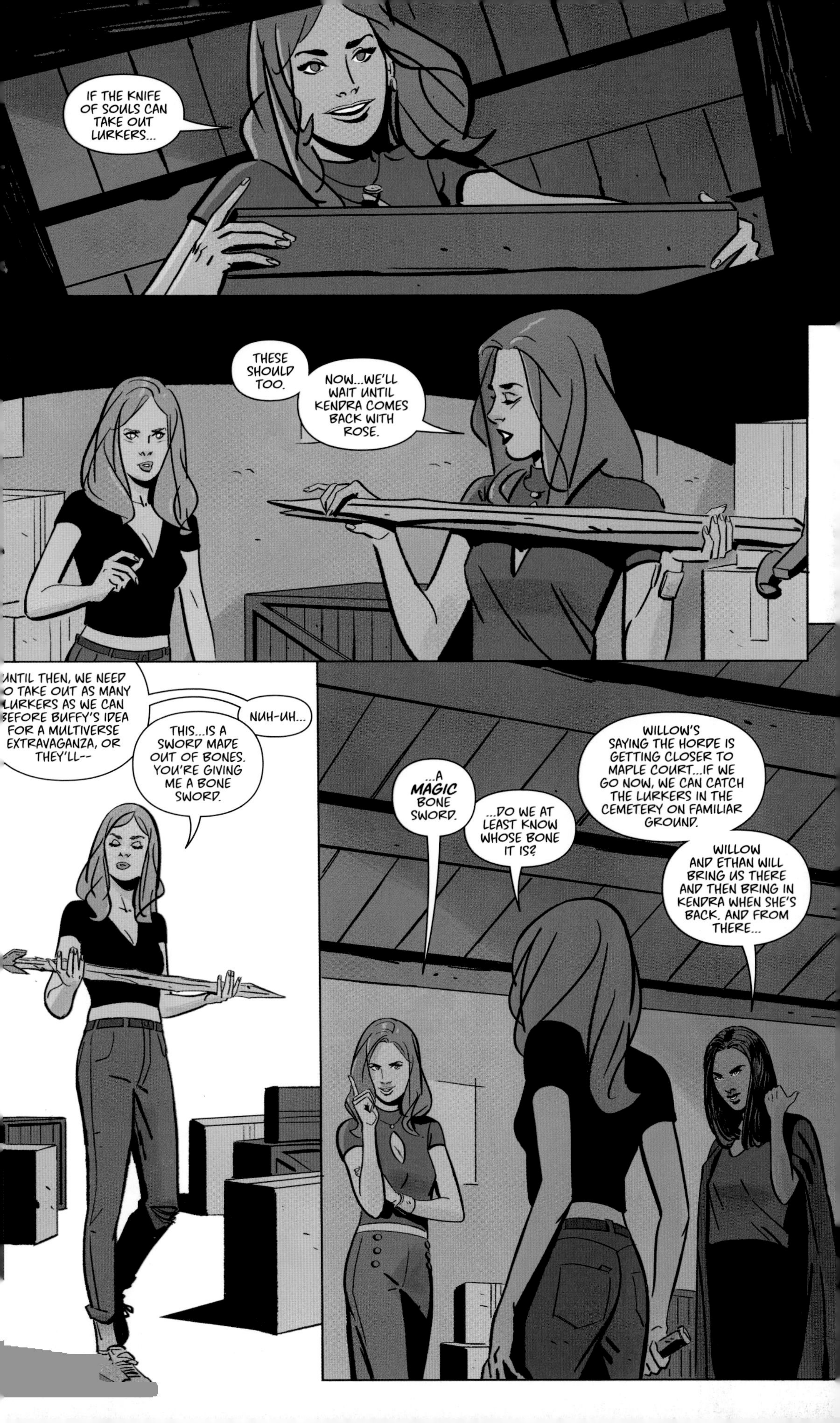
IF THE KNIFE OF SOULS CAN TAKE OUT LURKERS...
THESE SHOULD TOO.
NOW...WE'LL WAIT UNTIL KENDRA COMES BACK WITH ROSE.
UNTIL THEN, WE NEED TO TAKE OUT AS MANY LURKERS AS WE CAN BEFORE BUFFY'S IDEA FOR A MULTIVERSE EXTRAVAGANZA, OR THEY'LL--
NUH-UH...
THIS...IS A SWORD MADE OUT OF BONES. YOU'RE GIVING ME A BONE SWORD.
...A *MAGIC* BONE SWORD.
...DO WE AT LEAST KNOW WHOSE BONE IT IS?
WILLOW'S SAYING THE HORDE IS GETTING CLOSER TO MAPLE COURT...IF WE GO NOW, WE CAN CATCH THE LURKERS IN THE CEMETERY ON FAMILIAR GROUND.
WILLOW AND ETHAN WILL BRING US THERE AND THEN BRING IN KENDRA WHEN SHE'S BACK. AND FROM THERE...

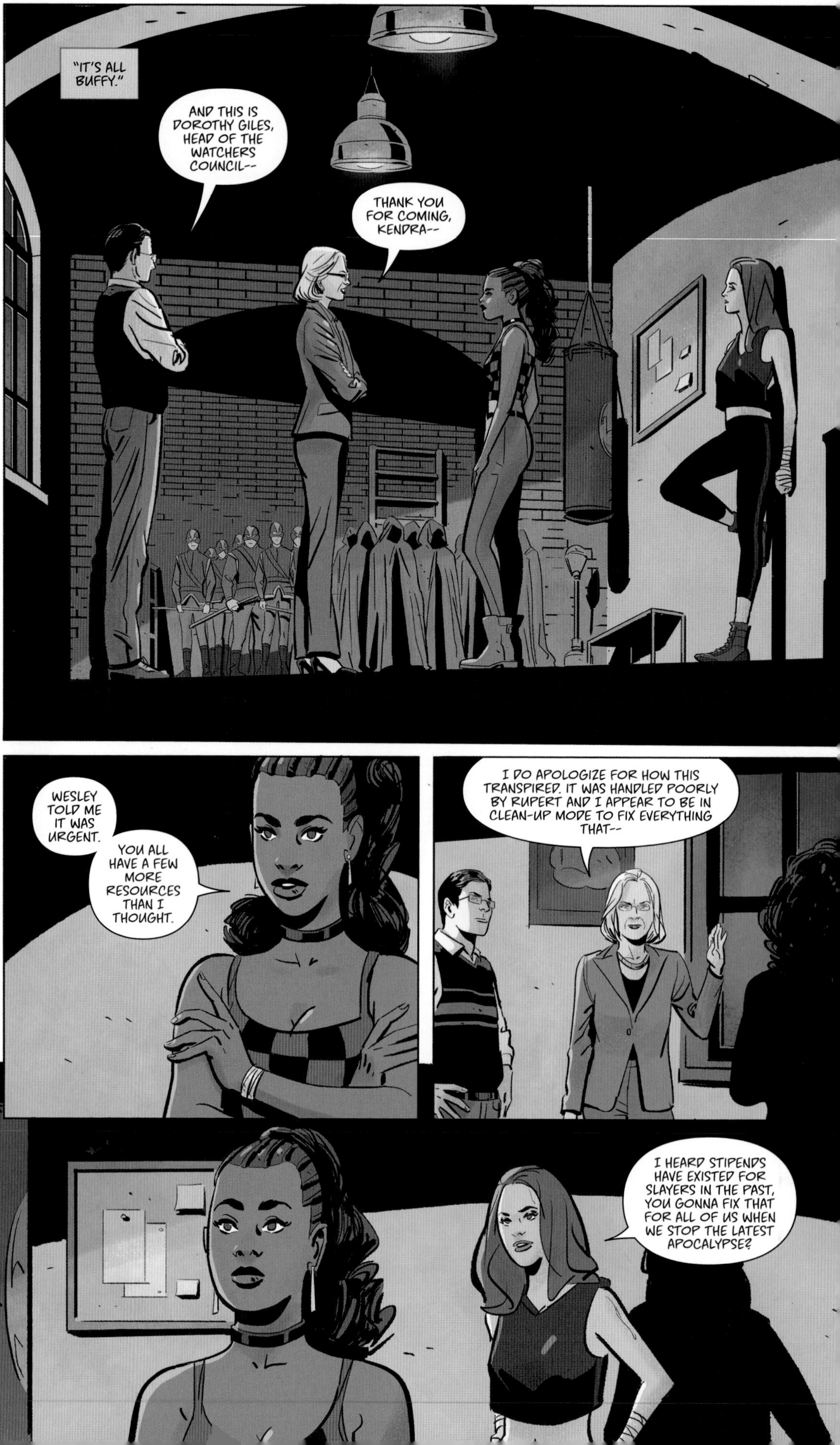
"IT'S ALL BUFFY."
AND THIS IS DOROTHY GILES, HEAD OF THE WATCHERS COUNCIL--
THANK YOU FOR COMING, KENDRA--
WESLEY TOLD ME IT WAS URGENT.
YOU ALL HAVE A FEW MORE RESOURCES THAN I THOUGHT.
I DO APOLOGIZE FOR HOW THIS TRANSPIRED. IT WAS HANDLED POORLY BY RUPERT AND I APPEAR TO BE IN CLEAN-UP MODE TO FIX EVERYTHING THAT--
I HEARD STIPENDS HAVE EXISTED FOR SLAYERS IN THE PAST, YOU GONNA FIX THAT FOR ALL OF US WHEN WE STOP THE LATEST APOCALYPSE?

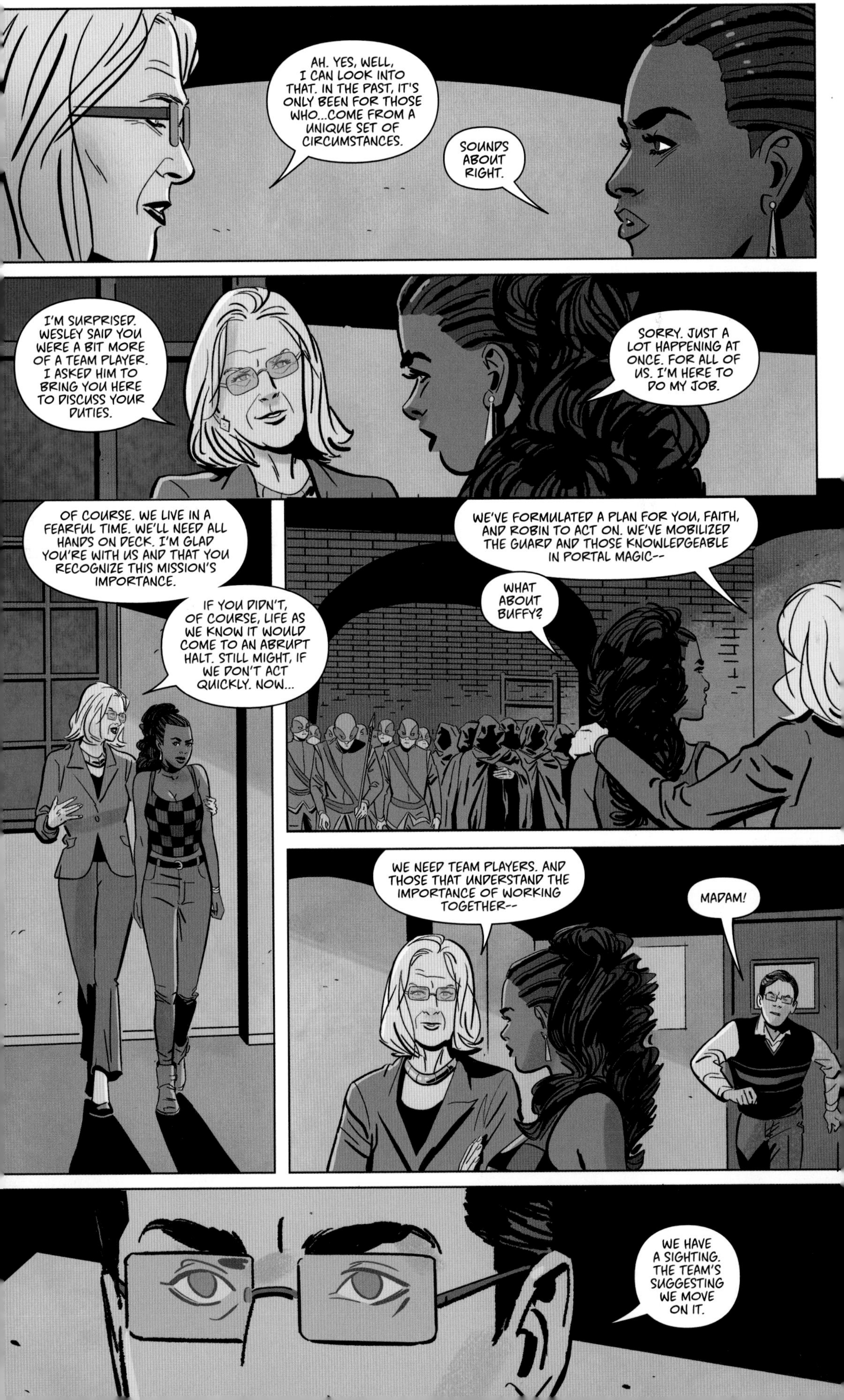
AH. YES, WELL, I CAN LOOK INTO THAT. IN THE PAST, IT'S ONLY BEEN FOR THOSE WHO...COME FROM A UNIQUE SET OF CIRCUMSTANCES.
SOUNDS ABOUT RIGHT.
I'M SURPRISED. WESLEY SAID YOU WERE A BIT MORE OF A TEAM PLAYER. I ASKED HIM TO BRING YOU HERE TO DISCUSS YOUR DUTIES.
SORRY. JUST A LOT HAPPENING AT ONCE. FOR ALL OF US. I'M HERE TO DO MY JOB.
OF COURSE. WE LIVE IN A FEARFUL TIME. WE'LL NEED ALL HANDS ON DECK. I'M GLAD YOU'RE WITH US AND THAT YOU RECOGNIZE THIS MISSION'S IMPORTANCE.
IF YOU DIDN'T, OF COURSE, LIFE AS WE KNOW IT WOULD COME TO AN ABRUPT HALT. STILL MIGHT, IF WE DON'T ACT QUICKLY. NOW...
WE'VE FORMULATED A PLAN FOR YOU, FAITH, AND ROBIN TO ACT ON. WE'VE MOBILIZED THE GUARD AND THOSE KNOWLEDGEABLE IN PORTAL MAGIC--
WHAT ABOUT BUFFY?
WE NEED TEAM PLAYERS. AND THOSE THAT UNDERSTAND THE IMPORTANCE OF WORKING TOGETHER--
MADAM!
WE HAVE A SIGHTING. THE TEAM'S SUGGESTING WE MOVE ON IT.

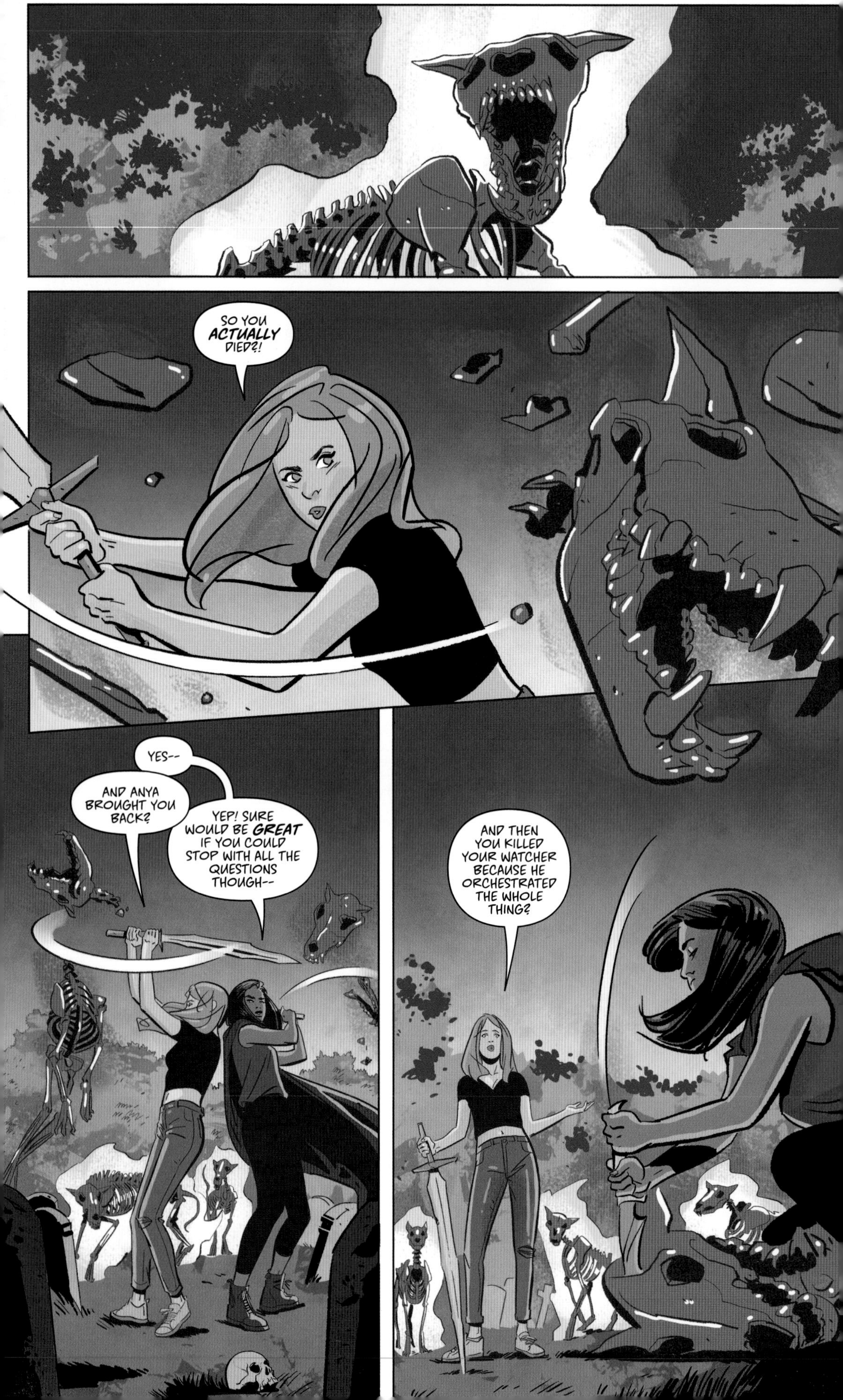
SO YOU ACTUALLY DIED?!
YES--
AND ANYA BROUGHT YOU BACK?
YEP! SURE WOULD BE GREAT IF YOU COULD STOP WITH ALL THE QUESTIONS THOUGH--
AND THEN YOU KILLED YOUR WATCHER BECAUSE HE ORCHESTRATED THE WHOLE THING?

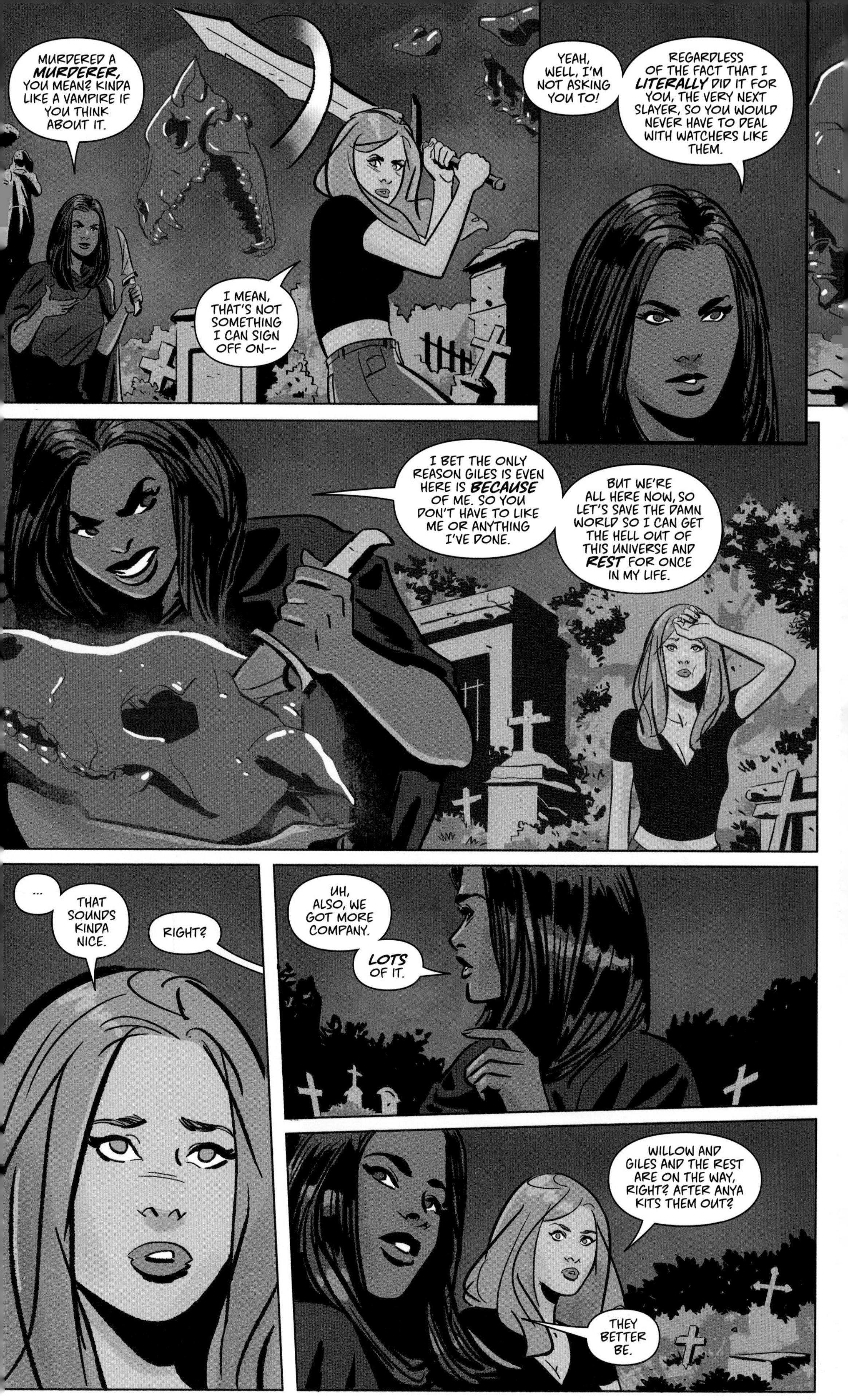
MURDERED A **MURDERER**, YOU MEAN? KINDA LIKE A VAMPIRE IF YOU THINK ABOUT IT.
I MEAN, THAT'S NOT SOMETHING I CAN SIGN OFF ON--
YEAH, WELL, I'M NOT ASKING YOU TO!
REGARDLESS OF THE FACT THAT I **LITERALLY** DID IT FOR YOU, THE VERY NEXT SLAYER, SO YOU WOULD NEVER HAVE TO DEAL WITH WATCHERS LIKE THEM.
I BET THE ONLY REASON GILES IS EVEN HERE IS **BECAUSE** OF ME. SO YOU DON'T HAVE TO LIKE ME OR ANYTHING I'VE DONE.
BUT WE'RE ALL HERE NOW, SO LET'S SAVE THE DAMN WORLD SO I CAN GET THE HELL OUT OF THIS UNIVERSE AND **REST** FOR ONCE IN MY LIFE.
...
THAT SOUNDS KINDA NICE.
RIGHT?
UH, ALSO, WE GOT MORE COMPANY.
LOTS OF IT.
WILLOW AND GILES AND THE REST ARE ON THE WAY, RIGHT? AFTER ANYA KITS THEM OUT?
THEY BETTER BE.

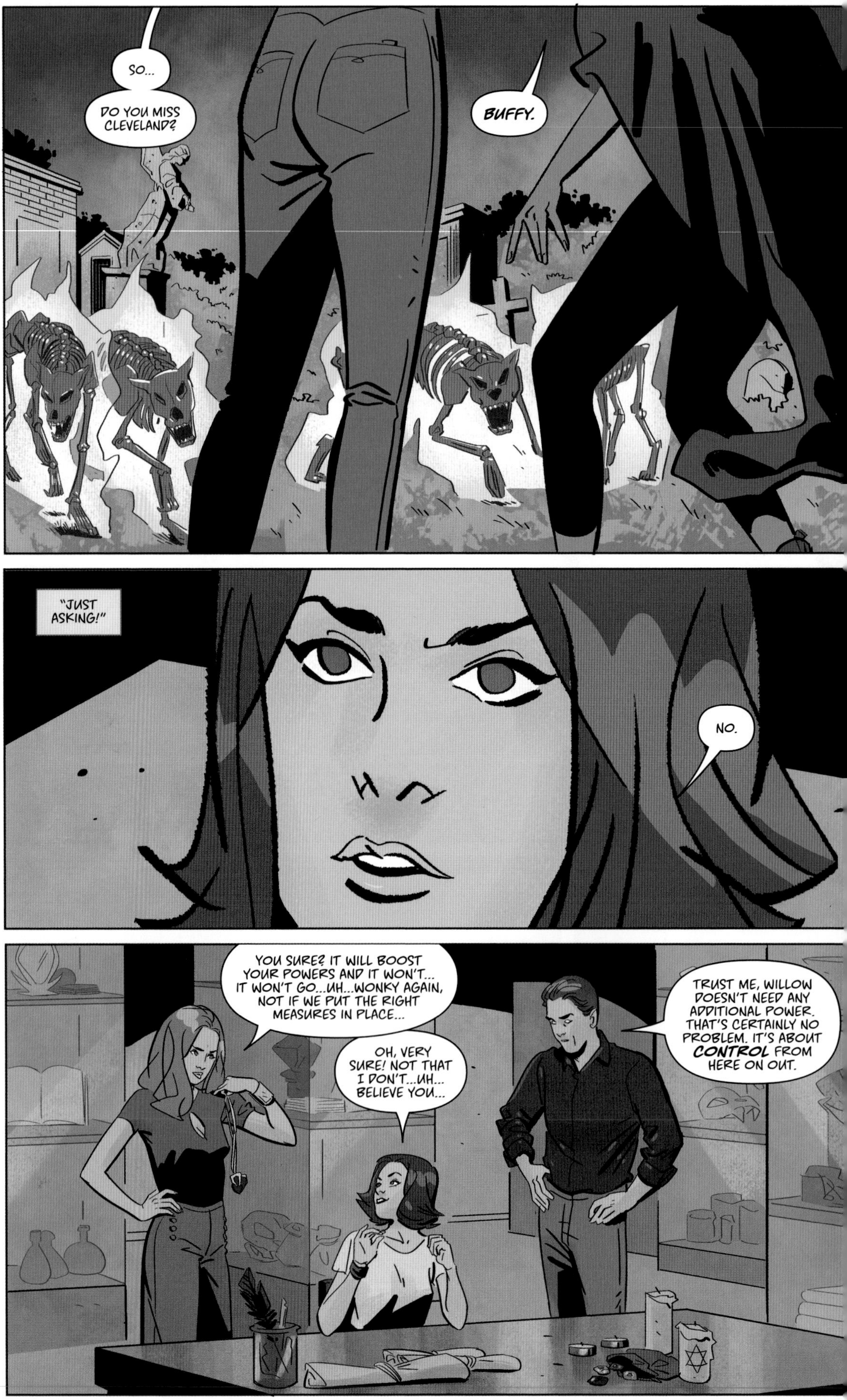
SO...
DO YOU MISS CLEVELAND?
BUFFY.
"JUST ASKING!"
NO.
YOU SURE? IT WILL BOOST YOUR POWERS AND IT WON'T... IT WON'T GO...UH...WONKY AGAIN, NOT IF WE PUT THE RIGHT MEASURES IN PLACE...
OH, VERY SURE! NOT THAT I DON'T...UH... BELIEVE YOU...
TRUST ME, WILLOW DOESN'T NEED ANY ADDITIONAL POWER. THAT'S CERTAINLY NO PROBLEM. IT'S ABOUT *CONTROL* FROM HERE ON OUT.

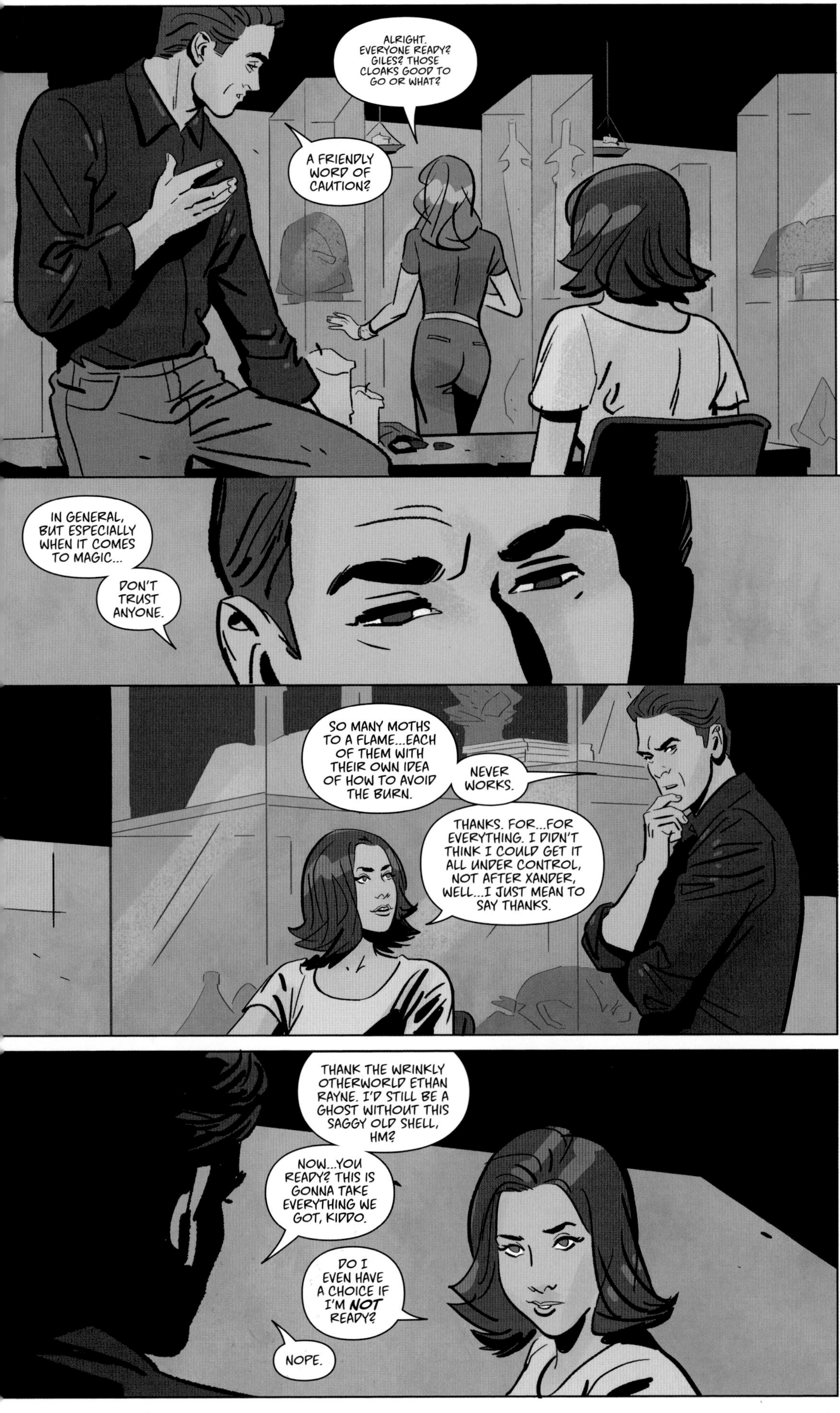
ALRIGHT. EVERYONE READY? GILES? THOSE CLOAKS GOOD TO GO OR WHAT?
A FRIENDLY WORD OF CAUTION?
IN GENERAL, BUT ESPECIALLY WHEN IT COMES TO MAGIC...
DON'T TRUST ANYONE.
SO MANY MOTHS TO A FLAME...EACH OF THEM WITH THEIR OWN IDEA OF HOW TO AVOID THE BURN.
NEVER WORKS.
THANKS. FOR...FOR EVERYTHING. I DIDN'T THINK I COULD GET IT ALL UNDER CONTROL, NOT AFTER XANDER, WELL...I JUST MEAN TO SAY THANKS.
THANK THE WRINKLY OTHERWORLD ETHAN RAYNE. I'D STILL BE A GHOST WITHOUT THIS SAGGY OLD SHELL, HM?
NOW...YOU READY? THIS IS GONNA TAKE EVERYTHING WE GOT, KIDDO.
DO I EVEN HAVE A CHOICE IF I'M ***NOT*** READY?
NOPE.

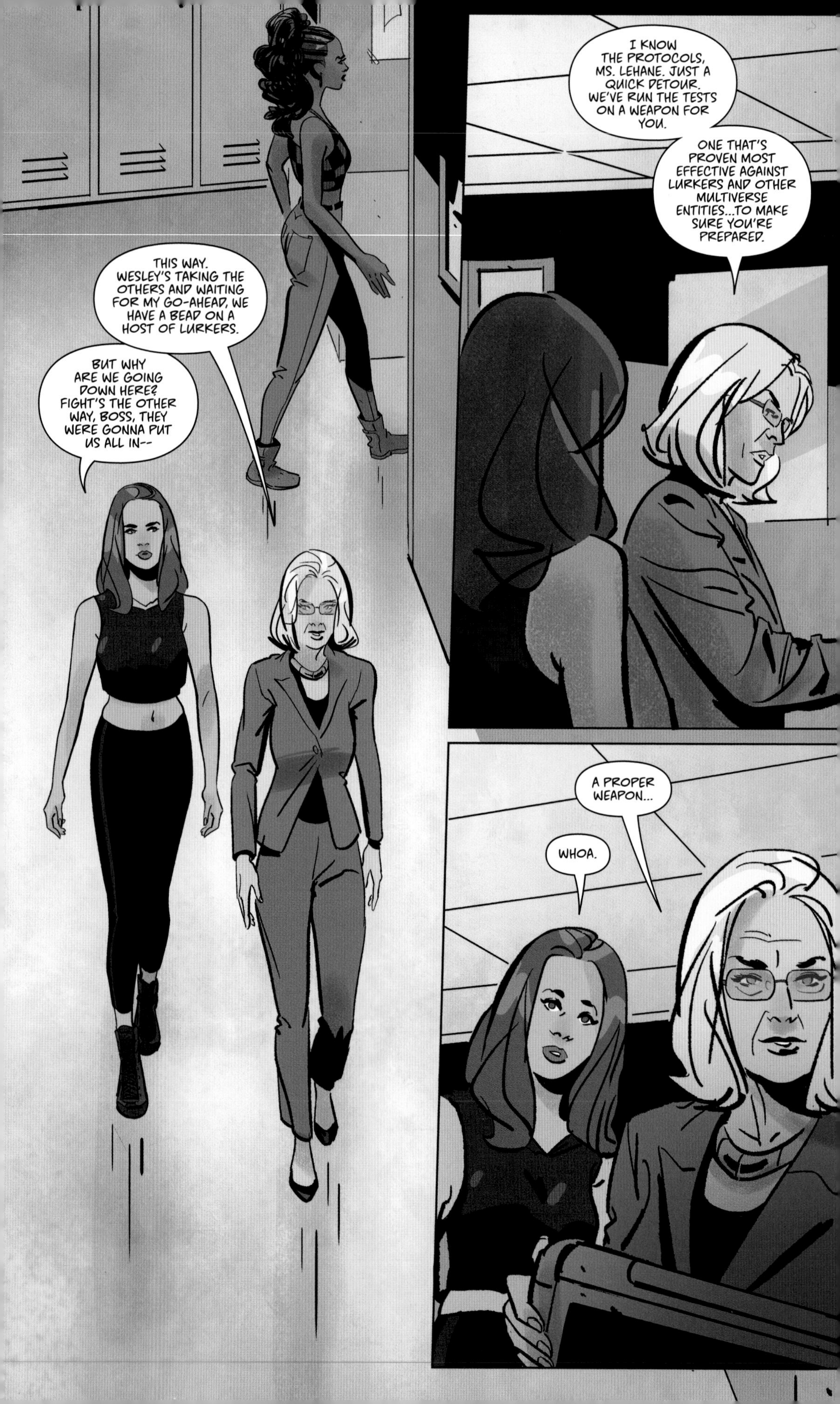
THIS WAY. WESLEY'S TAKING THE OTHERS AND WAITING FOR MY GO-AHEAD, WE HAVE A BEAD ON A HOST OF LURKERS.
BUT WHY ARE WE GOING DOWN HERE? FIGHT'S THE OTHER WAY, BOSS, THEY WERE GONNA PUT US ALL IN--
I KNOW THE PROTOCOLS, MS. LEHANE. JUST A QUICK DETOUR. WE'VE RUN THE TESTS ON A WEAPON FOR YOU.
ONE THAT'S PROVEN MOST EFFECTIVE AGAINST LURKERS AND OTHER MULTIVERSE ENTITIES...TO MAKE SURE YOU'RE PREPARED.
A PROPER WEAPON...
WHOA.

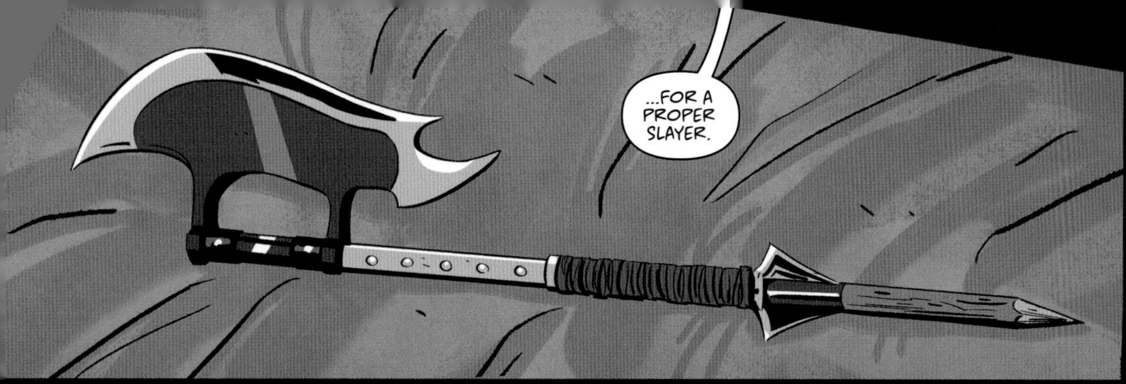
...FOR A PROPER SLAYER.
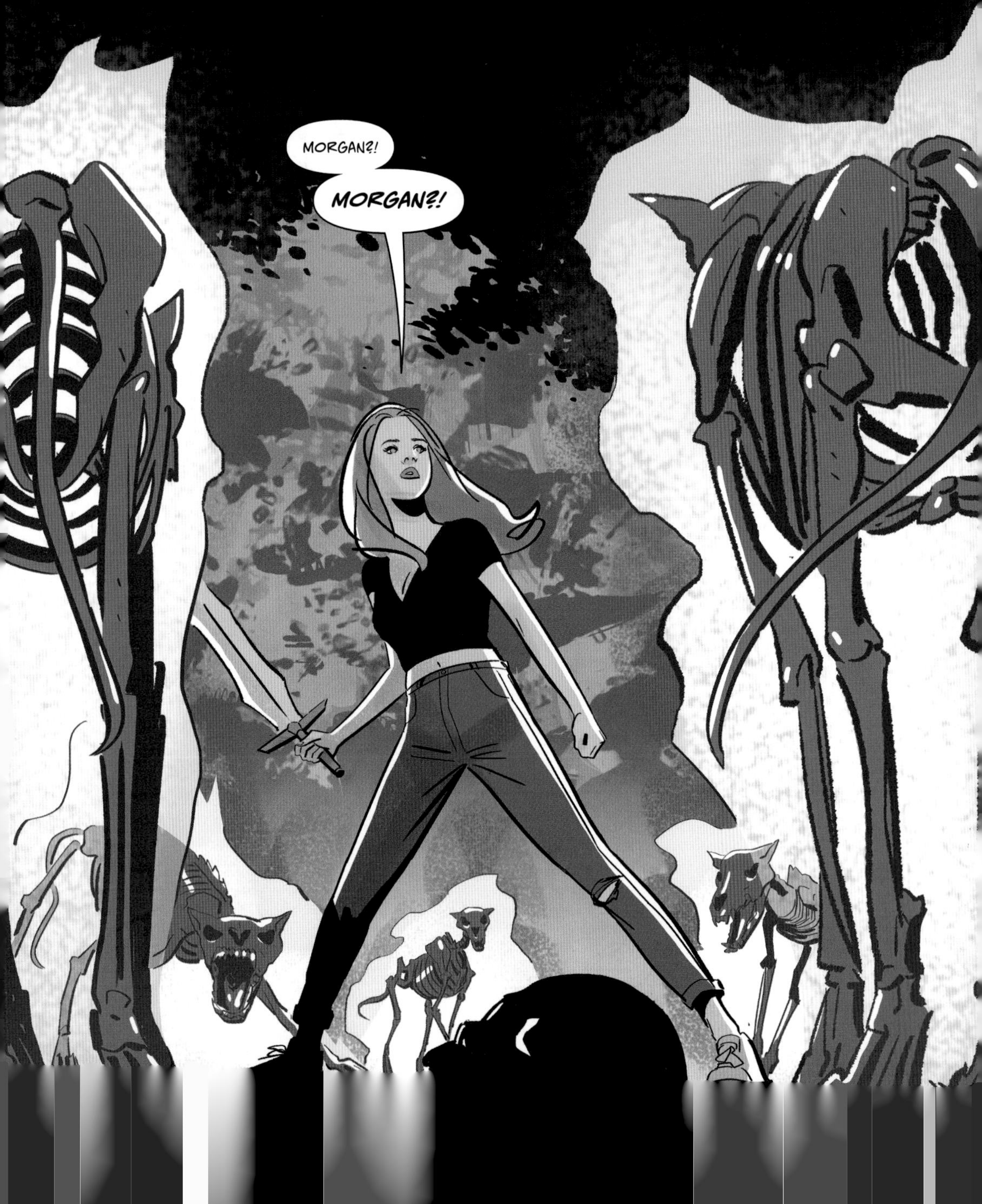
MORGAN?!
MORGAN?!

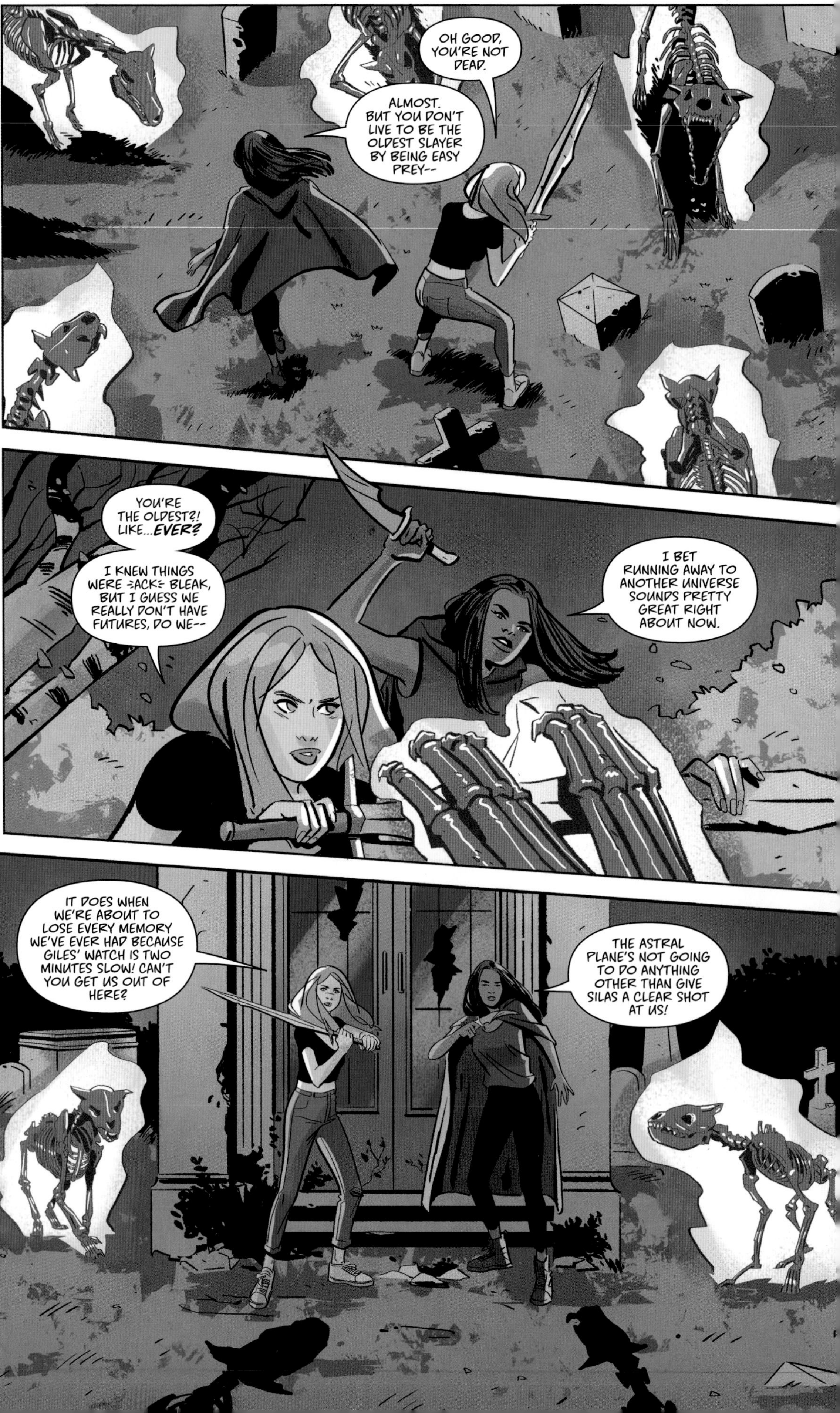
OH GOOD, YOU'RE NOT DEAD.
ALMOST. BUT YOU DON'T LIVE TO BE THE OLDEST SLAYER BY BEING EASY PREY--
YOU'RE THE OLDEST?! LIKE...**EVER?**
I KNEW THINGS WERE =ACK= BLEAK, BUT I GUESS WE REALLY DON'T HAVE FUTURES, DO WE--
I BET RUNNING AWAY TO ANOTHER UNIVERSE SOUNDS PRETTY GREAT RIGHT ABOUT NOW.
IT DOES WHEN WE'RE ABOUT TO LOSE EVERY MEMORY WE'VE EVER HAD BECAUSE GILES' WATCH IS TWO MINUTES SLOW! CAN'T YOU GET US OUT OF HERE?
THE ASTRAL PLANE'S NOT GOING TO DO ANYTHING OTHER THAN GIVE SILAS A CLEAR SHOT AT US!

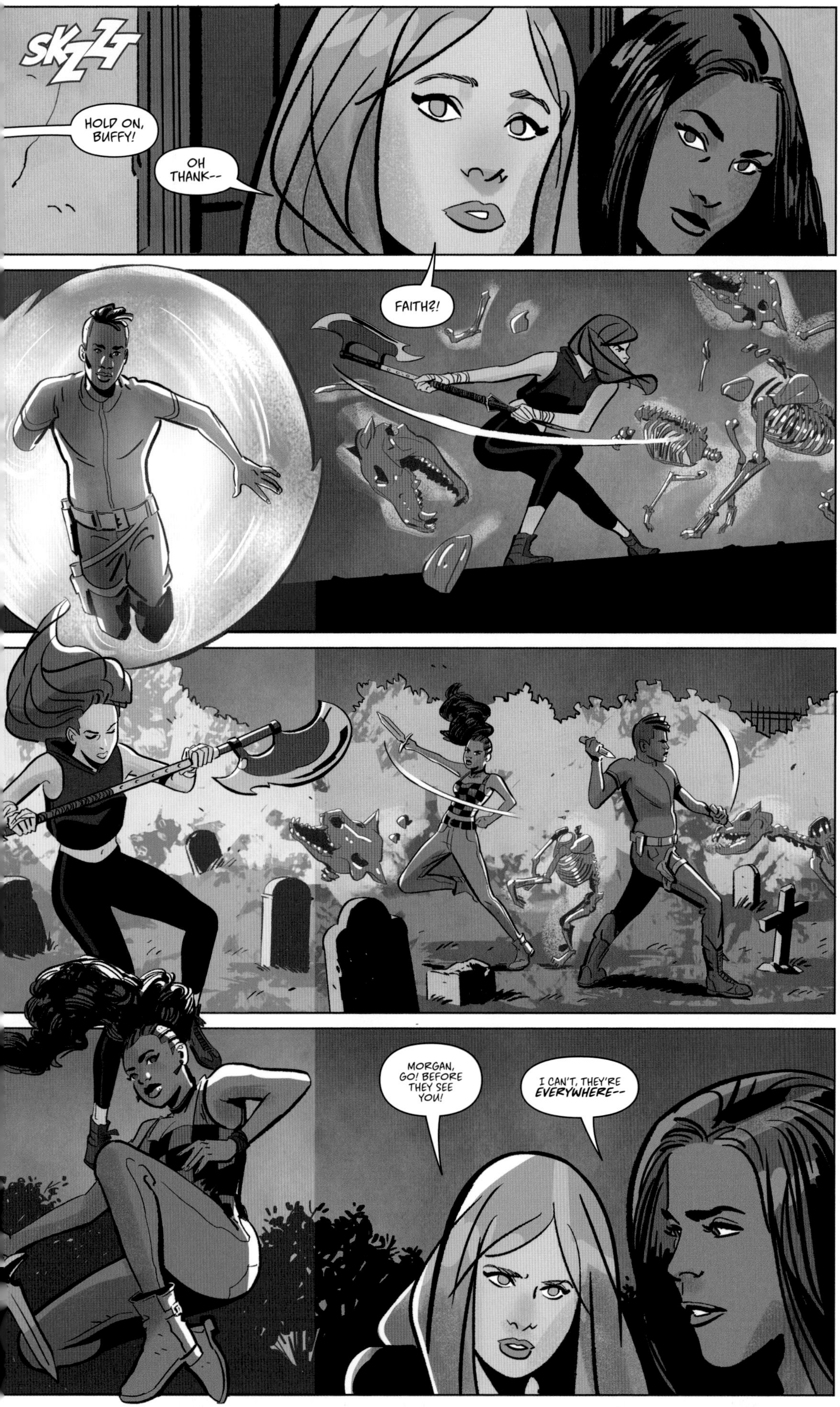
SKZZT
HOLD ON, BUFFY!
OH THANK--
FAITH?!
MORGAN, GO! BEFORE THEY SEE YOU!
I CAN'T, THEY'RE *EVERYWHERE*--

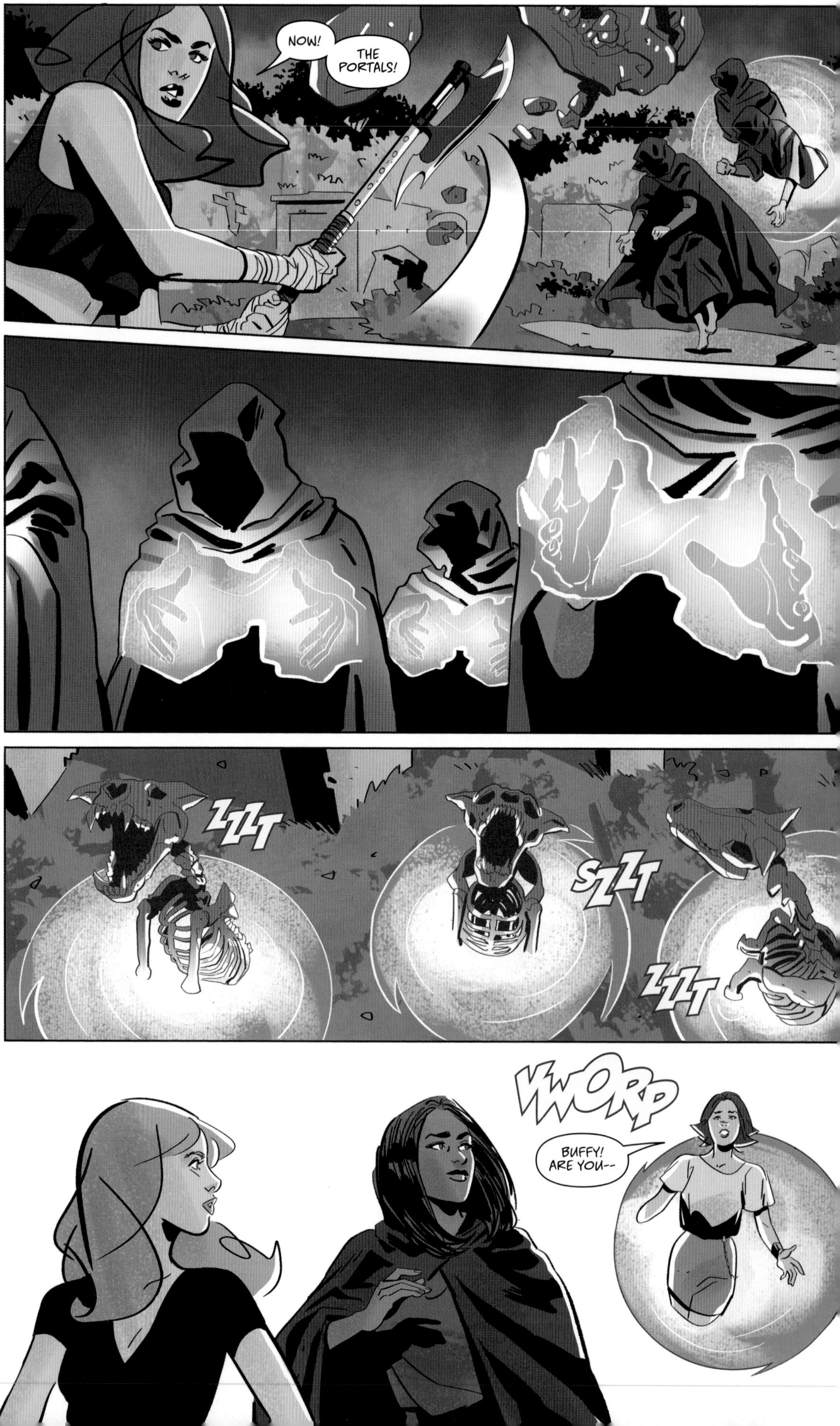
NOW!
THE PORTALS!
ZZZT
SZZT
ZZZT
VWORP
BUFFY! ARE YOU--

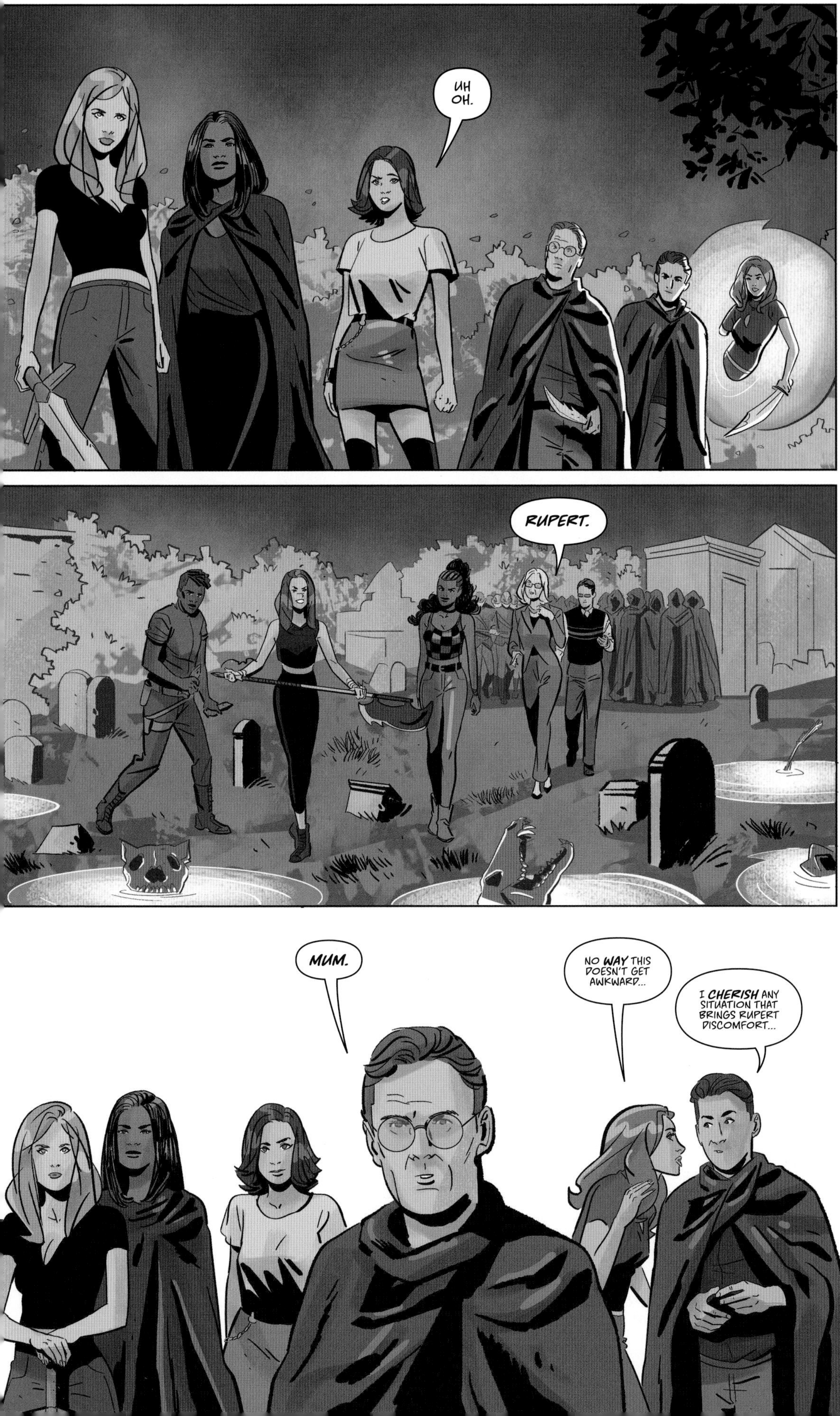
UH OH.
RUPERT.
MUM.
NO WAY THIS DOESN'T GET AWKWARD...
I CHERISH ANY SITUATION THAT BRINGS RUPERT DISCOMFORT...

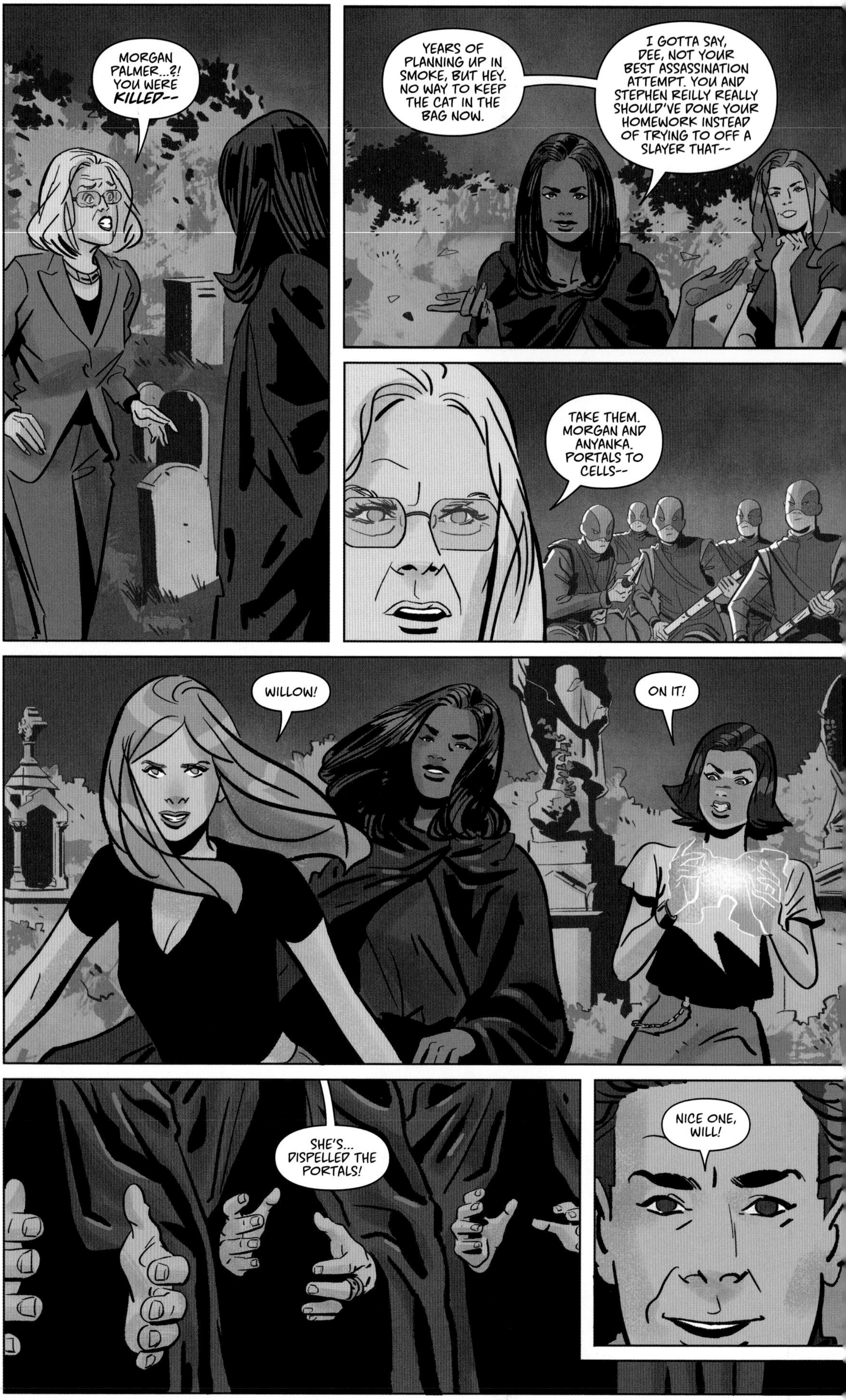
MORGAN PALMER...?! YOU WERE **KILLED**--
YEARS OF PLANNING UP IN SMOKE, BUT HEY. NO WAY TO KEEP THE CAT IN THE BAG NOW.
I GOTTA SAY, DEE, NOT YOUR BEST ASSASSINATION ATTEMPT. YOU AND STEPHEN REILLY REALLY SHOULD'VE DONE YOUR HOMEWORK INSTEAD OF TRYING TO OFF A SLAYER THAT--
TAKE THEM. MORGAN AND ANYANKA. PORTALS TO CELLS--
WILLOW!
ON IT!
SHE'S... DISPELLED THE PORTALS!
NICE ONE, WILL!

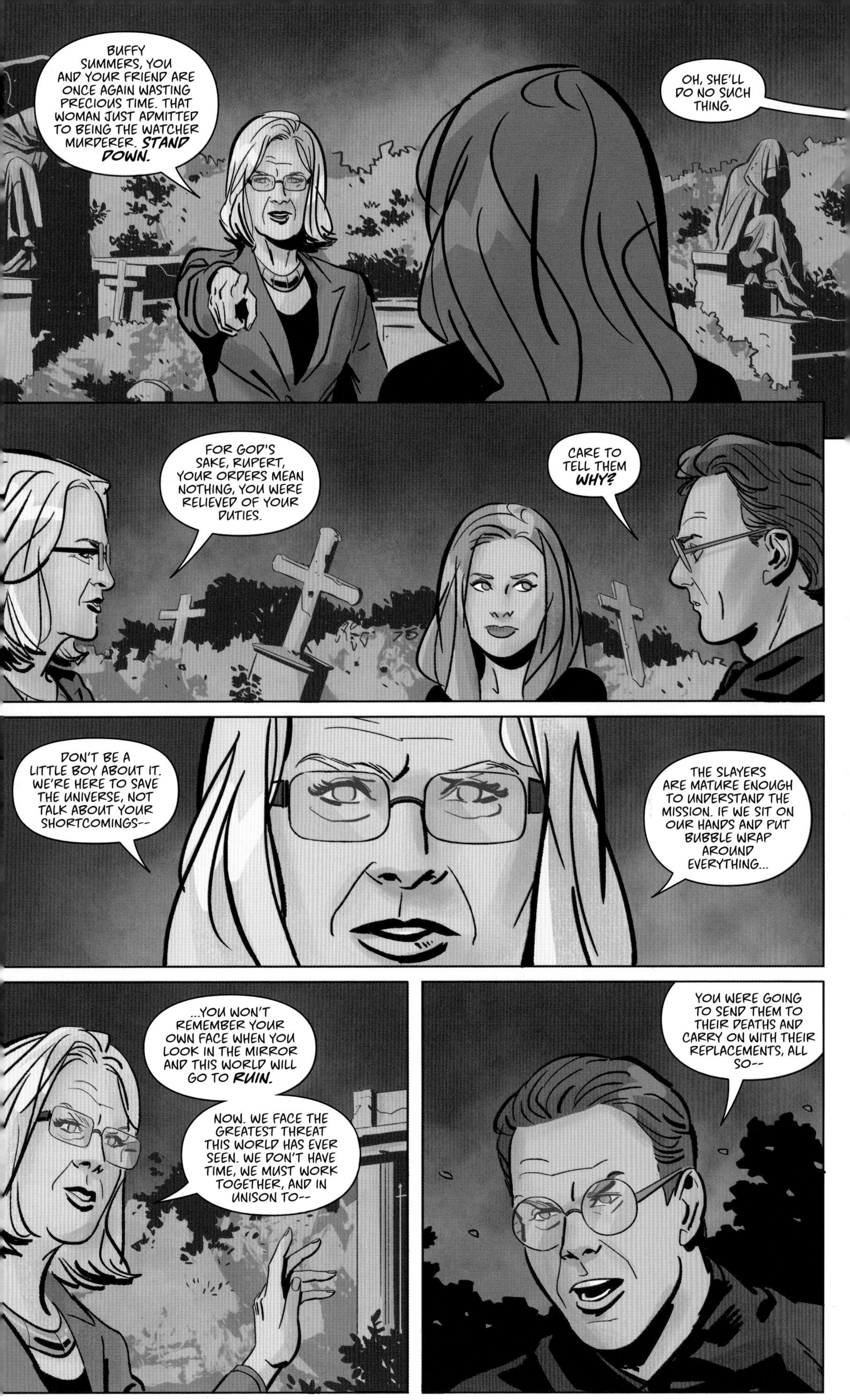
BUFFY SUMMERS, YOU AND YOUR FRIEND ARE ONCE AGAIN WASTING PRECIOUS TIME. THAT WOMAN JUST ADMITTED TO BEING THE WATCHER MURDERER. STAND DOWN.
OH, SHE'LL DO NO SUCH THING.
FOR GOD'S SAKE, RUPERT, YOUR ORDERS MEAN NOTHING, YOU WERE RELIEVED OF YOUR DUTIES.
CARE TO TELL THEM WHY?
DON'T BE A LITTLE BOY ABOUT IT. WE'RE HERE TO SAVE THE UNIVERSE, NOT TALK ABOUT YOUR SHORTCOMINGS--
THE SLAYERS ARE MATURE ENOUGH TO UNDERSTAND THE MISSION. IF WE SIT ON OUR HANDS AND PUT BUBBLE WRAP AROUND EVERYTHING...
...YOU WON'T REMEMBER YOUR OWN FACE WHEN YOU LOOK IN THE MIRROR AND THIS WORLD WILL GO TO RUIN.
NOW. WE FACE THE GREATEST THREAT THIS WORLD HAS EVER SEEN. WE DON'T HAVE TIME, WE MUST WORK TOGETHER, AND IN UNISON TO--
YOU WERE GOING TO SEND THEM TO THEIR DEATHS AND CARRY ON WITH THEIR REPLACEMENTS, ALL SO--

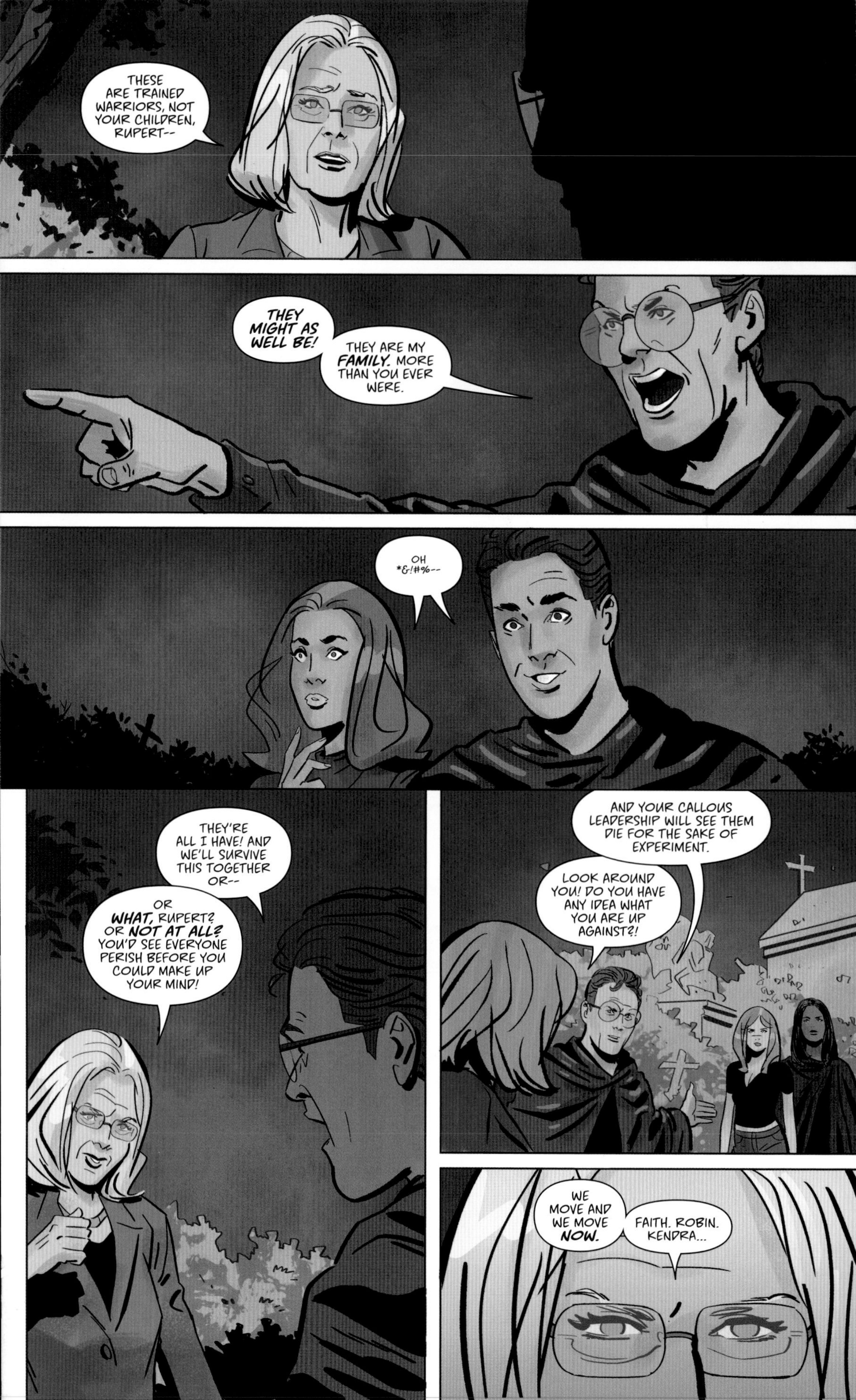

THESE ARE TRAINED WARRIORS, NOT YOUR CHILDREN, RUPERT--
THEY MIGHT AS WELL BE!
THEY ARE MY FAMILY. MORE THAN YOU EVER WERE.
OH *&!#%--
THEY'RE ALL I HAVE! AND WE'LL SURVIVE THIS TOGETHER OR--
OR WHAT, RUPERT? OR NOT AT ALL? YOU'D SEE EVERYONE PERISH BEFORE YOU COULD MAKE UP YOUR MIND!
AND YOUR CALLOUS LEADERSHIP WILL SEE THEM DIE FOR THE SAKE OF EXPERIMENT.
LOOK AROUND YOU! DO YOU HAVE ANY IDEA WHAT YOU ARE UP AGAINST?!
WE MOVE AND WE MOVE NOW.
FAITH. ROBIN. KENDRA...

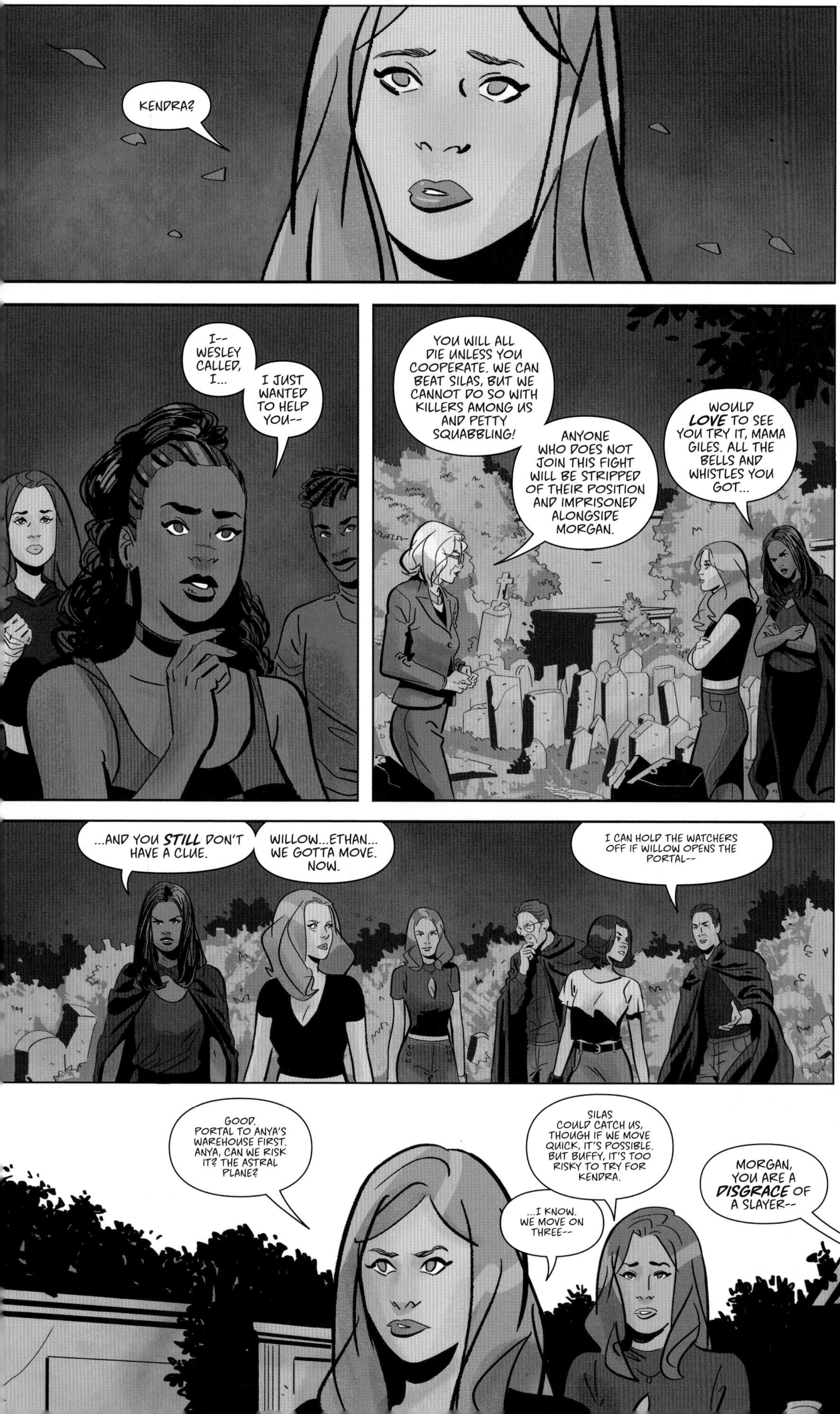

KENDRA?
I-- WESLEY CALLED, I...
I JUST WANTED TO HELP YOU--
YOU WILL ALL DIE UNLESS YOU COOPERATE. WE CAN BEAT SILAS, BUT WE CANNOT DO SO WITH KILLERS AMONG US AND PETTY SQUABBLING!
ANYONE WHO DOES NOT JOIN THIS FIGHT WILL BE STRIPPED OF THEIR POSITION AND IMPRISONED ALONGSIDE MORGAN.
WOULD LOVE TO SEE YOU TRY IT, MAMA GILES. ALL THE BELLS AND WHISTLES YOU GOT...
...AND YOU STILL DON'T HAVE A CLUE.
WILLOW...ETHAN... WE GOTTA MOVE. NOW.
I CAN HOLD THE WATCHERS OFF IF WILLOW OPENS THE PORTAL--
GOOD. PORTAL TO ANYA'S WAREHOUSE FIRST. ANYA, CAN WE RISK IT? THE ASTRAL PLANE?
SILAS COULD CATCH US, THOUGH IF WE MOVE QUICK, IT'S POSSIBLE. BUT BUFFY, IT'S TOO RISKY TO TRY FOR KENDRA.
...I KNOW. WE MOVE ON THREE--
MORGAN, YOU ARE A DISGRACE OF A SLAYER--

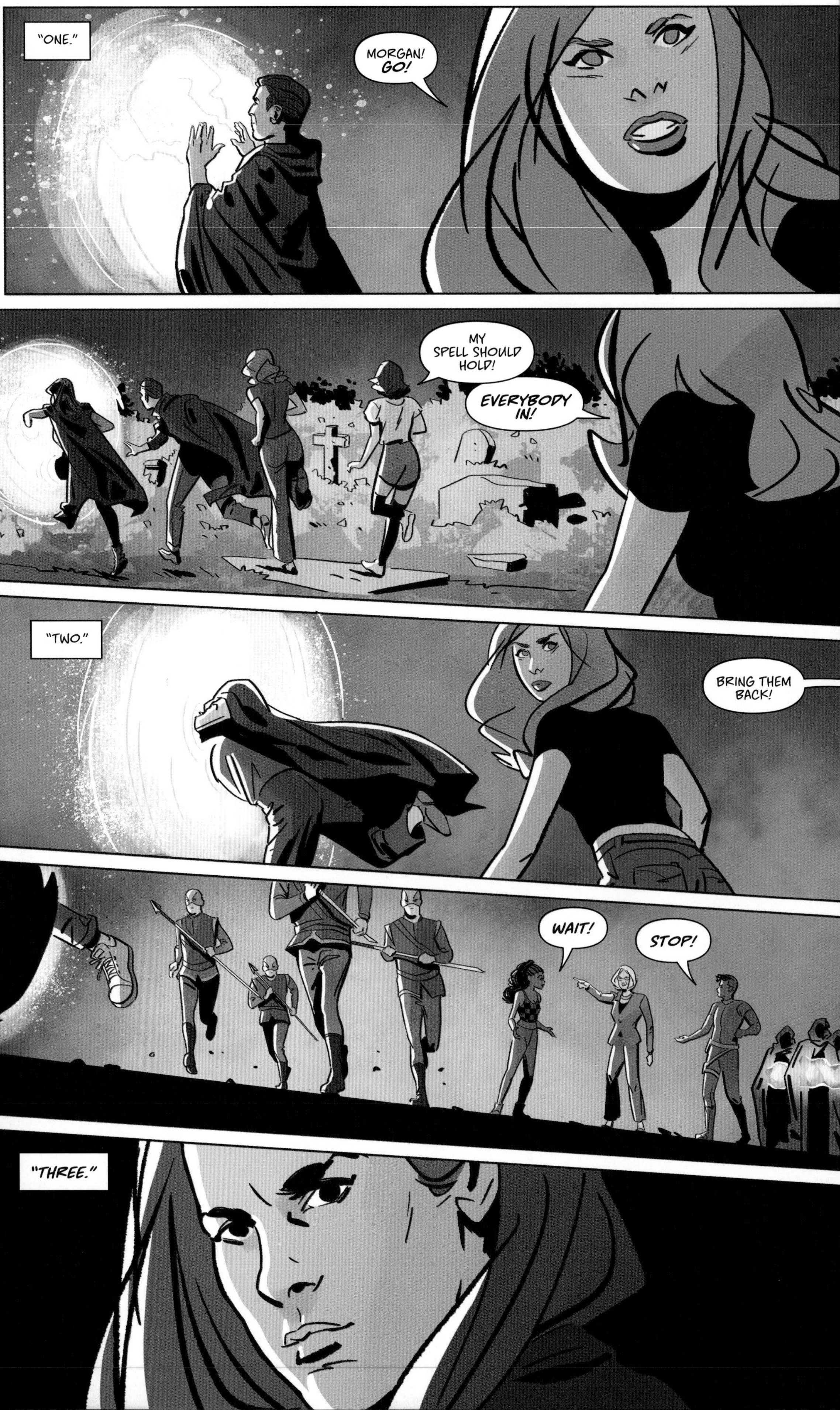
"ONE."
MORGAN! GO!
MY SPELL SHOULD HOLD!
EVERYBODY IN!
"TWO."
BRING THEM BACK!
WAIT!
STOP!
"THREE."

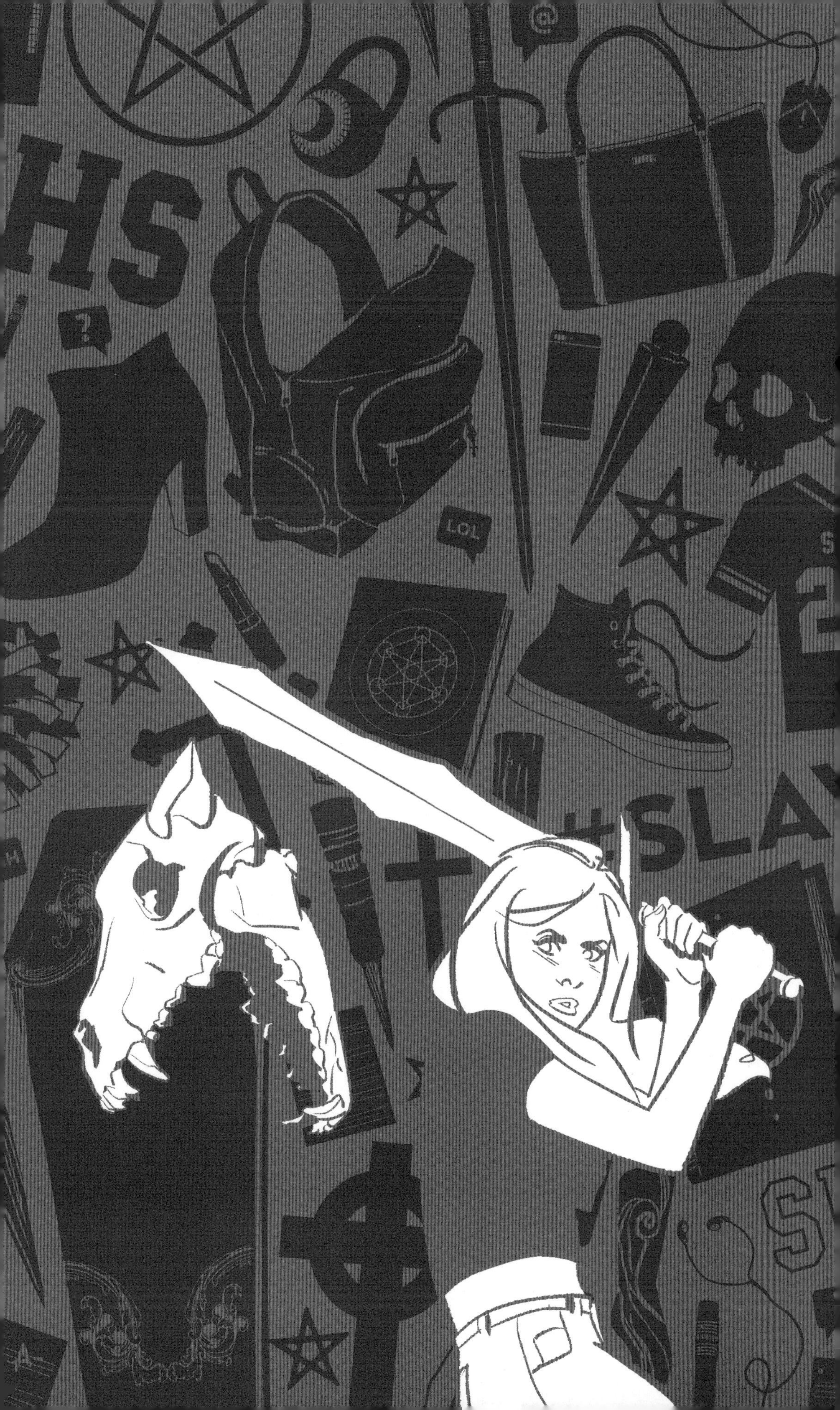
LOL

CHAPTER
THIRTY

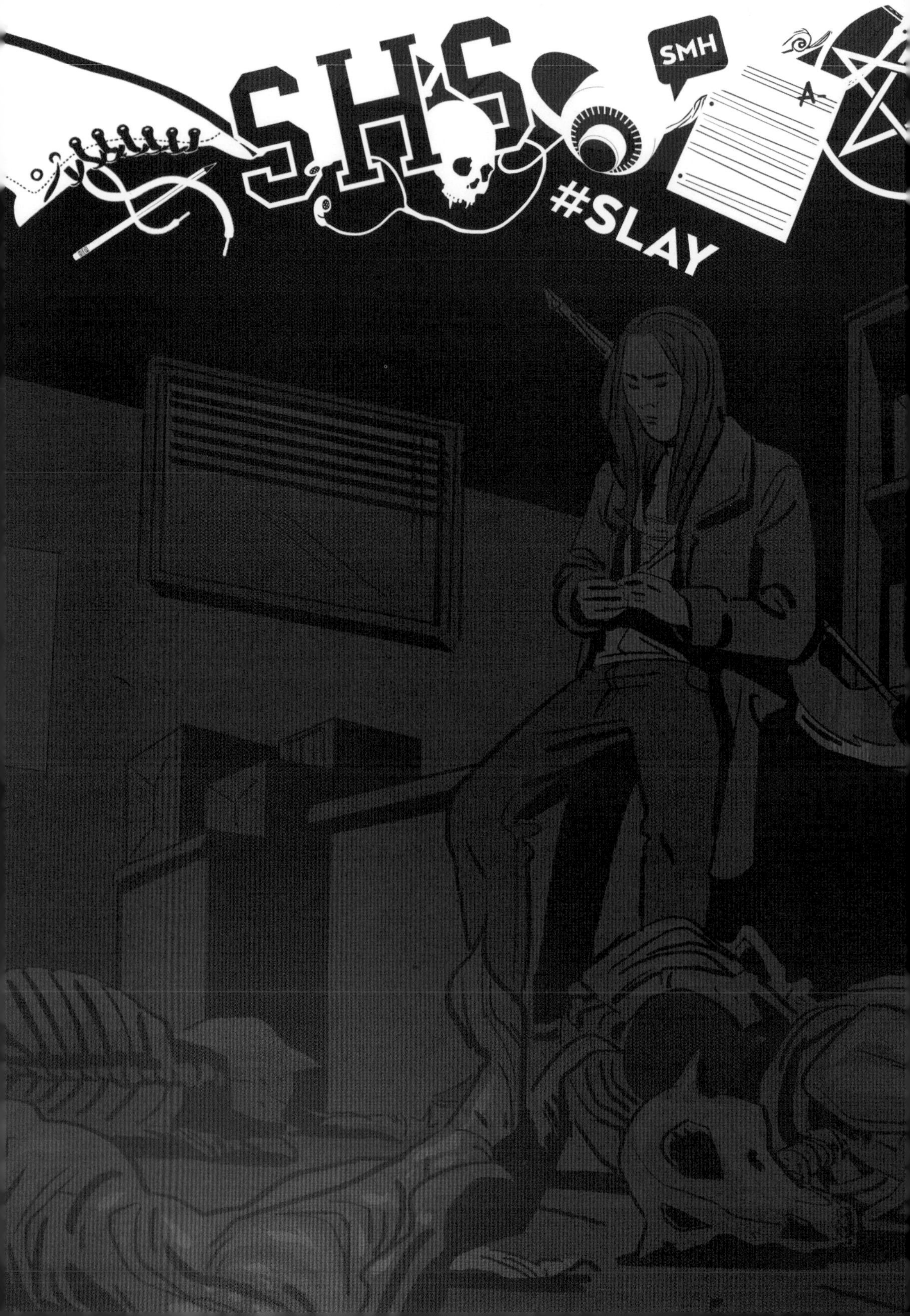
SHS
SMH
A-
#SLAY

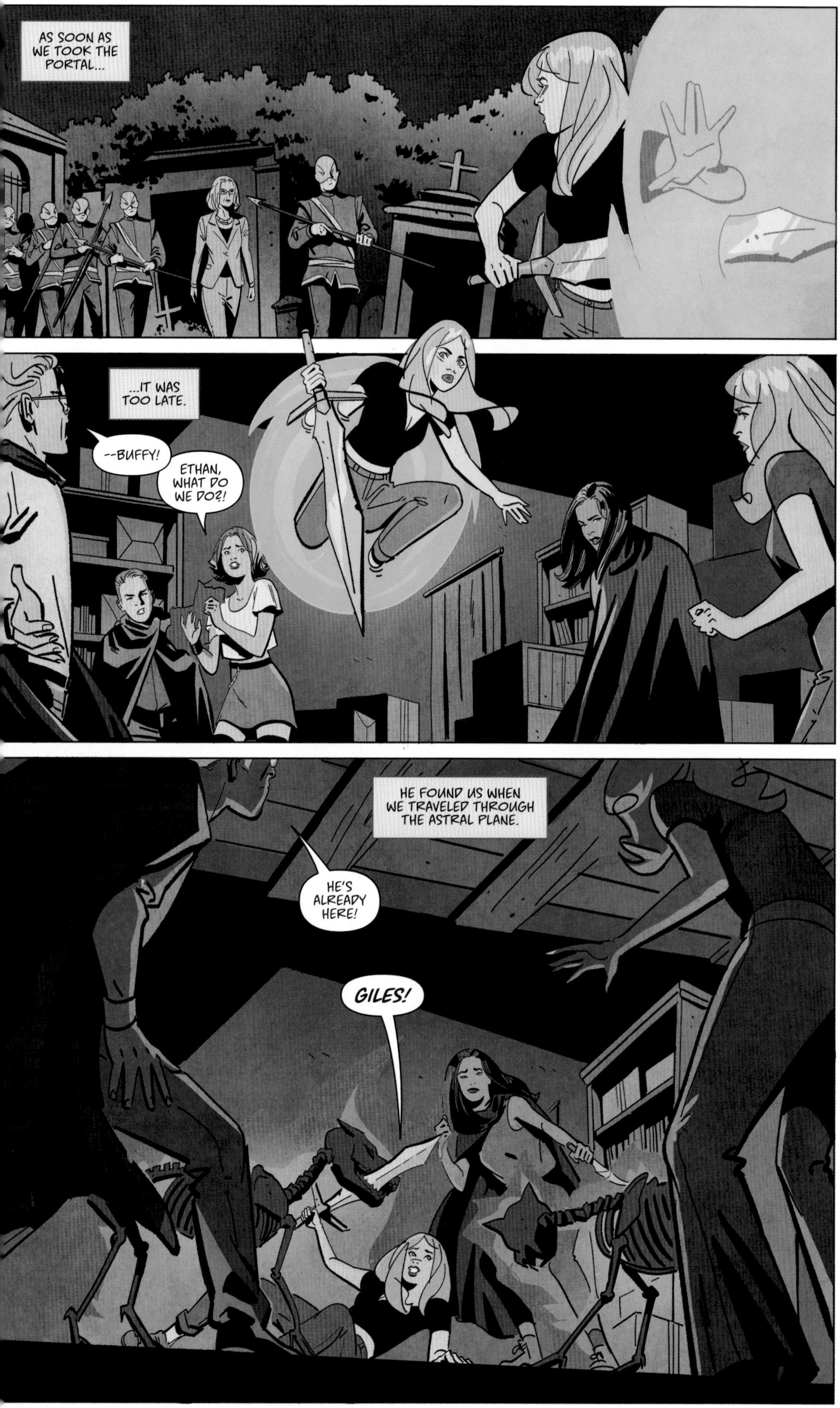
AS SOON AS WE TOOK THE PORTAL...
...IT WAS TOO LATE.
--BUFFY!
ETHAN, WHAT DO WE DO?!
HE FOUND US WHEN WE TRAVELED THROUGH THE ASTRAL PLANE.
HE'S ALREADY HERE!
GILES!

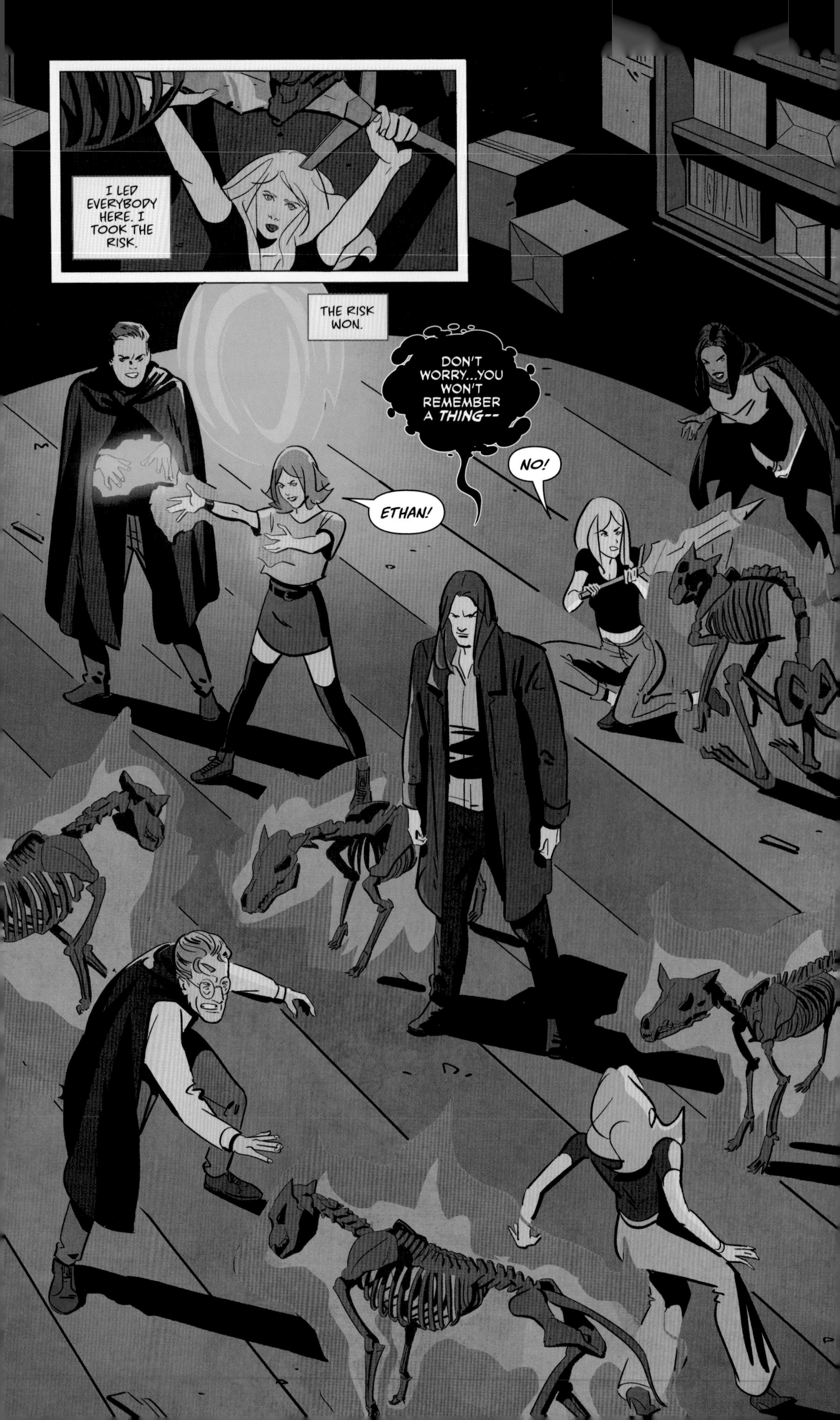
I LED EVERYBODY HERE. I TOOK THE RISK.
THE RISK WON.
DON'T WORRY...YOU WON'T REMEMBER A *THING*--
ETHAN!
NO!

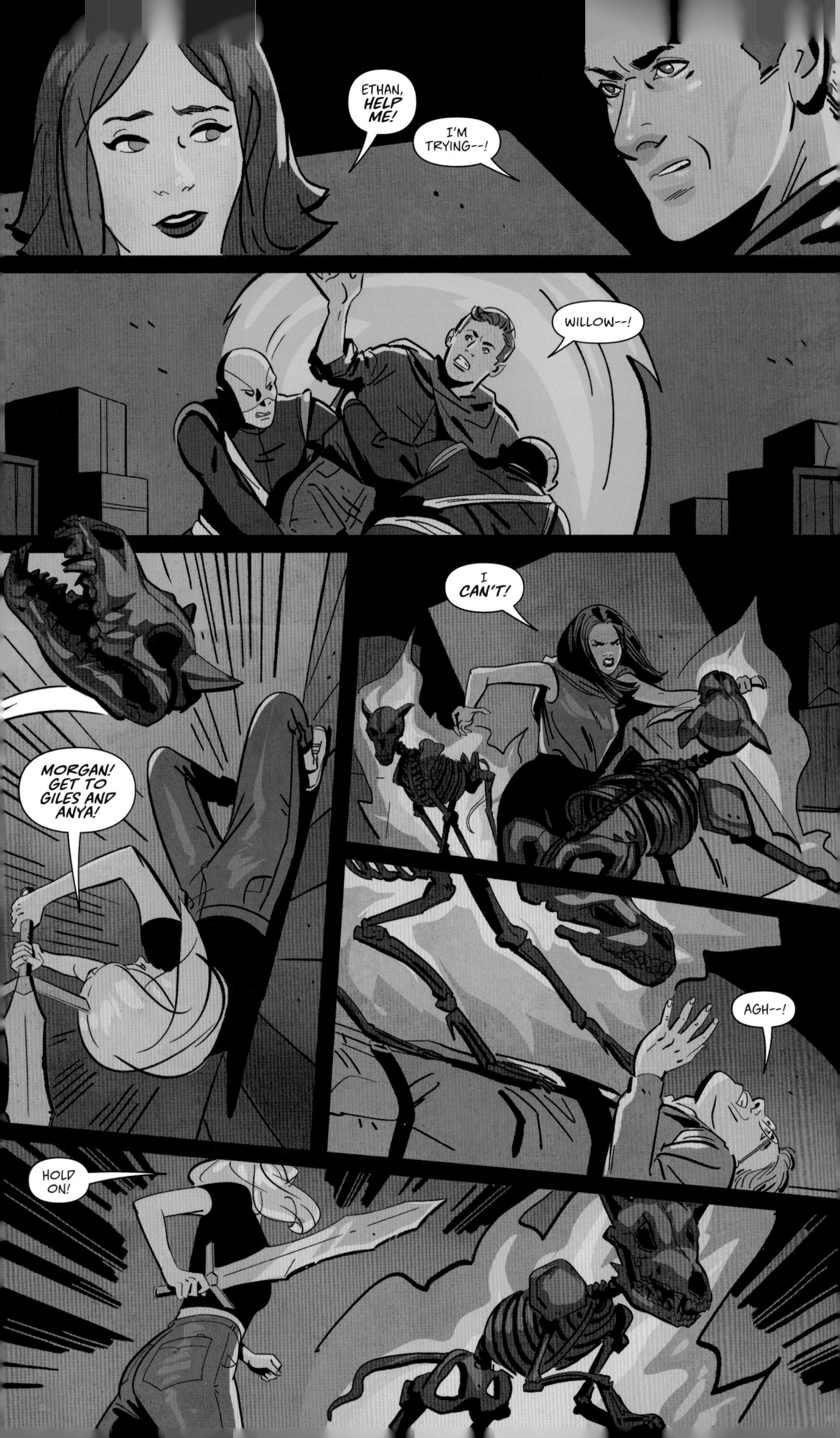
ETHAN, HELP ME!
I'M TRYING--!
WILLOW--!
MORGAN! GET TO GILES AND ANYA!
I CAN'T!
AGH--!
HOLD ON!

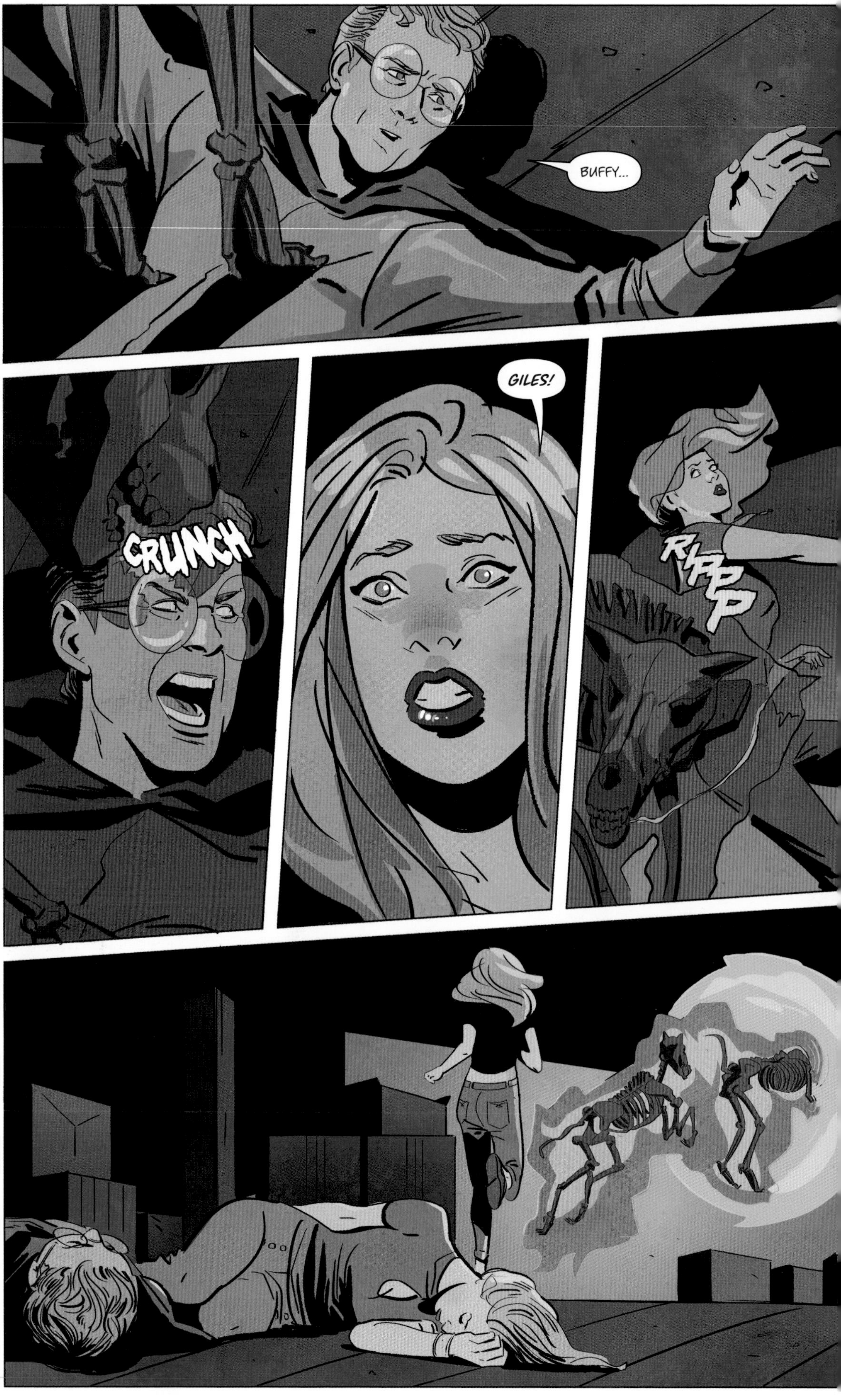
BUFFY...
CRUNCH
GILES!
RIPPP

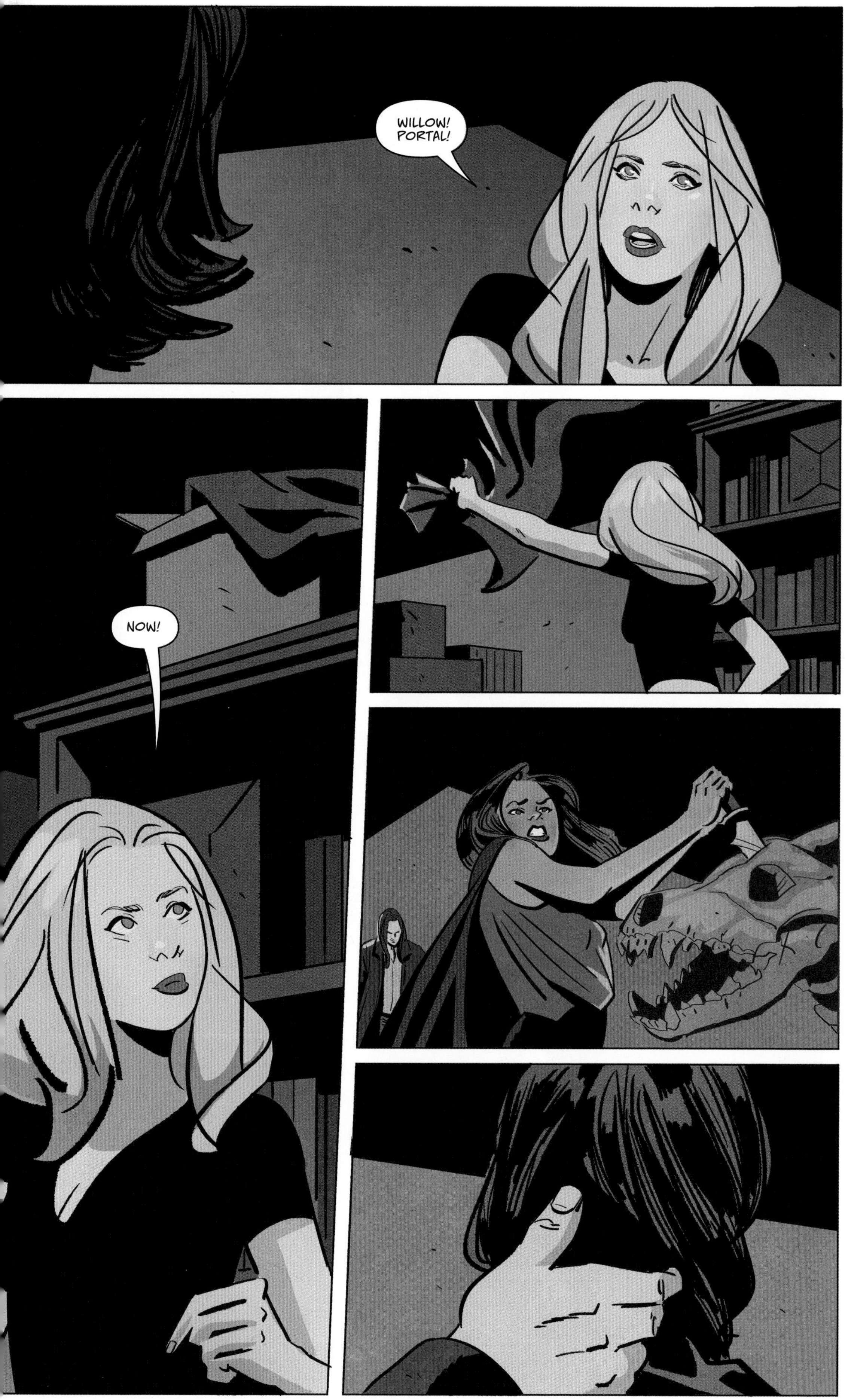
WILLOW! PORTAL!
NOW!

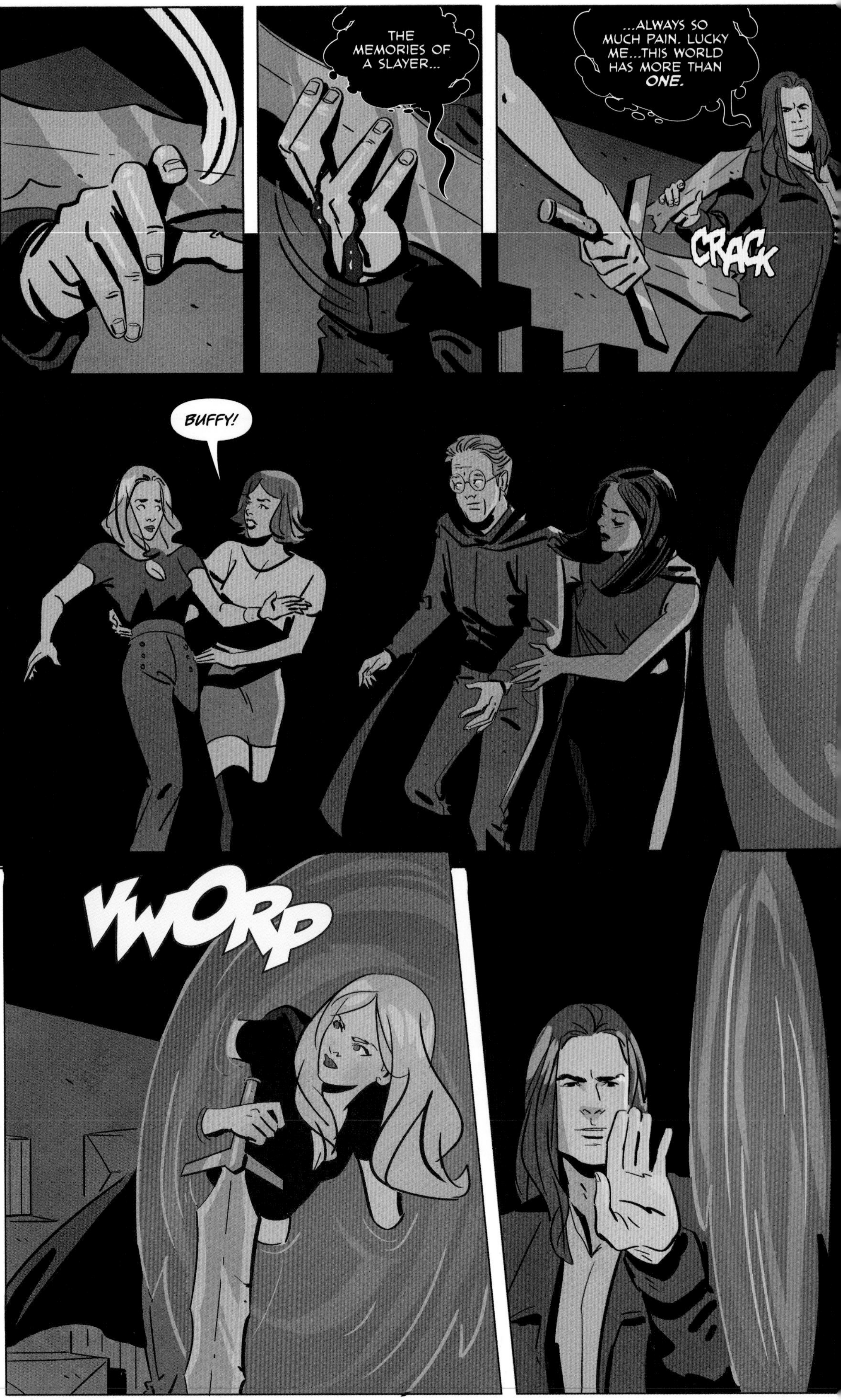
THE MEMORIES OF A SLAYER...
...ALWAYS SO MUCH PAIN. LUCKY ME...THIS WORLD HAS MORE THAN ONE.
CRACK
BUFFY!
VWORP

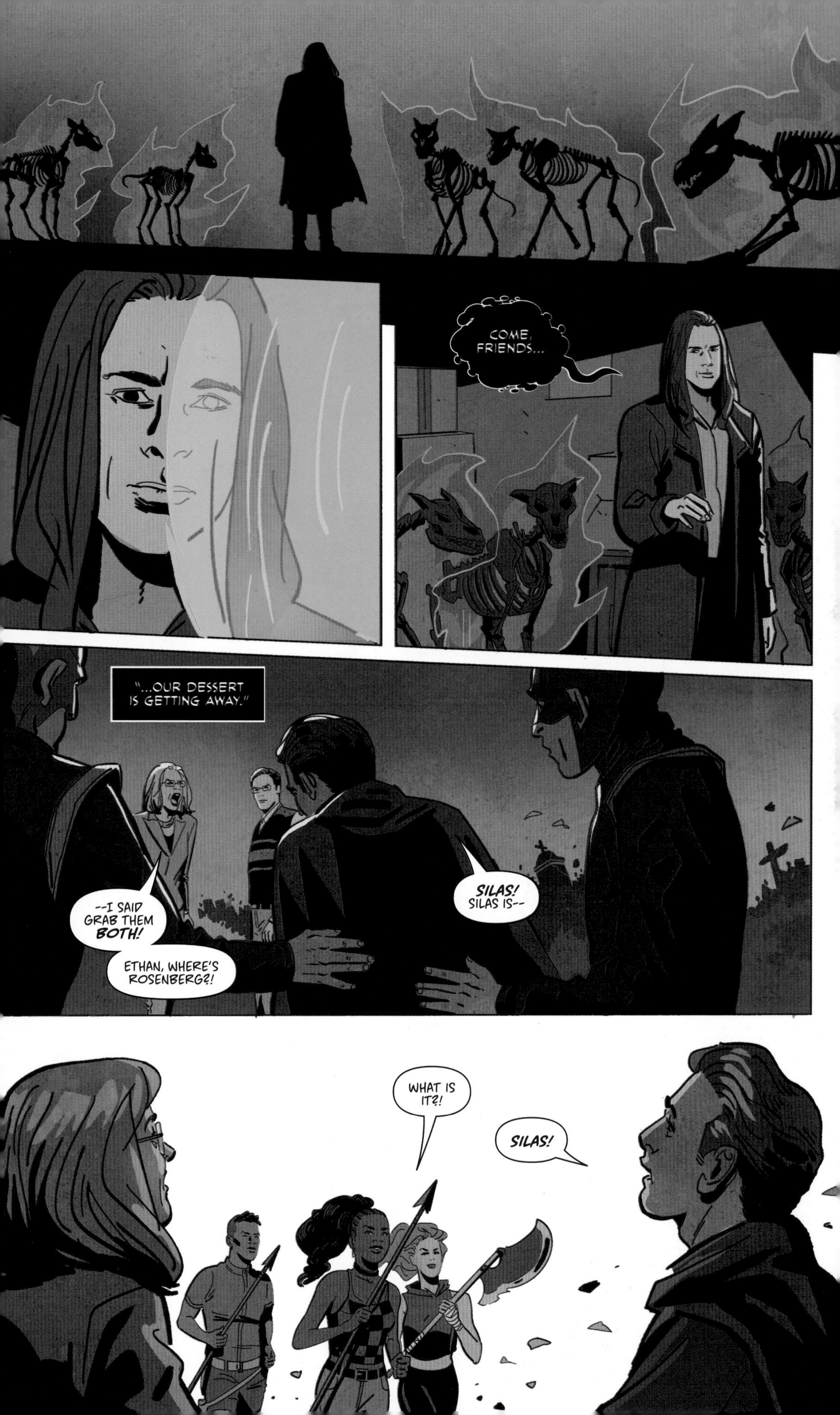
COME, FRIENDS...
"...OUR DESSERT IS GETTING AWAY."
--I SAID GRAB THEM BOTH!
ETHAN, WHERE'S ROSENBERG?!
SILAS! SILAS IS--
WHAT IS IT?!
SILAS!

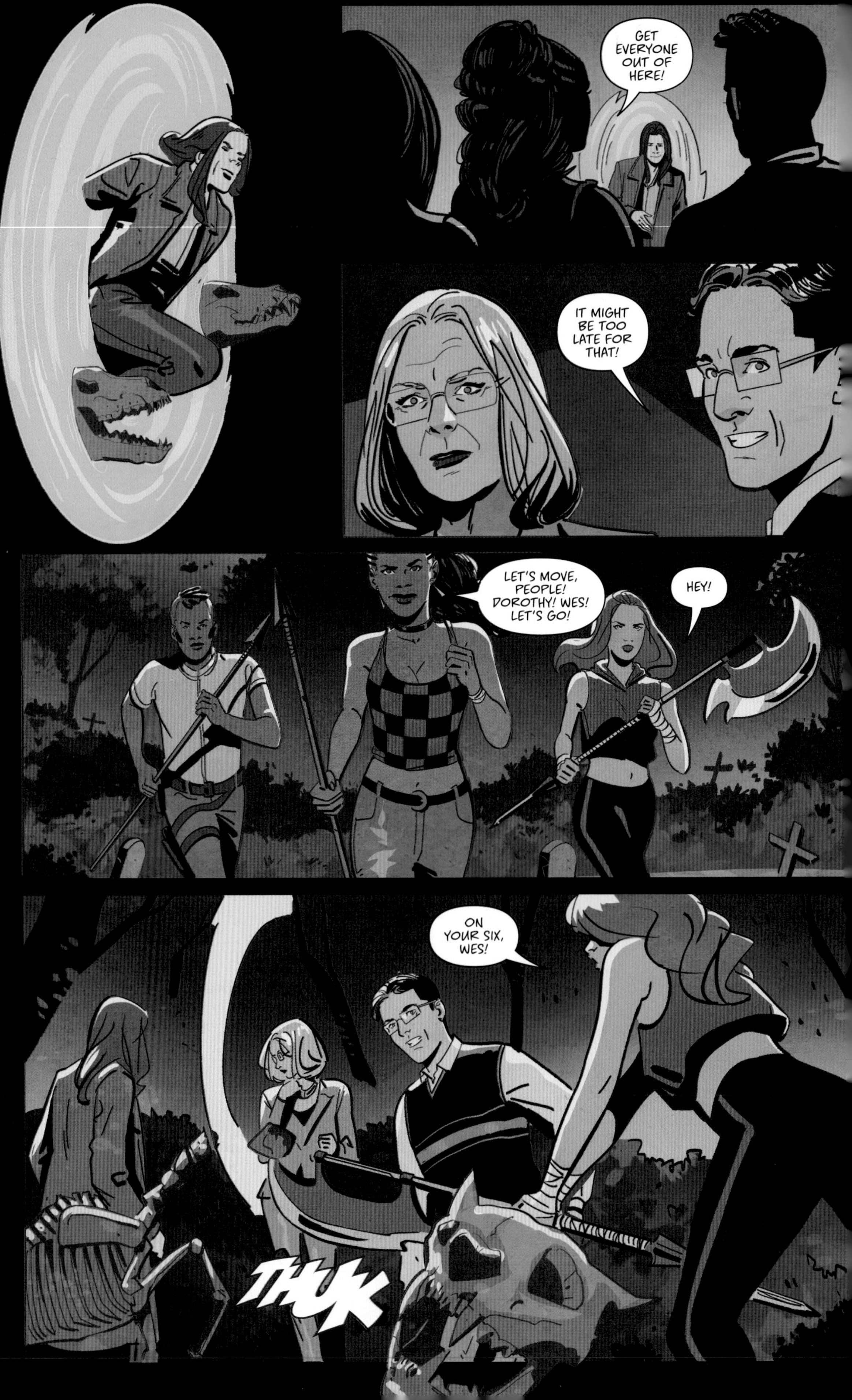
GET EVERYONE OUT OF HERE!
IT MIGHT BE TOO LATE FOR THAT!
LET'S MOVE, PEOPLE! DOROTHY! WES! LET'S GO!
HEY!
ON YOUR SIX, WES!
THUK

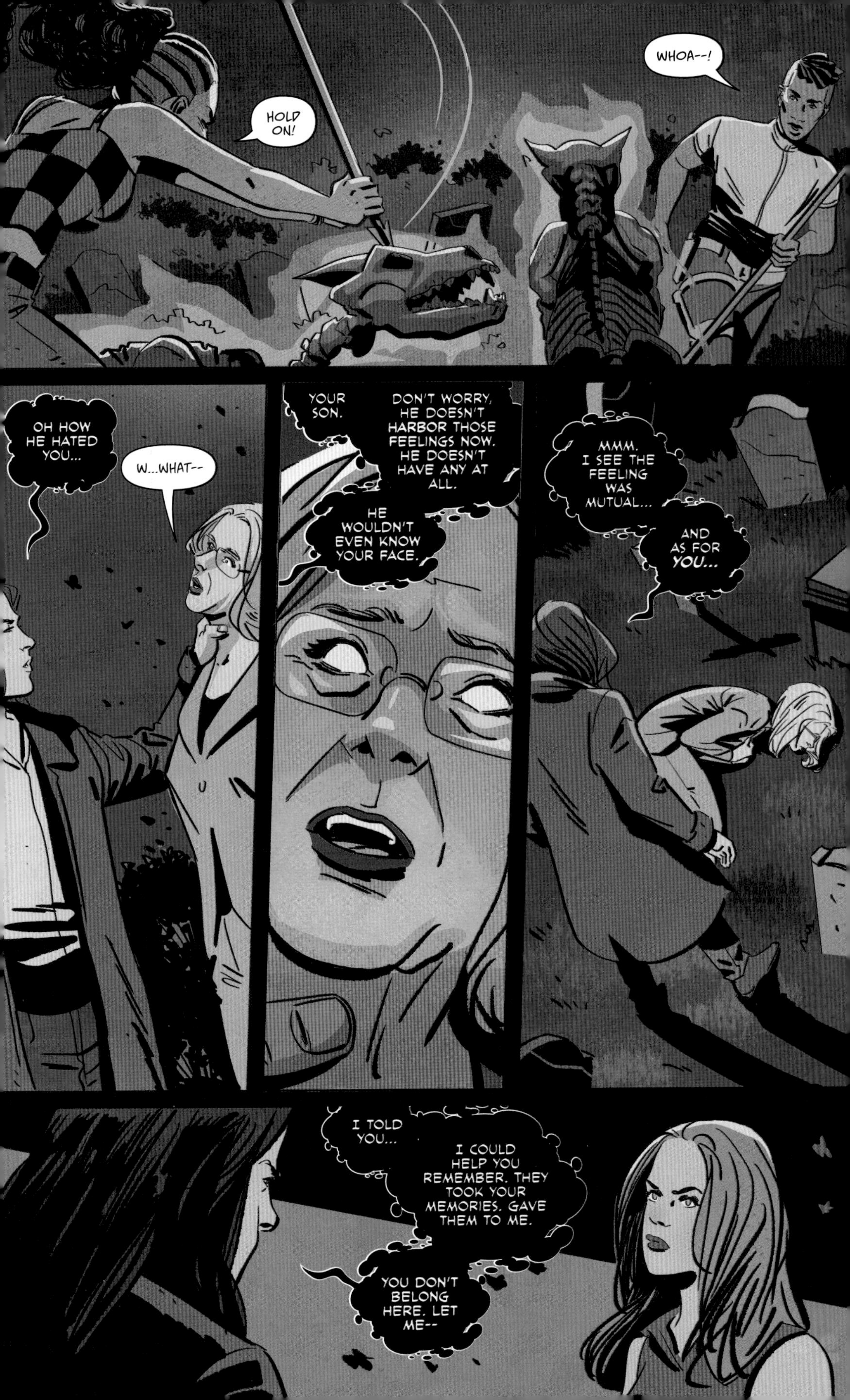
HOLD ON!
WHOA--!
OH HOW HE HATED YOU...
W...WHAT--
YOUR SON.
DON'T WORRY, HE DOESN'T HARBOR THOSE FEELINGS NOW. HE DOESN'T HAVE ANY AT ALL.
HE WOULDN'T EVEN KNOW YOUR FACE.
MMM. I SEE THE FEELING WAS MUTUAL...
AND AS FOR *YOU...*
I TOLD YOU...
I COULD HELP YOU REMEMBER. THEY TOOK YOUR MEMORIES. GAVE THEM TO ME.
YOU DON'T BELONG HERE. LET ME--

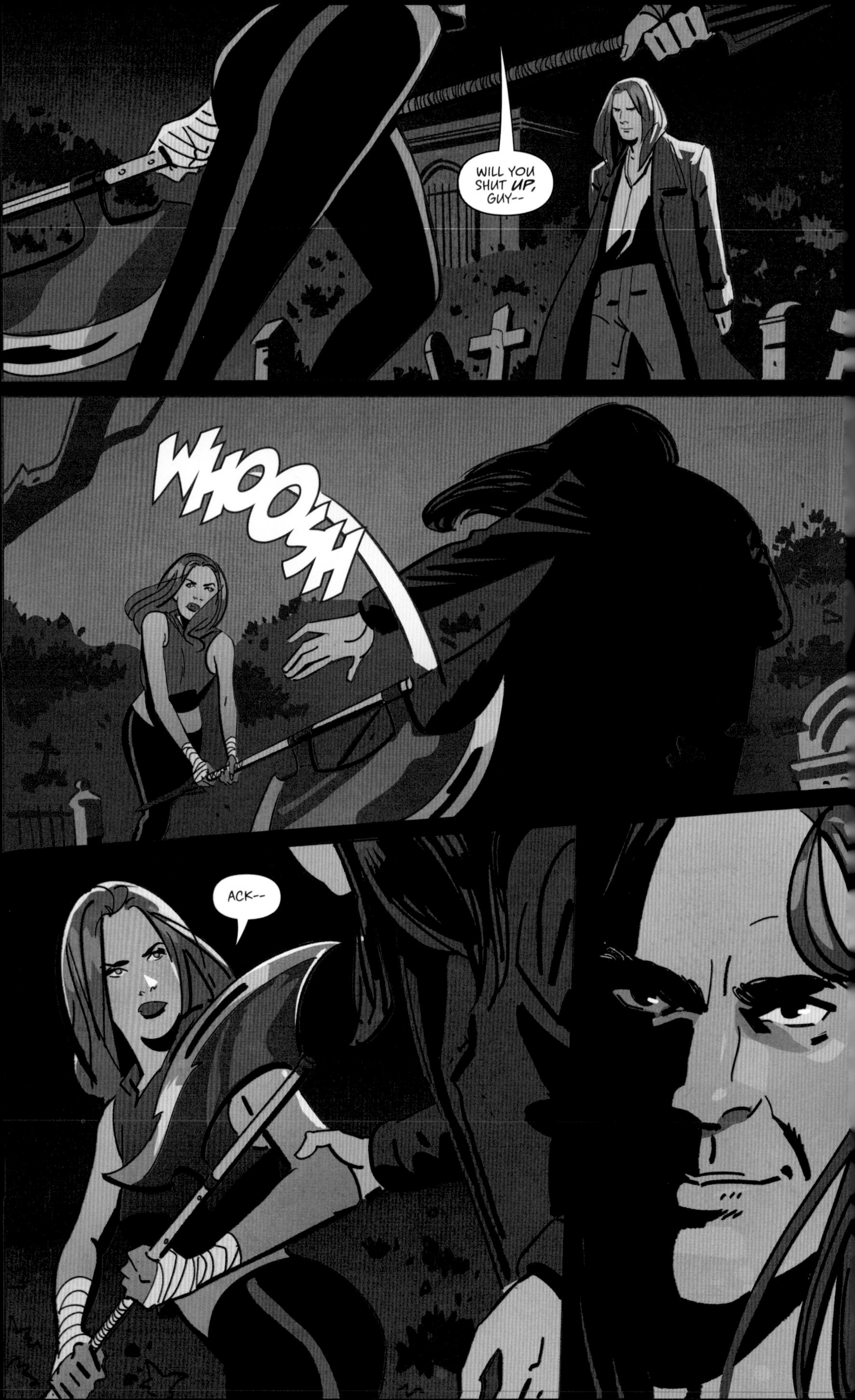
WILL YOU SHUT UP, GUY--
WHOOSH
ACK--

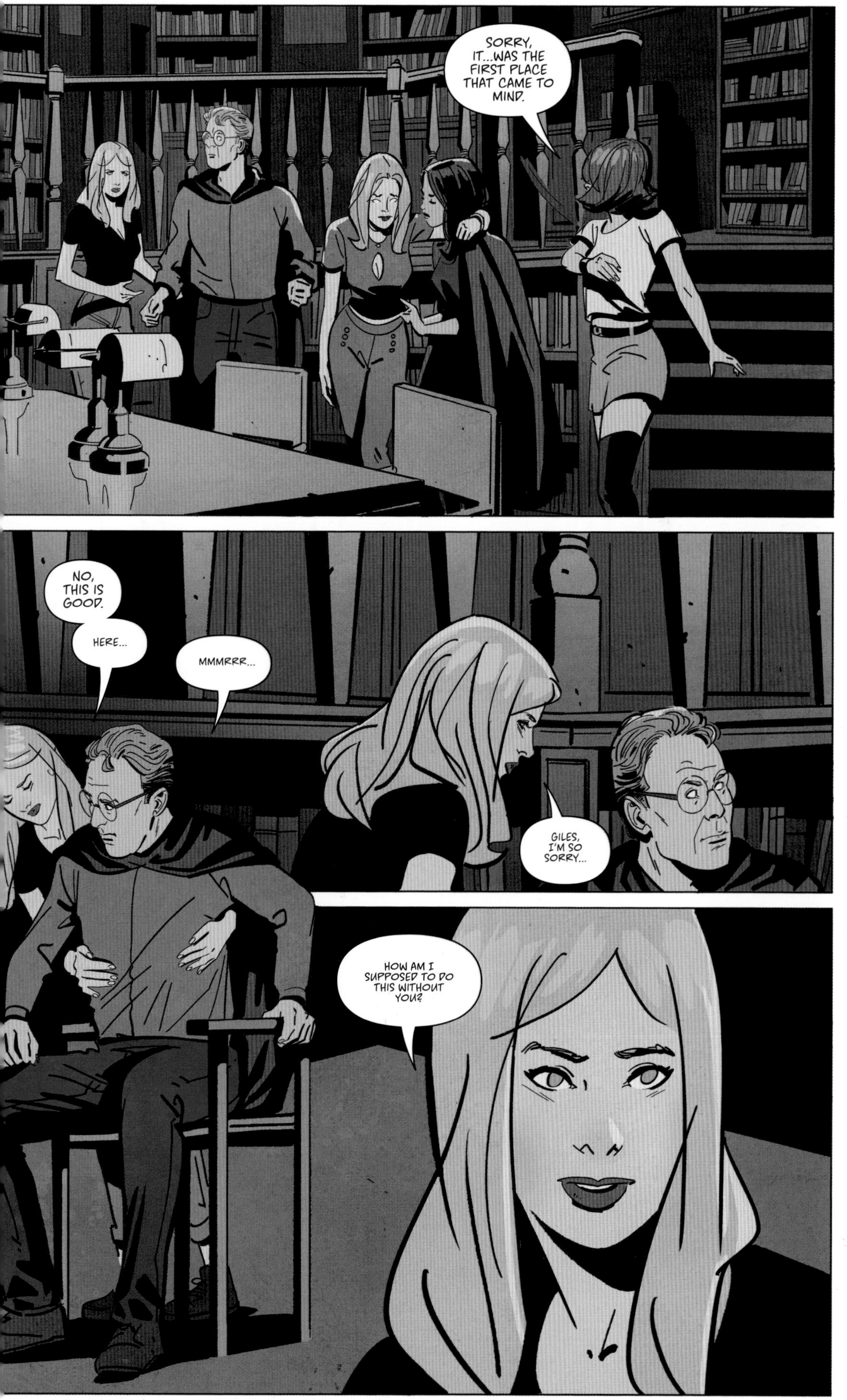
SORRY, IT...WAS THE FIRST PLACE THAT CAME TO MIND.
NO, THIS IS GOOD.
HERE...
MMMRRR...
GILES, I'M SO SORRY...
HOW AM I SUPPOSED TO DO THIS WITHOUT YOU?

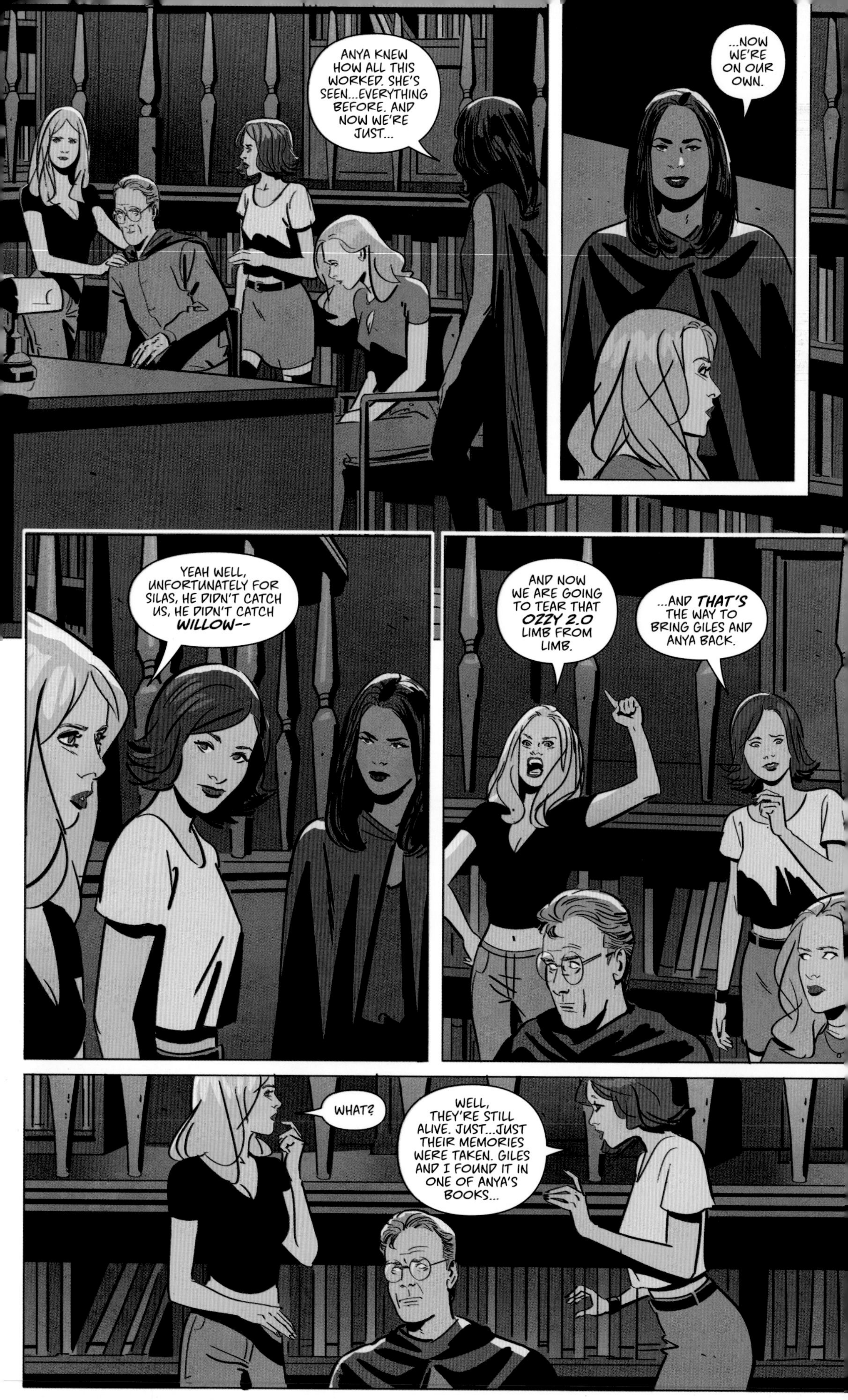
ANYA KNEW HOW ALL THIS WORKED. SHE'S SEEN...EVERYTHING BEFORE. AND NOW WE'RE JUST...
...NOW WE'RE ON OUR OWN.
YEAH WELL, UNFORTUNATELY FOR SILAS, HE DIDN'T CATCH US, HE DIDN'T CATCH WILLOW--
AND NOW WE ARE GOING TO TEAR THAT OZZY 2.0 LIMB FROM LIMB.
...AND THAT'S THE WAY TO BRING GILES AND ANYA BACK.
WHAT?
WELL, THEY'RE STILL ALIVE. JUST...JUST THEIR MEMORIES WERE TAKEN. GILES AND I FOUND IT IN ONE OF ANYA'S BOOKS...

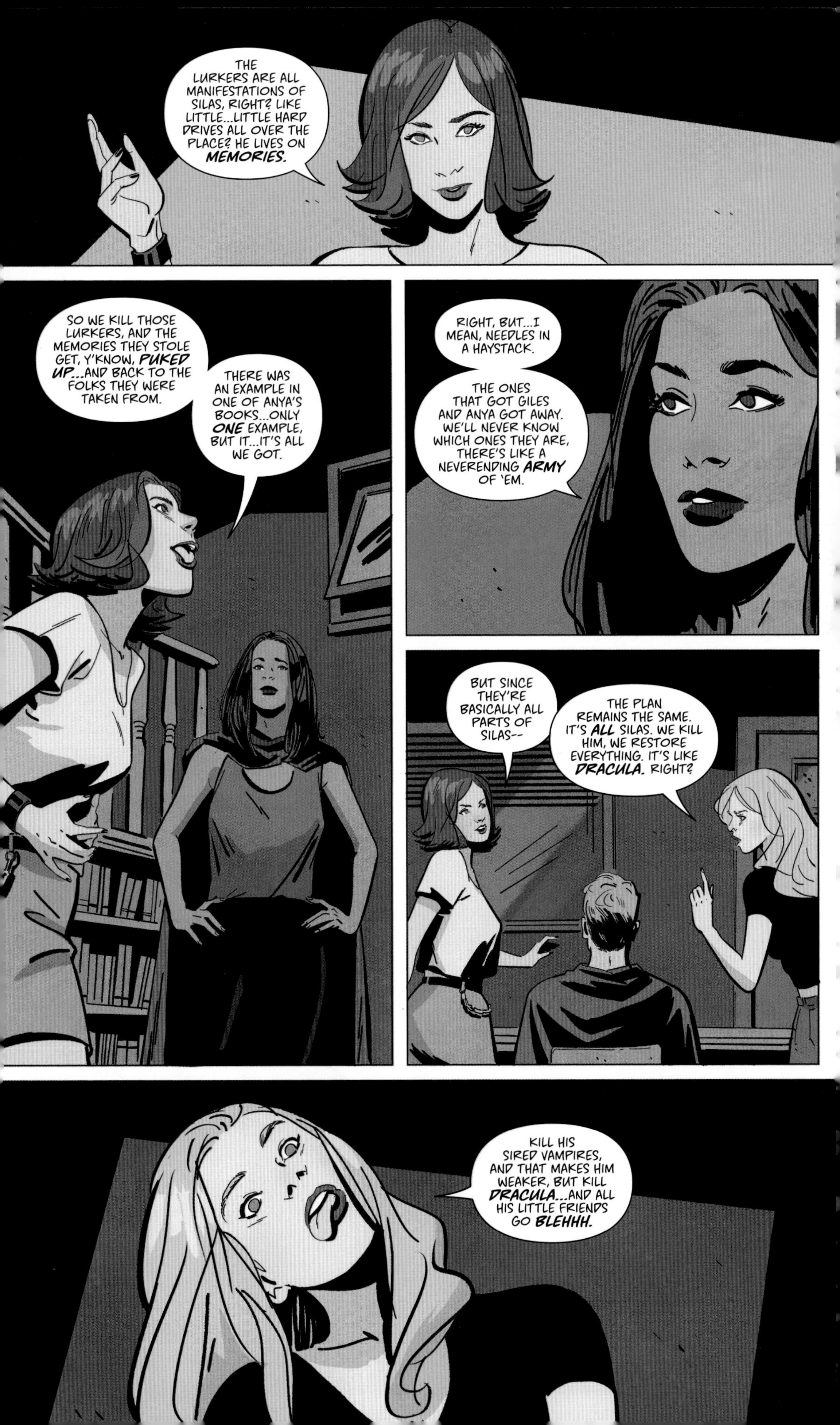
THE LURKERS ARE ALL MANIFESTATIONS OF SILAS, RIGHT? LIKE LITTLE...LITTLE HARD DRIVES ALL OVER THE PLACE? HE LIVES ON MEMORIES.
SO WE KILL THOSE LURKERS, AND THE MEMORIES THEY STOLE GET, Y'KNOW, PUKED UP...AND BACK TO THE FOLKS THEY WERE TAKEN FROM.
THERE WAS AN EXAMPLE IN ONE OF ANYA'S BOOKS...ONLY ONE EXAMPLE, BUT IT...IT'S ALL WE GOT.
RIGHT, BUT...I MEAN, NEEDLES IN A HAYSTACK.
THE ONES THAT GOT GILES AND ANYA GOT AWAY. WE'LL NEVER KNOW WHICH ONES THEY ARE, THERE'S LIKE A NEVERENDING ARMY OF 'EM.
BUT SINCE THEY'RE BASICALLY ALL PARTS OF SILAS--
THE PLAN REMAINS THE SAME. IT'S ALL SILAS. WE KILL HIM, WE RESTORE EVERYTHING. IT'S LIKE DRACULA. RIGHT?
KILL HIS SIRED VAMPIRES, AND THAT MAKES HIM WEAKER, BUT KILL DRACULA...AND ALL HIS LITTLE FRIENDS GO BLEHHH.

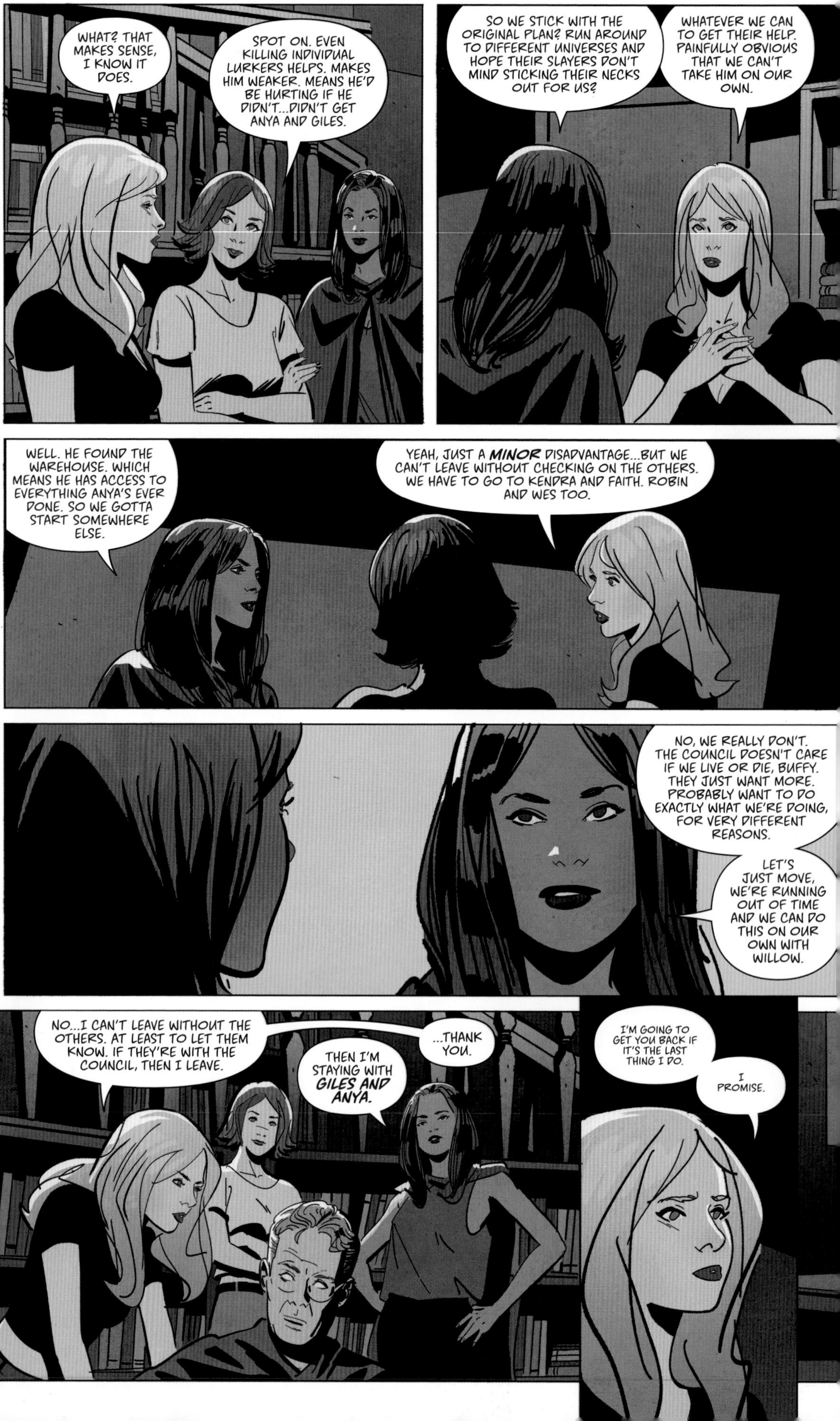
WHAT? THAT MAKES SENSE, I KNOW IT DOES.
SPOT ON. EVEN KILLING INDIVIDUAL LURKERS HELPS. MAKES HIM WEAKER. MEANS HE'D BE HURTING IF HE DIDN'T...DIDN'T GET ANYA AND GILES.
SO WE STICK WITH THE ORIGINAL PLAN? RUN AROUND TO DIFFERENT UNIVERSES AND HOPE THEIR SLAYERS DON'T MIND STICKING THEIR NECKS OUT FOR US?
WHATEVER WE CAN TO GET THEIR HELP. PAINFULLY OBVIOUS THAT WE CAN'T TAKE HIM ON OUR OWN.
WELL. HE FOUND THE WAREHOUSE. WHICH MEANS HE HAS ACCESS TO EVERYTHING ANYA'S EVER DONE. SO WE GOTTA START SOMEWHERE ELSE.
YEAH, JUST A ***MINOR*** DISADVANTAGE...BUT WE CAN'T LEAVE WITHOUT CHECKING ON THE OTHERS. WE HAVE TO GO TO KENDRA AND FAITH. ROBIN AND WES TOO.
NO, WE REALLY DON'T. THE COUNCIL DOESN'T CARE IF WE LIVE OR DIE, BUFFY. THEY JUST WANT MORE. PROBABLY WANT TO DO EXACTLY WHAT WE'RE DOING, FOR VERY DIFFERENT REASONS.
LET'S JUST MOVE, WE'RE RUNNING OUT OF TIME AND WE CAN DO THIS ON OUR OWN WITH WILLOW.
NO...I CAN'T LEAVE WITHOUT THE OTHERS. AT LEAST TO LET THEM KNOW. IF THEY'RE WITH THE COUNCIL, THEN I LEAVE.
...THANK YOU.
THEN I'M STAYING WITH ***GILES AND ANYA.***
I'M GOING TO GET YOU BACK IF IT'S THE LAST THING I DO.
I PROMISE.

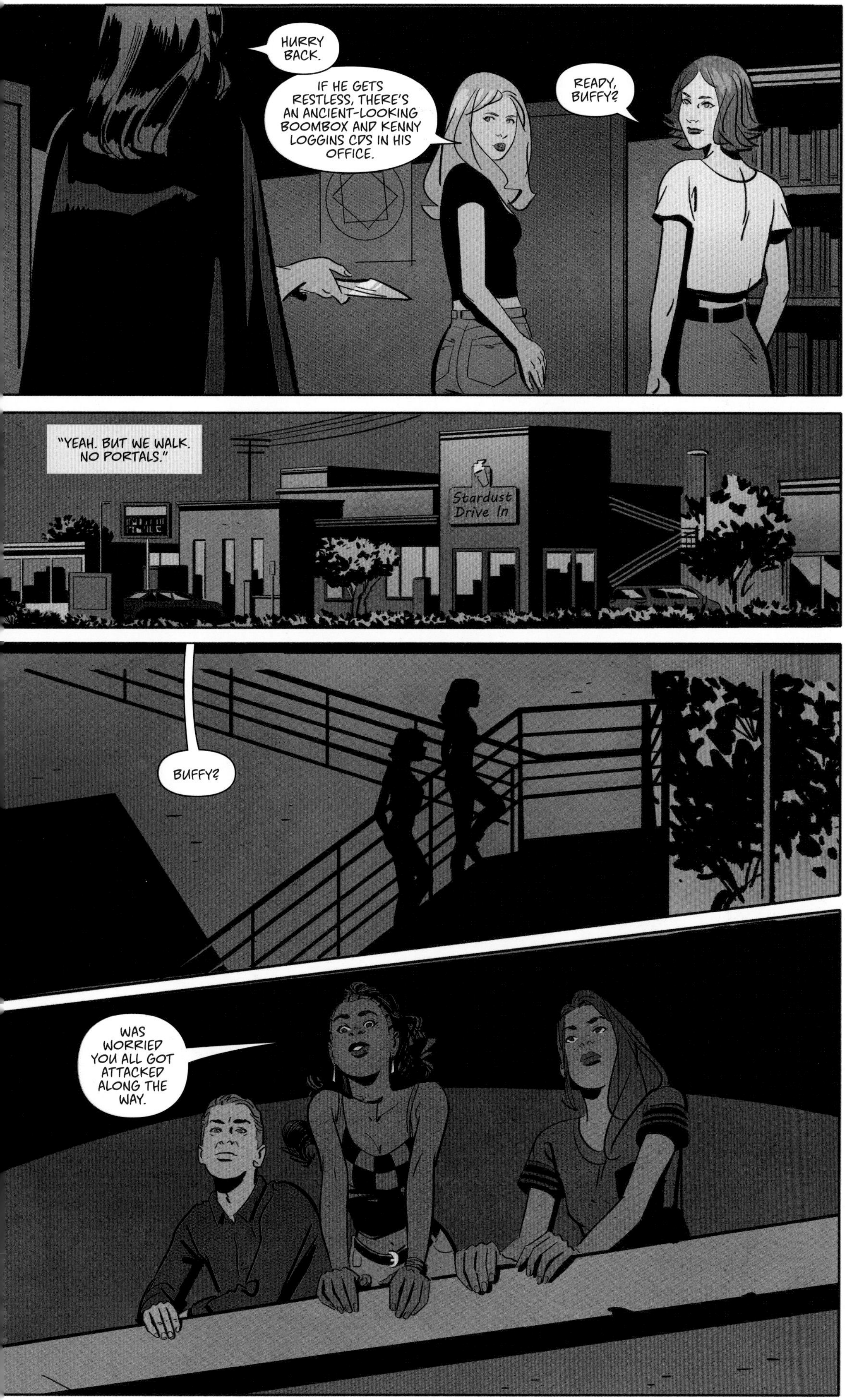
HURRY BACK.
IF HE GETS RESTLESS, THERE'S AN ANCIENT-LOOKING BOOMBOX AND KENNY LOGGINS CDS IN HIS OFFICE.
READY, BUFFY?
"YEAH. BUT WE WALK. NO PORTALS."
Stardust Drive In
BUFFY?
WAS WORRIED YOU ALL GOT ATTACKED ALONG THE WAY.

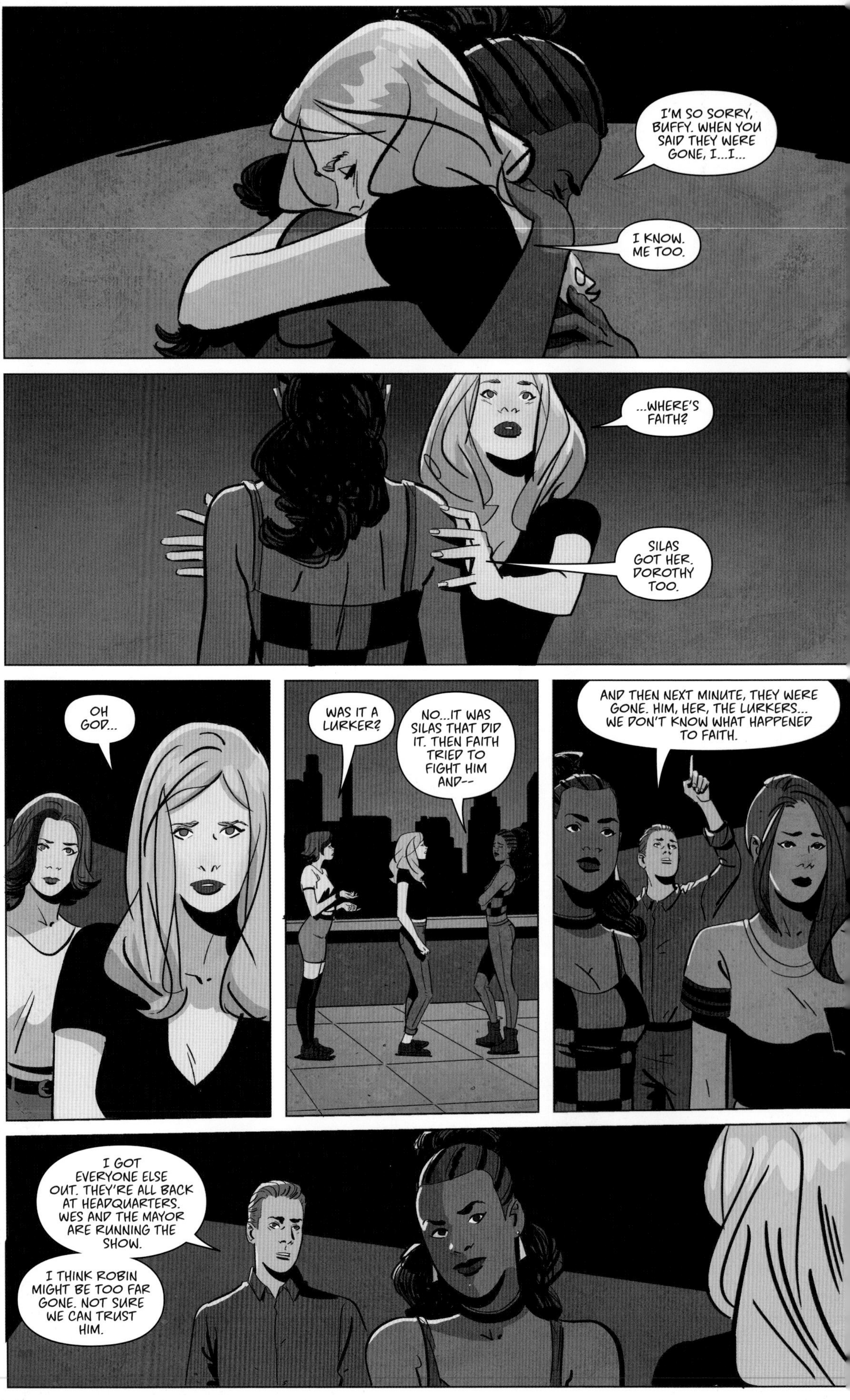
I'M SO SORRY, BUFFY. WHEN YOU SAID THEY WERE GONE, I...I...
I KNOW. ME TOO.
...WHERE'S FAITH?
SILAS GOT HER. DOROTHY TOO.
OH GOD...
WAS IT A LURKER?
NO...IT WAS SILAS THAT DID IT. THEN FAITH TRIED TO FIGHT HIM AND--
AND THEN NEXT MINUTE, THEY WERE GONE. HIM, HER, THE LURKERS... WE DON'T KNOW WHAT HAPPENED TO FAITH.
I GOT EVERYONE ELSE OUT. THEY'RE ALL BACK AT HEADQUARTERS. WES AND THE MAYOR ARE RUNNING THE SHOW.
I THINK ROBIN MIGHT BE TOO FAR GONE. NOT SURE WE CAN TRUST HIM.

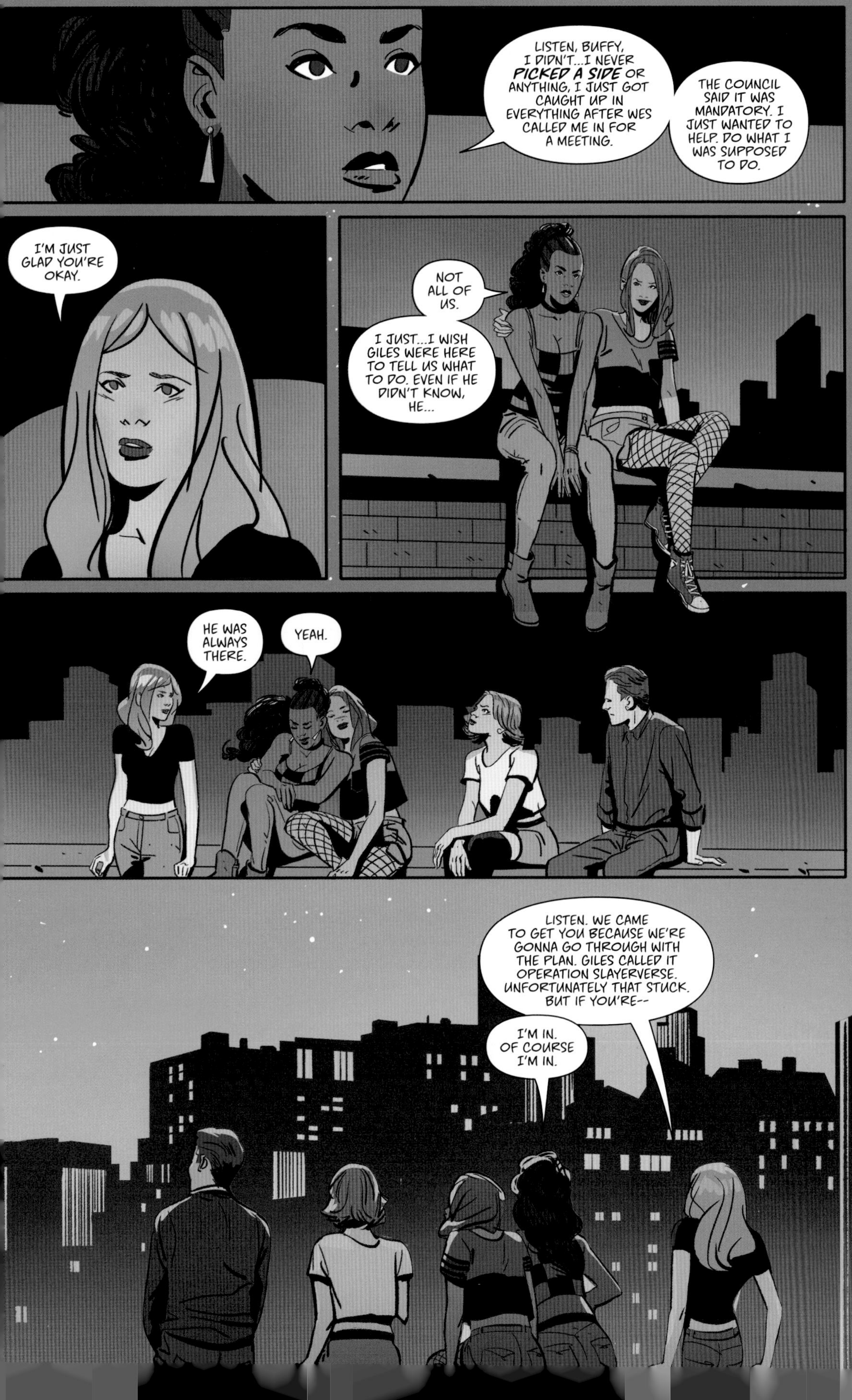
LISTEN, BUFFY, I DIDN'T...I NEVER PICKED A SIDE OR ANYTHING, I JUST GOT CAUGHT UP IN EVERYTHING AFTER WES CALLED ME IN FOR A MEETING.
THE COUNCIL SAID IT WAS MANDATORY. I JUST WANTED TO HELP. DO WHAT I WAS SUPPOSED TO DO.
I'M JUST GLAD YOU'RE OKAY.
NOT ALL OF US.
I JUST...I WISH GILES WERE HERE TO TELL US WHAT TO DO. EVEN IF HE DIDN'T KNOW, HE...
HE WAS ALWAYS THERE.
YEAH.
LISTEN. WE CAME TO GET YOU BECAUSE WE'RE GONNA GO THROUGH WITH THE PLAN. GILES CALLED IT OPERATION SLAYERVERSE. UNFORTUNATELY THAT STUCK. BUT IF YOU'RE--
I'M IN. OF COURSE I'M IN.

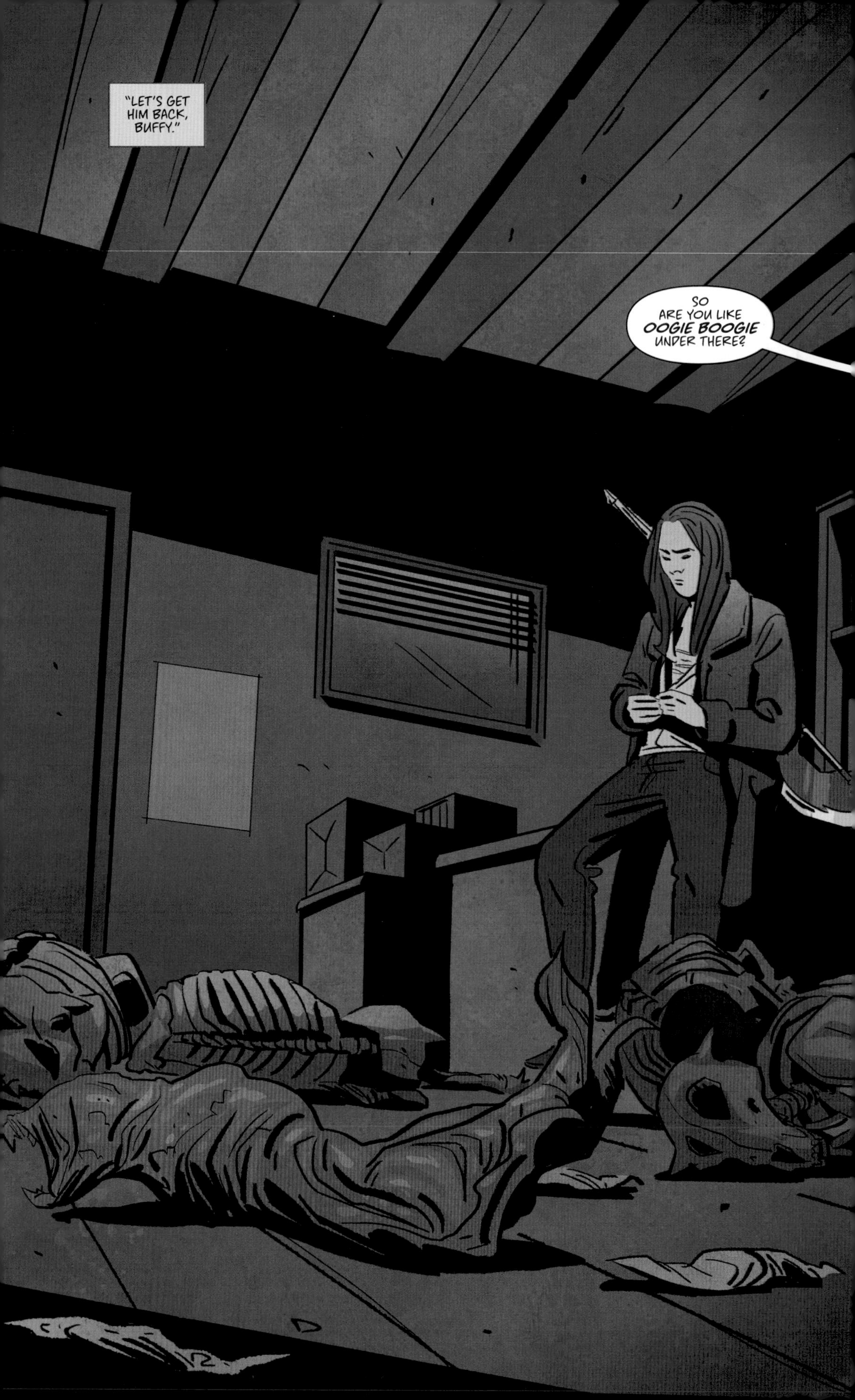
"LET'S GET HIM BACK, BUFFY."
SO ARE YOU LIKE OOGIE BOOGIE UNDER THERE?

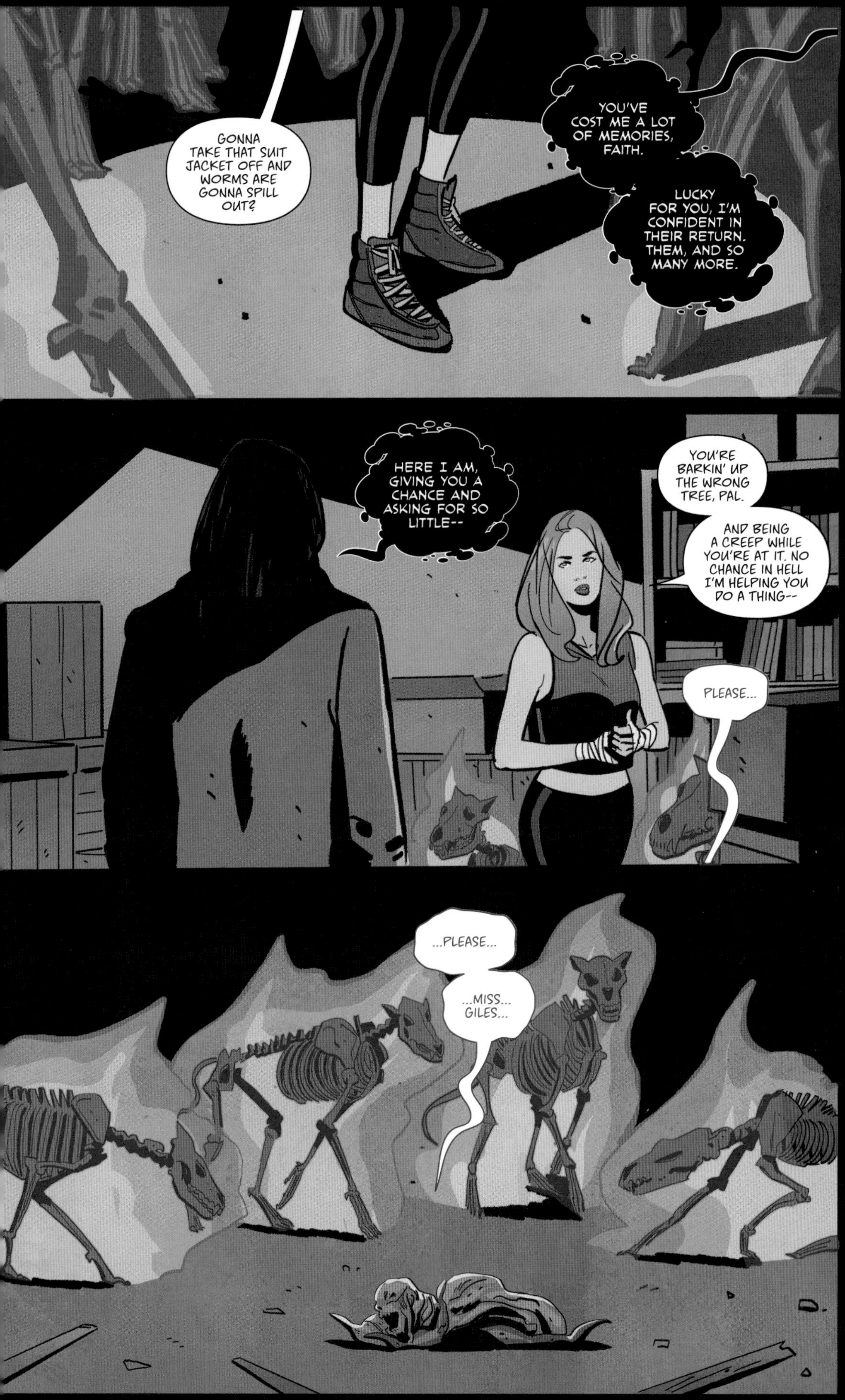
GONNA TAKE THAT SUIT JACKET OFF AND WORMS ARE GONNA SPILL OUT?
YOU'VE COST ME A LOT OF MEMORIES, FAITH.
LUCKY FOR YOU, I'M CONFIDENT IN THEIR RETURN. THEM, AND SO MANY MORE.
HERE I AM, GIVING YOU A CHANCE AND ASKING FOR SO LITTLE--
YOU'RE BARKIN' UP THE WRONG TREE, PAL.
AND BEING A CREEP WHILE YOU'RE AT IT. NO CHANCE IN HELL I'M HELPING YOU DO A THING--
PLEASE...
...PLEASE...
...MISS... GILES...

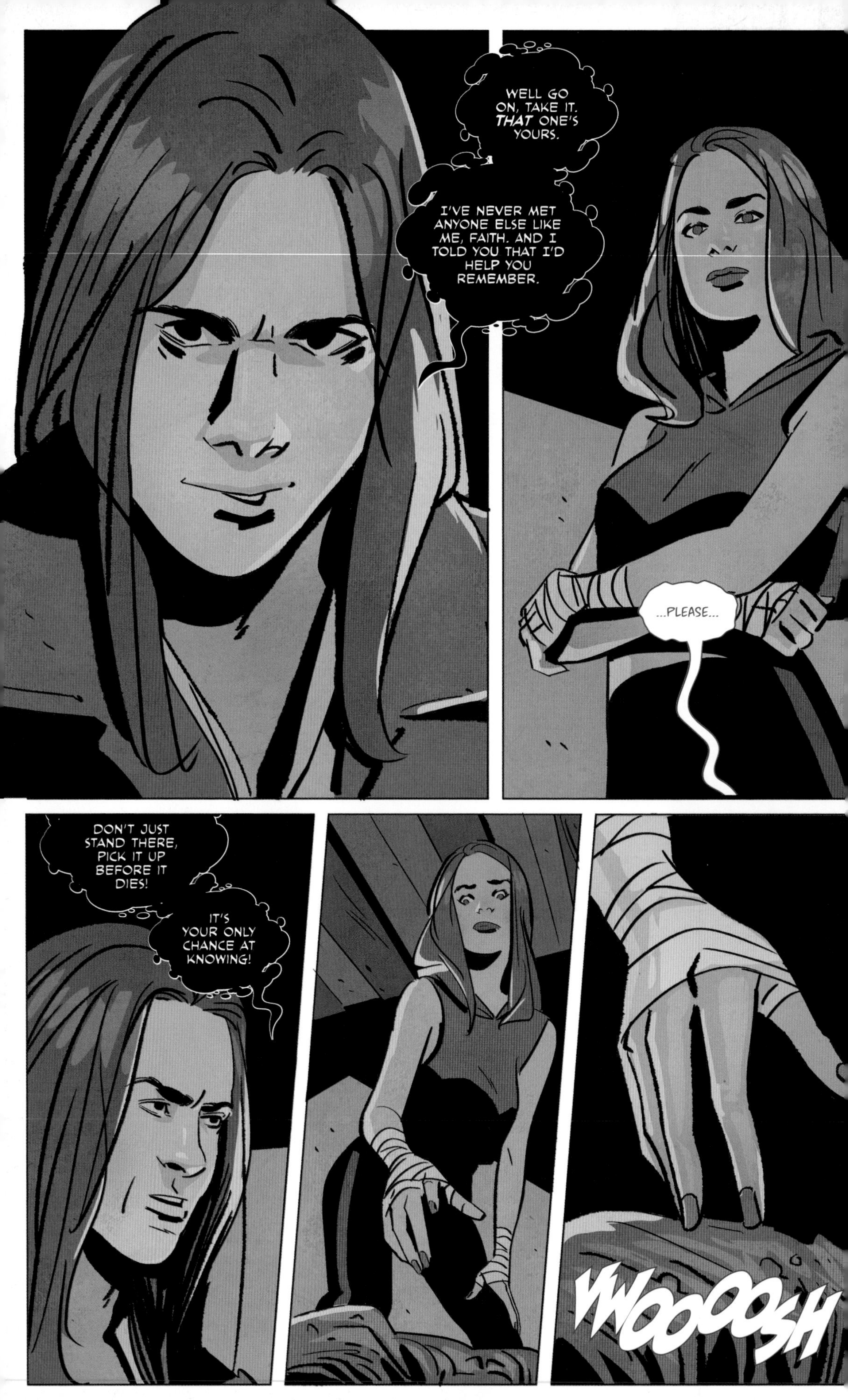
WELL GO ON, TAKE IT. *THAT* ONE'S YOURS.
I'VE NEVER MET ANYONE ELSE LIKE ME, FAITH. AND I TOLD YOU THAT I'D HELP YOU REMEMBER.
...PLEASE...
DON'T JUST STAND THERE, PICK IT UP BEFORE IT DIES!
IT'S YOUR ONLY CHANCE AT KNOWING!
WHOOOOSH

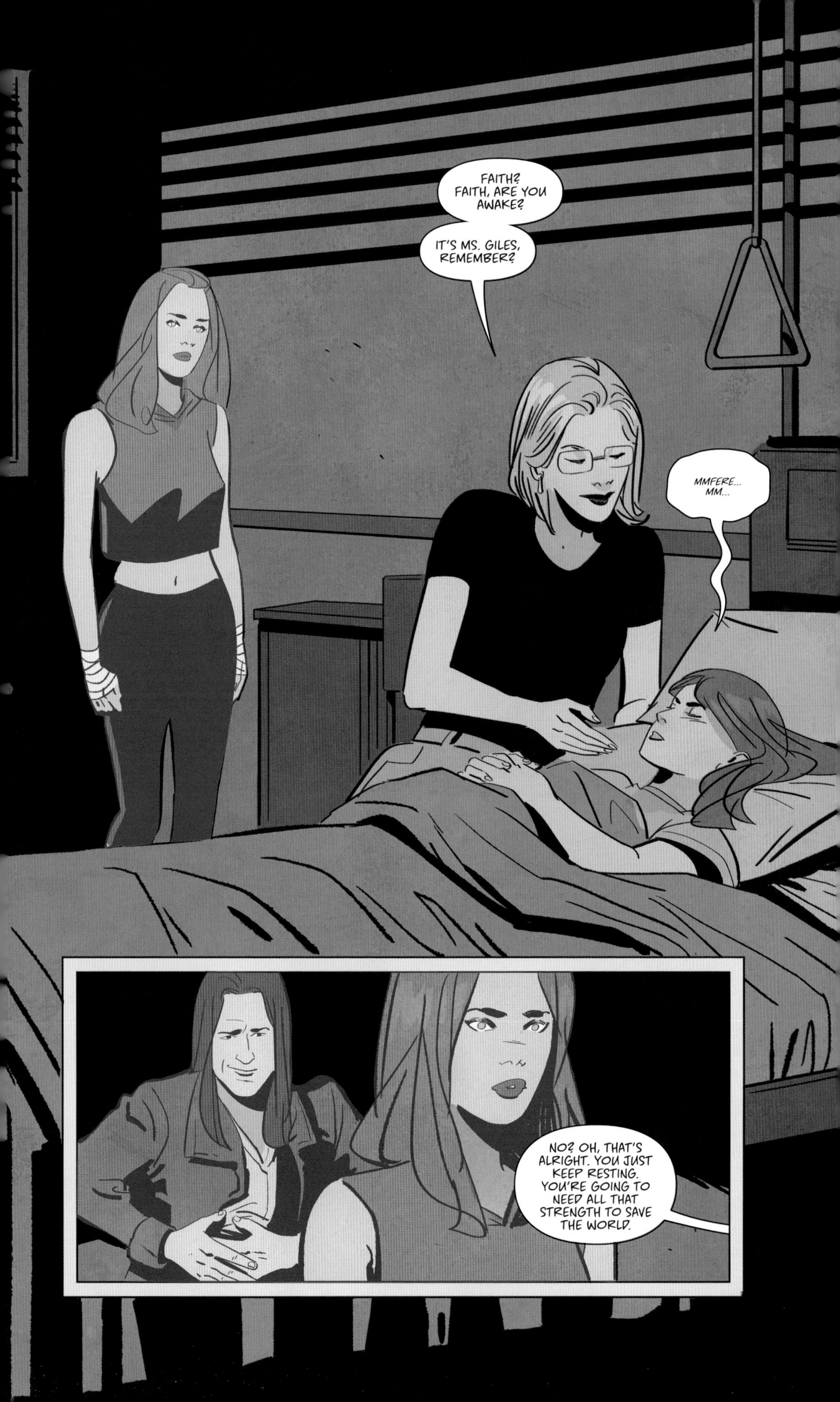

FAITH? FAITH, ARE YOU AWAKE?
IT'S MS. GILES, REMEMBER?
MMFERE... MM...
NO? OH, THAT'S ALRIGHT. YOU JUST KEEP RESTING. YOU'RE GOING TO NEED ALL THAT STRENGTH TO SAVE THE WORLD.

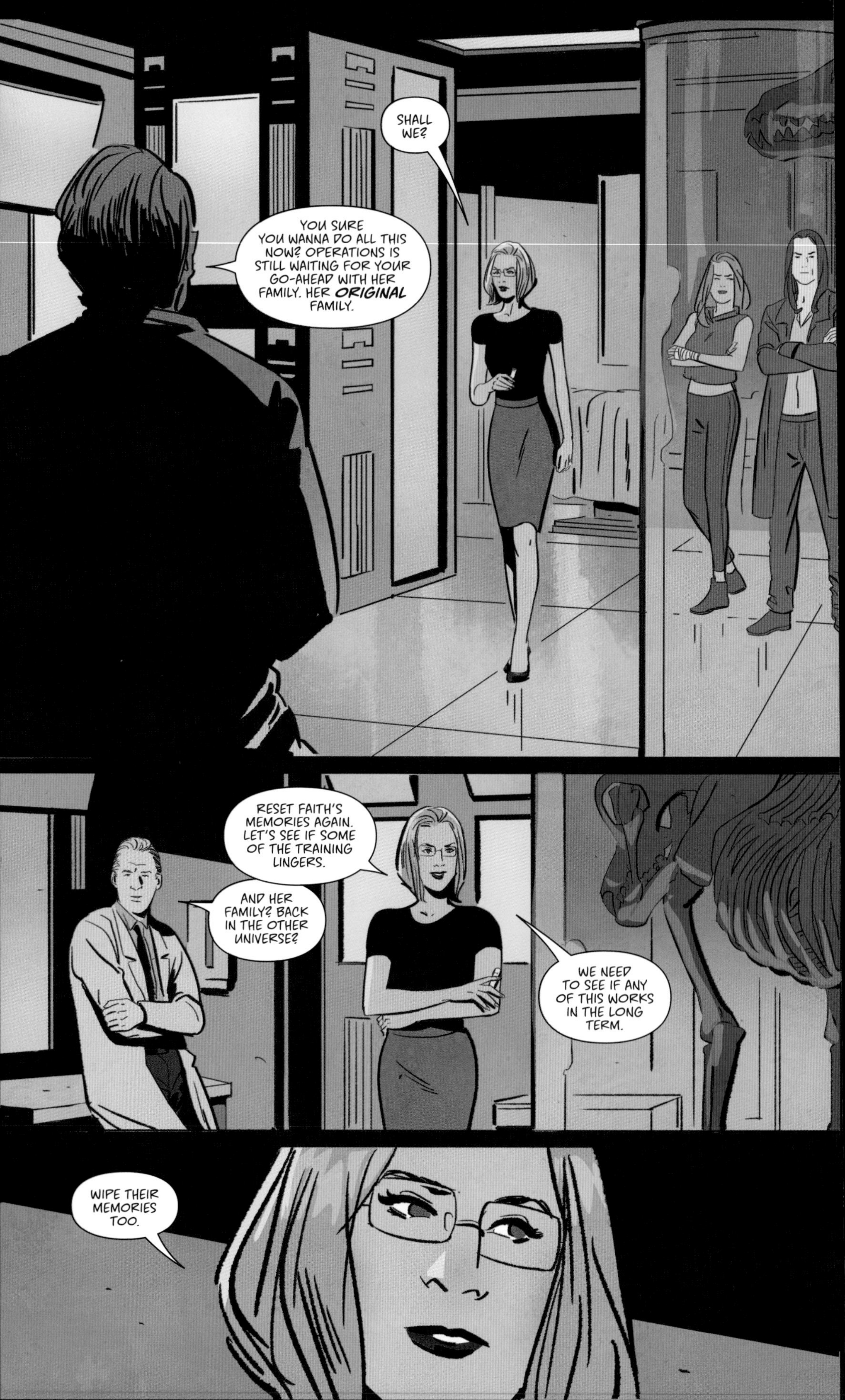
SHALL WE?
YOU SURE YOU WANNA DO ALL THIS NOW? OPERATIONS IS STILL WAITING FOR YOUR GO-AHEAD WITH HER FAMILY. HER ***ORIGINAL*** FAMILY.
RESET FAITH'S MEMORIES AGAIN. LET'S SEE IF SOME OF THE TRAINING LINGERS.
AND HER FAMILY? BACK IN THE OTHER UNIVERSE?
WE NEED TO SEE IF ANY OF THIS WORKS IN THE LONG TERM.
WIPE THEIR MEMORIES TOO.

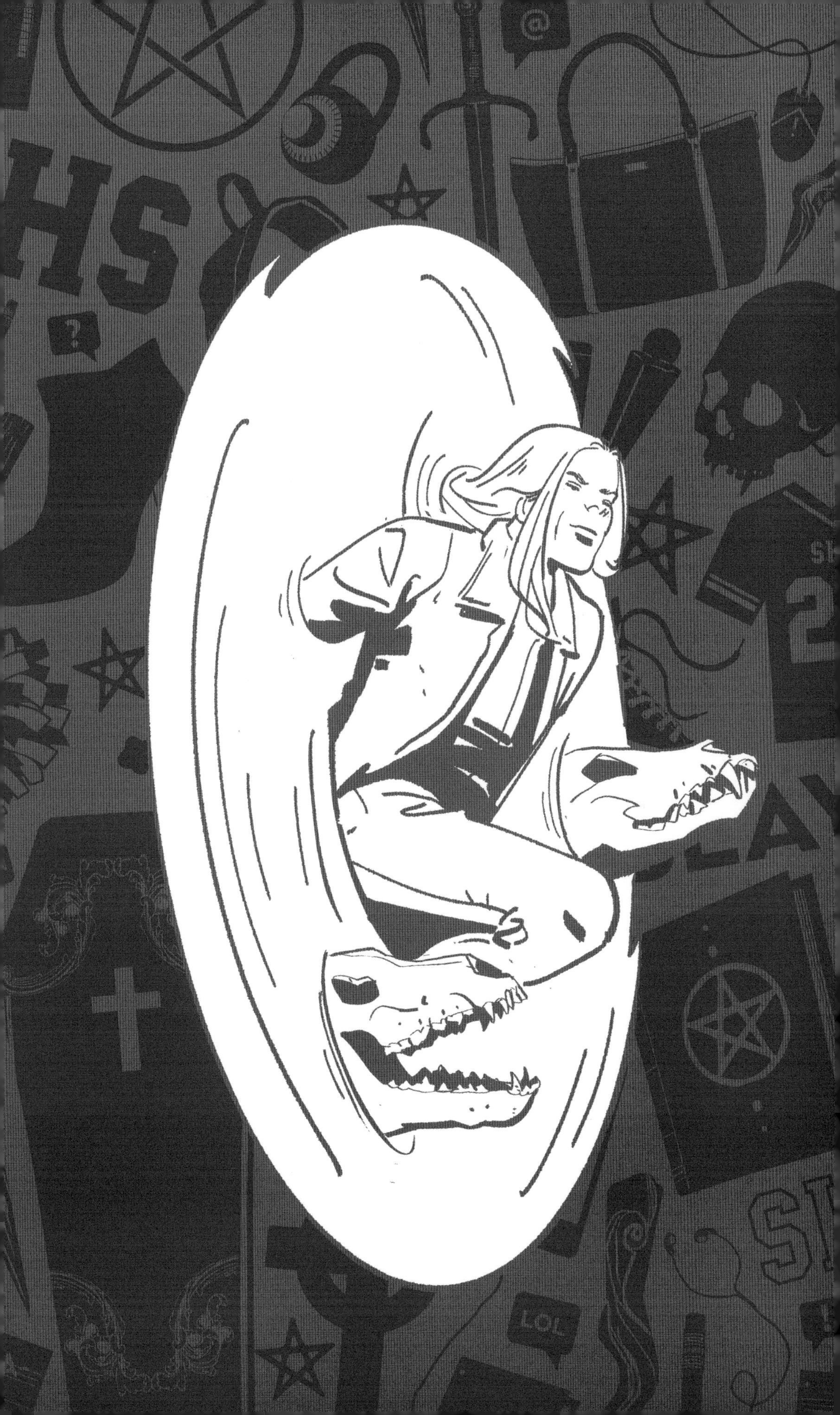
LOL

CHAPTER THIRTY-ONE

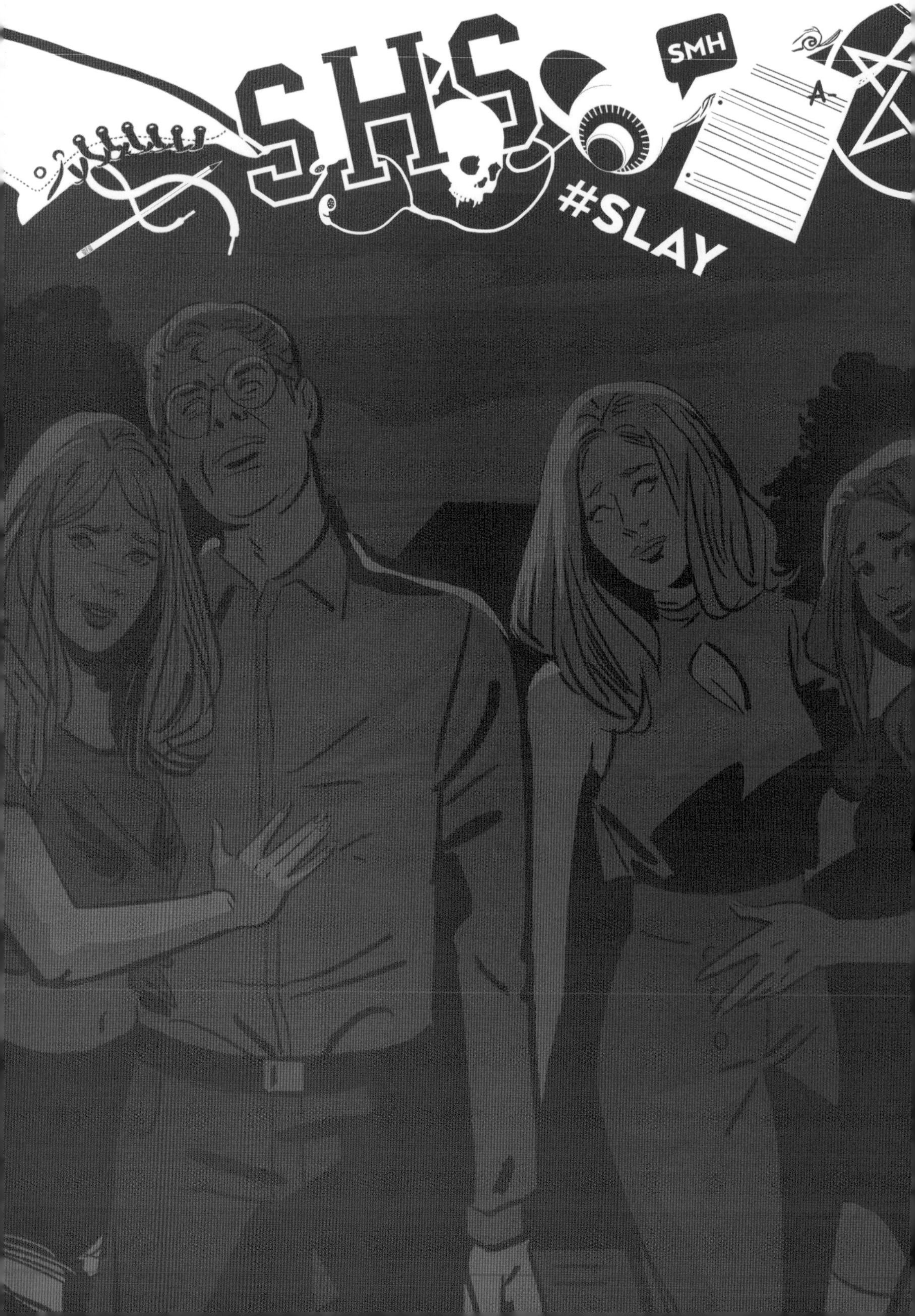
S.H.S.
SMH
#SLAY

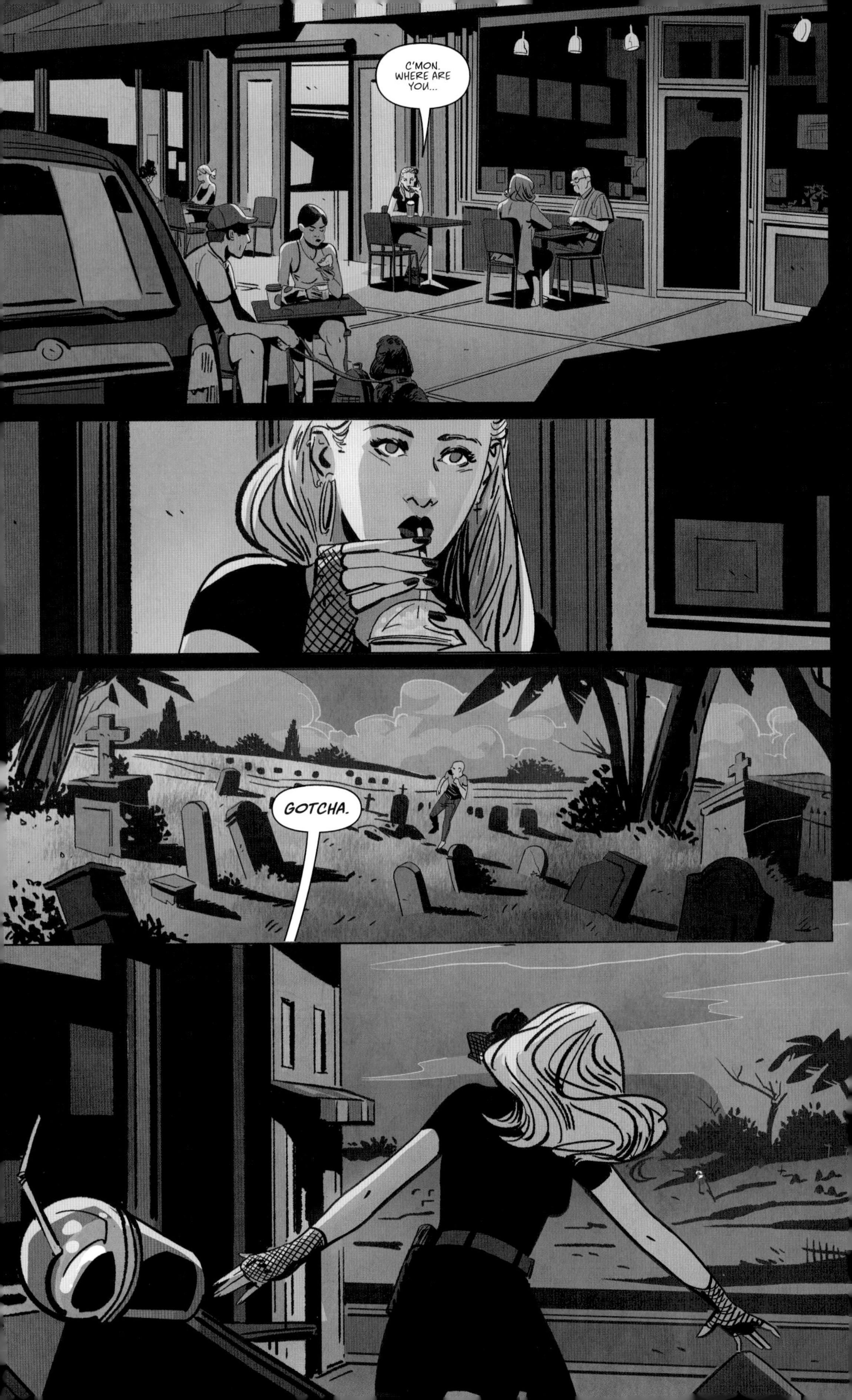
C'MON. WHERE ARE YOU...
GOTCHA.

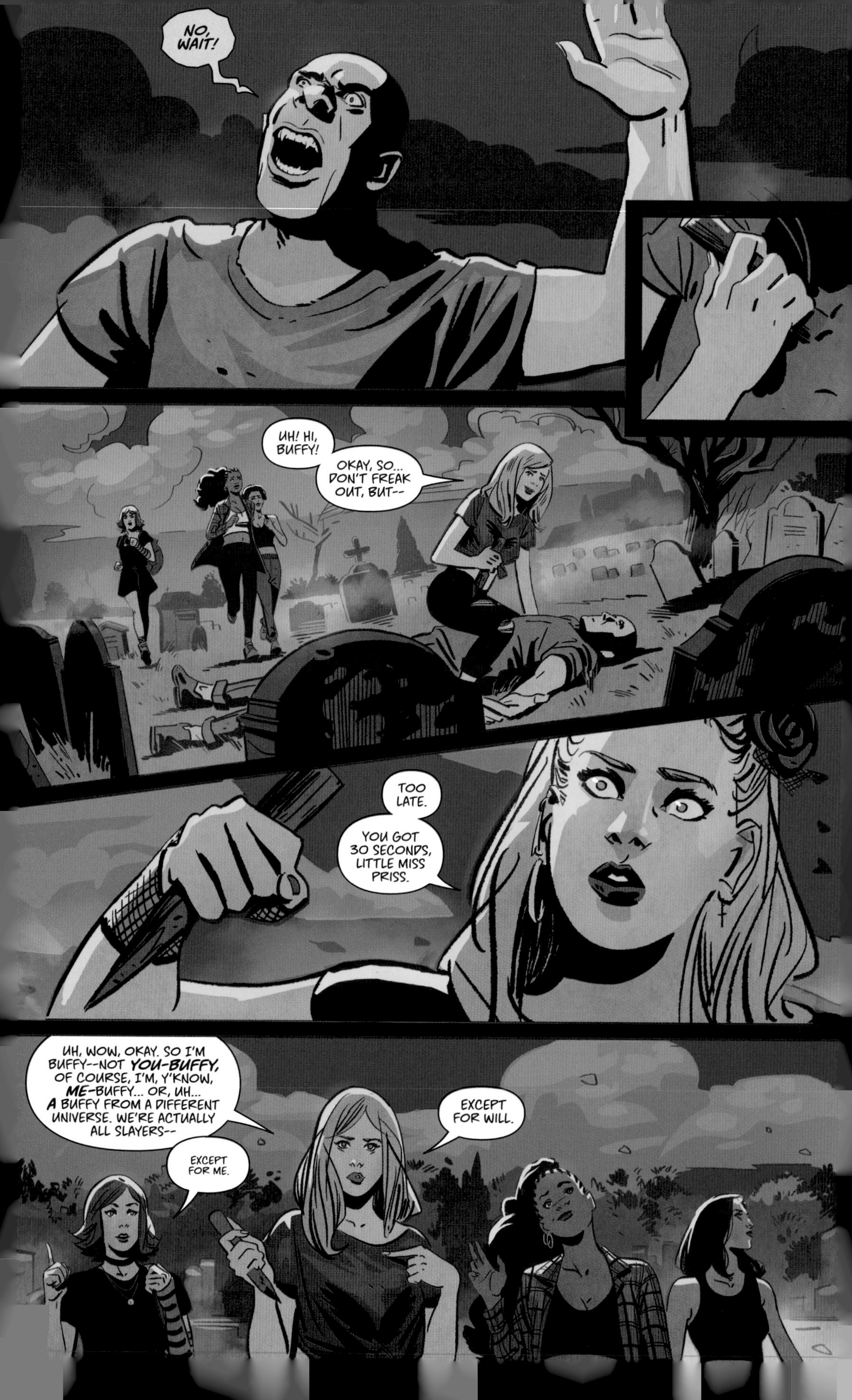
NO, WAIT!
UH! HI, BUFFY!
OKAY, SO... DON'T FREAK OUT, BUT--
TOO LATE.
YOU GOT 30 SECONDS, LITTLE MISS PRISS.
UH, WOW, OKAY. SO I'M BUFFY--NOT **YOU-BUFFY,** OF COURSE, I'M, Y'KNOW, **ME-**BUFFY... OR, UH... **A** BUFFY FROM A DIFFERENT UNIVERSE. WE'RE ACTUALLY ALL SLAYERS--
EXCEPT FOR ME.
EXCEPT FOR WILL.

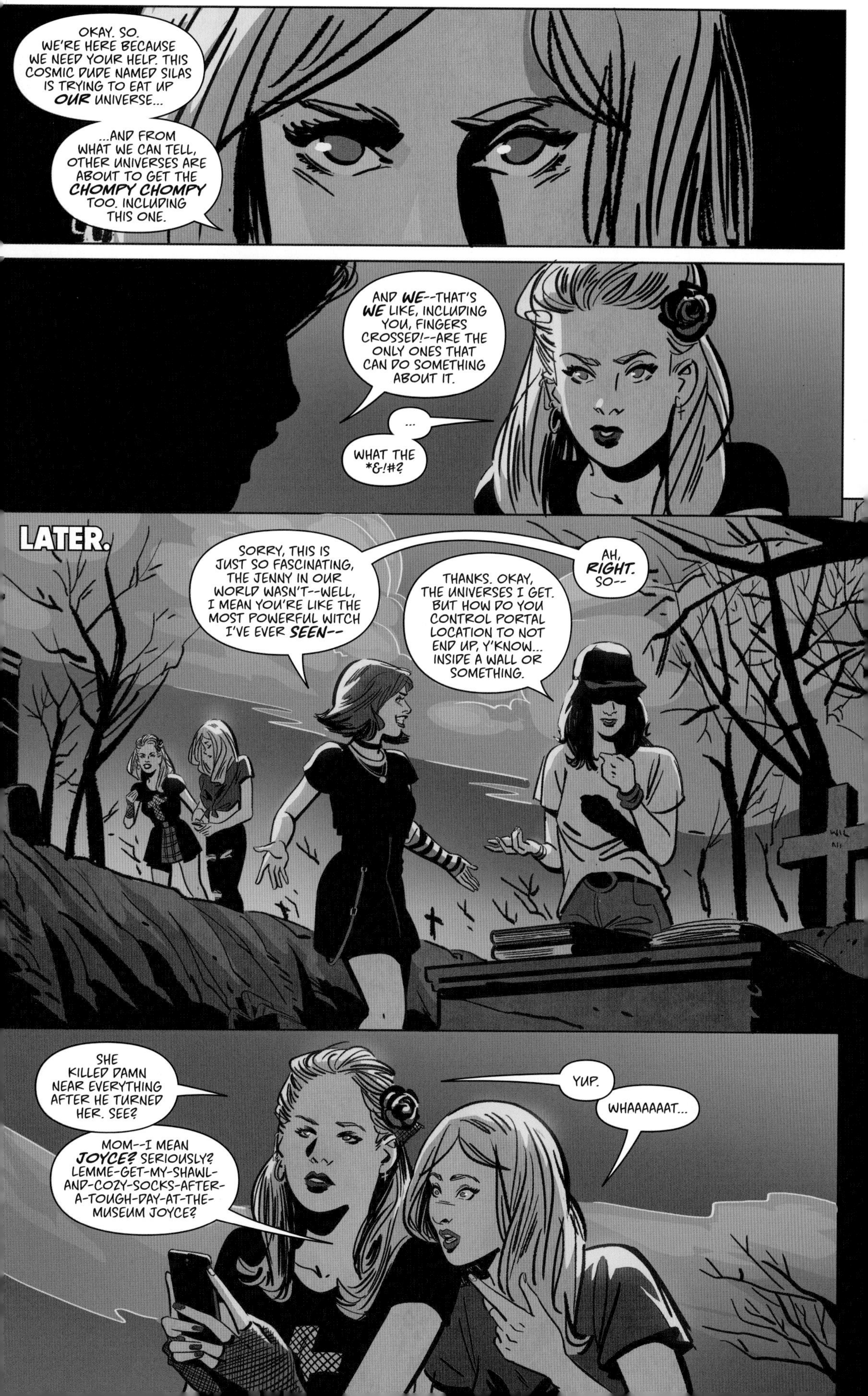
OKAY. SO. WE'RE HERE BECAUSE WE NEED YOUR HELP. THIS COSMIC DUDE NAMED SILAS IS TRYING TO EAT UP OUR UNIVERSE...
...AND FROM WHAT WE CAN TELL, OTHER UNIVERSES ARE ABOUT TO GET THE CHOMPY CHOMPY TOO. INCLUDING THIS ONE.
AND WE--THAT'S WE LIKE, INCLUDING YOU, FINGERS CROSSED!--ARE THE ONLY ONES THAT CAN DO SOMETHING ABOUT IT.
...
WHAT THE *&!#?
LATER.
SORRY, THIS IS JUST SO FASCINATING, THE JENNY IN OUR WORLD WASN'T--WELL, I MEAN YOU'RE LIKE THE MOST POWERFUL WITCH I'VE EVER SEEN--
AH, RIGHT. SO--
THANKS. OKAY, THE UNIVERSES I GET. BUT HOW DO YOU CONTROL PORTAL LOCATION TO NOT END UP, Y'KNOW... INSIDE A WALL OR SOMETHING.
SHE KILLED DAMN NEAR EVERYTHING AFTER HE TURNED HER. SEE?
MOM--I MEAN JOYCE? SERIOUSLY? LEMME-GET-MY-SHAWL-AND-COZY-SOCKS-AFTER-A-TOUGH-DAY-AT-THE-MUSEUM JOYCE?
YUP.
WHAAAAAAT...

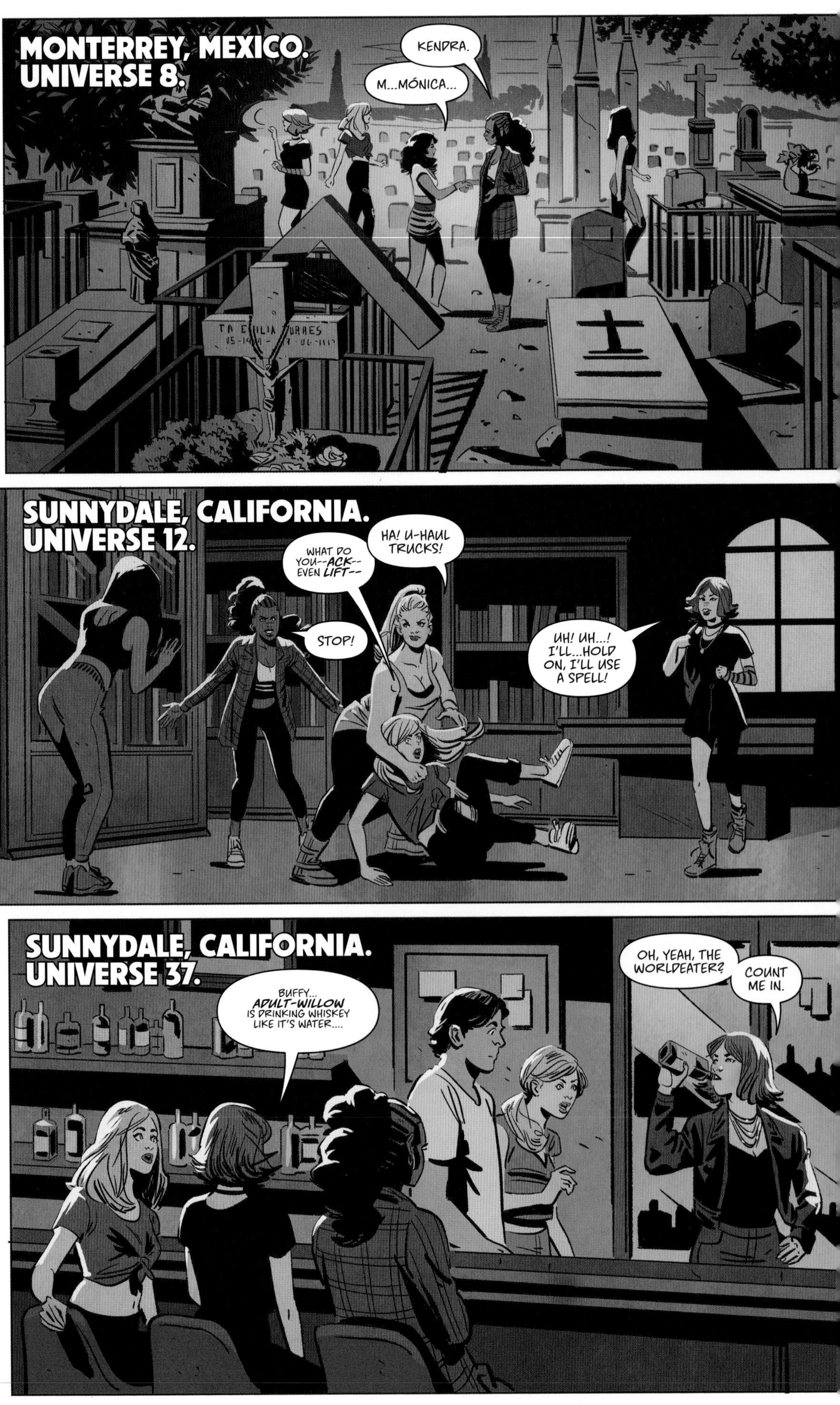
MONTERREY, MEXICO. UNIVERSE 8.
M...MÓNICA...
KENDRA.
SUNNYDALE, CALIFORNIA. UNIVERSE 12.
WHAT DO YOU--ACK--EVEN LIFT--
HA! U-HAUL TRUCKS!
STOP!
UH! UH...! I'LL...HOLD ON, I'LL USE A SPELL!
SUNNYDALE, CALIFORNIA. UNIVERSE 37.
BUFFY... ADULT-WILLOW IS DRINKING WHISKEY LIKE IT'S WATER....
OH, YEAH, THE WORLDEATER?
COUNT ME IN.

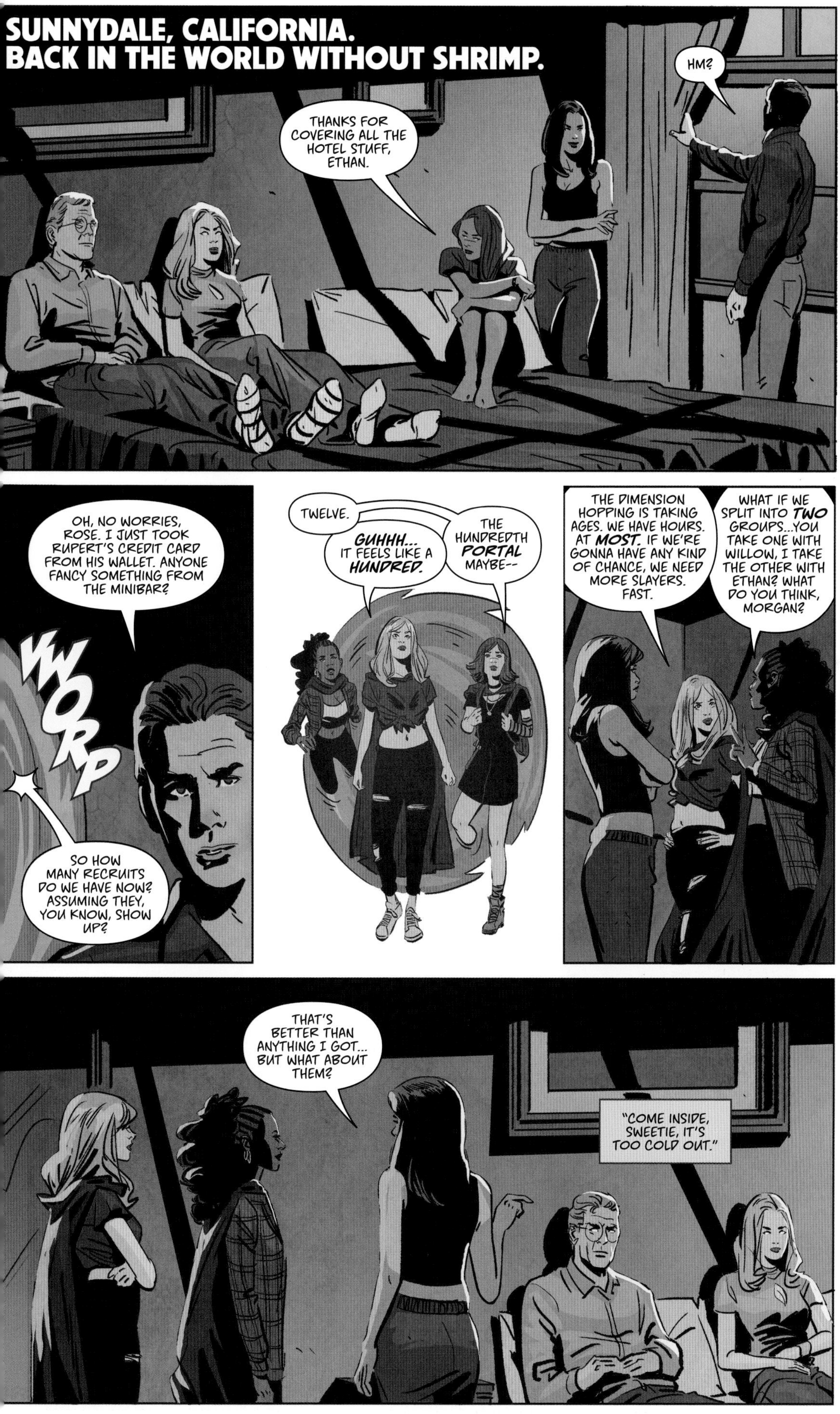
SUNNYDALE, CALIFORNIA.
BACK IN THE WORLD WITHOUT SHRIMP.
THANKS FOR COVERING ALL THE HOTEL STUFF, ETHAN.
HM?
OH, NO WORRIES, ROSE. I JUST TOOK RUPERT'S CREDIT CARD FROM HIS WALLET. ANYONE FANCY SOMETHING FROM THE MINIBAR?
WORP
SO HOW MANY RECRUITS DO WE HAVE NOW? ASSUMING THEY, YOU KNOW, SHOW UP?
TWELVE.
GUHHH... IT FEELS LIKE A HUNDRED.
THE HUNDREDTH PORTAL MAYBE--
THE DIMENSION HOPPING IS TAKING AGES. WE HAVE HOURS. AT MOST. IF WE'RE GONNA HAVE ANY KIND OF CHANCE, WE NEED MORE SLAYERS. FAST.
WHAT IF WE SPLIT INTO TWO GROUPS...YOU TAKE ONE WITH WILLOW, I TAKE THE OTHER WITH ETHAN? WHAT DO YOU THINK, MORGAN?
THAT'S BETTER THAN ANYTHING I GOT... BUT WHAT ABOUT THEM?
"COME INSIDE, SWEETIE, IT'S TOO COLD OUT."

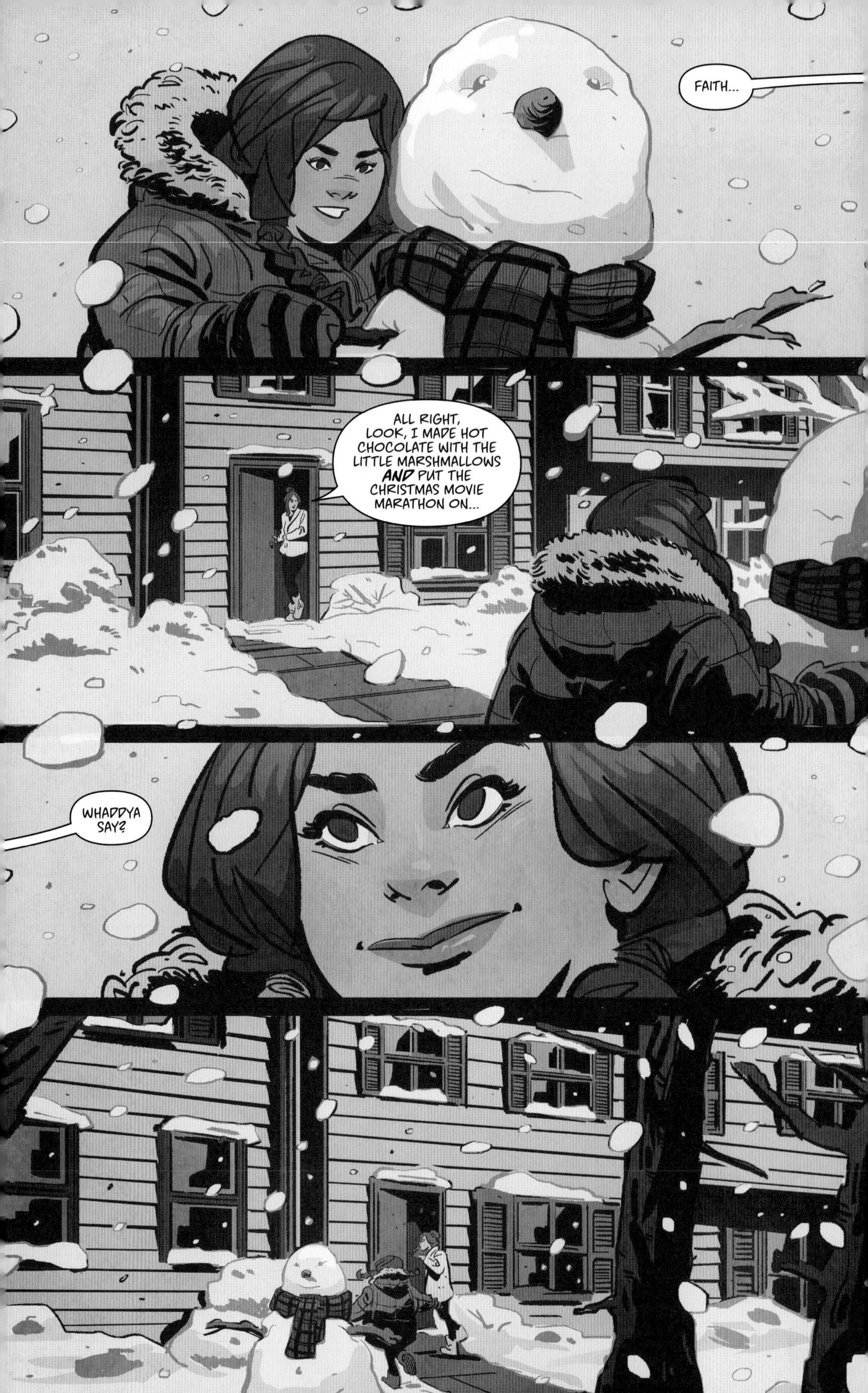
FAITH...
ALL RIGHT, LOOK, I MADE HOT CHOCOLATE WITH THE LITTLE MARSHMALLOWS **AND** PUT THE CHRISTMAS MOVIE MARATHON ON...
WHADDYA SAY?

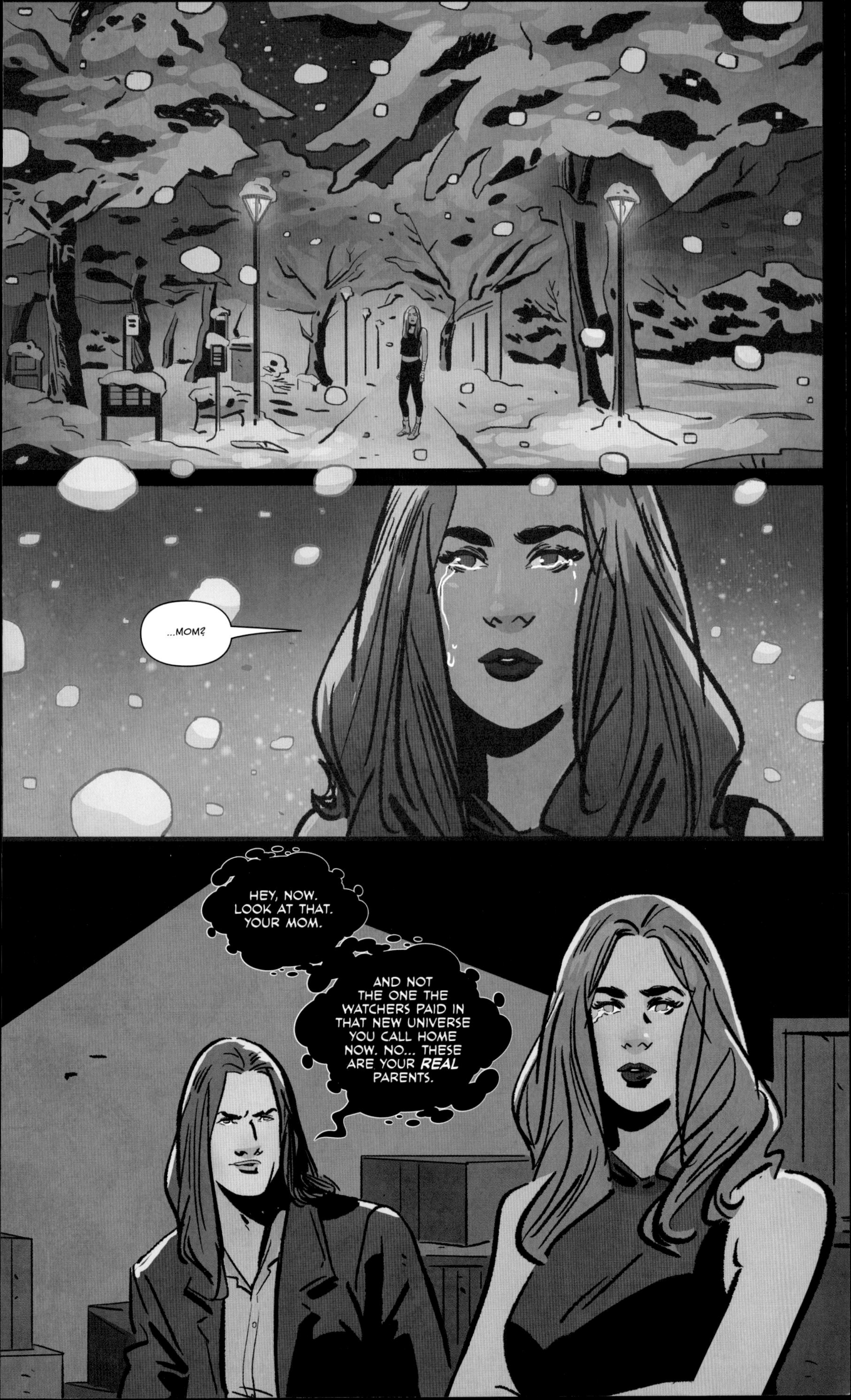
...MOM?
HEY, NOW. LOOK AT THAT. YOUR MOM.
AND NOT THE ONE THE WATCHERS PAID IN THAT NEW UNIVERSE YOU CALL HOME NOW. NO... THESE ARE YOUR *REAL* PARENTS.

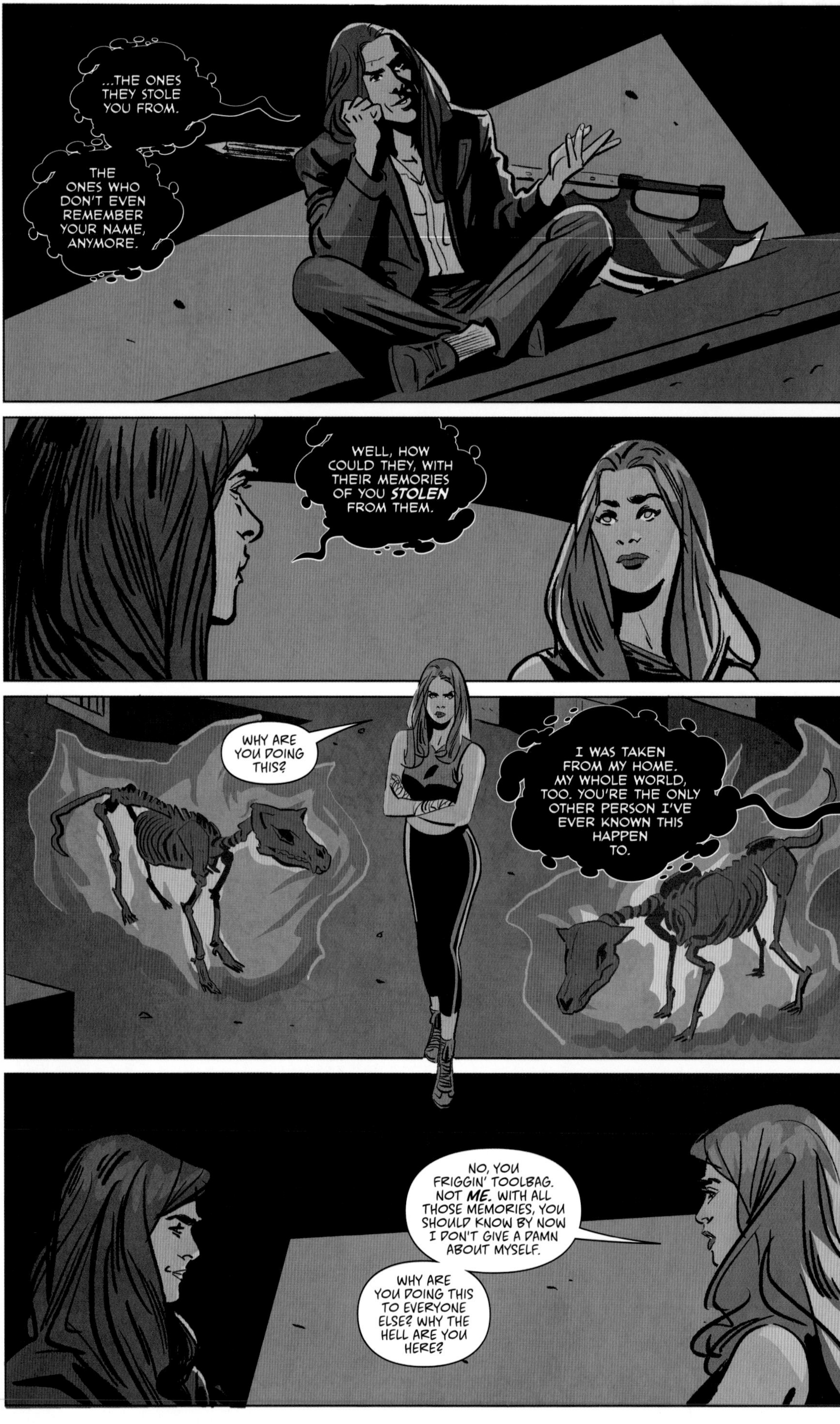
...THE ONES THEY STOLE YOU FROM.
THE ONES WHO DON'T EVEN REMEMBER YOUR NAME, ANYMORE.
WELL, HOW COULD THEY, WITH THEIR MEMORIES OF YOU *STOLEN* FROM THEM.
WHY ARE YOU DOING THIS?
I WAS TAKEN FROM MY HOME. MY WHOLE WORLD, TOO. YOU'RE THE ONLY OTHER PERSON I'VE EVER KNOWN THIS HAPPEN TO.
NO, YOU FRIGGIN' TOOLBAG. NOT *ME.* WITH ALL THOSE MEMORIES, YOU SHOULD KNOW BY NOW I DON'T GIVE A DAMN ABOUT MYSELF.
WHY ARE YOU DOING THIS TO EVERYONE ELSE? WHY THE HELL ARE YOU HERE?

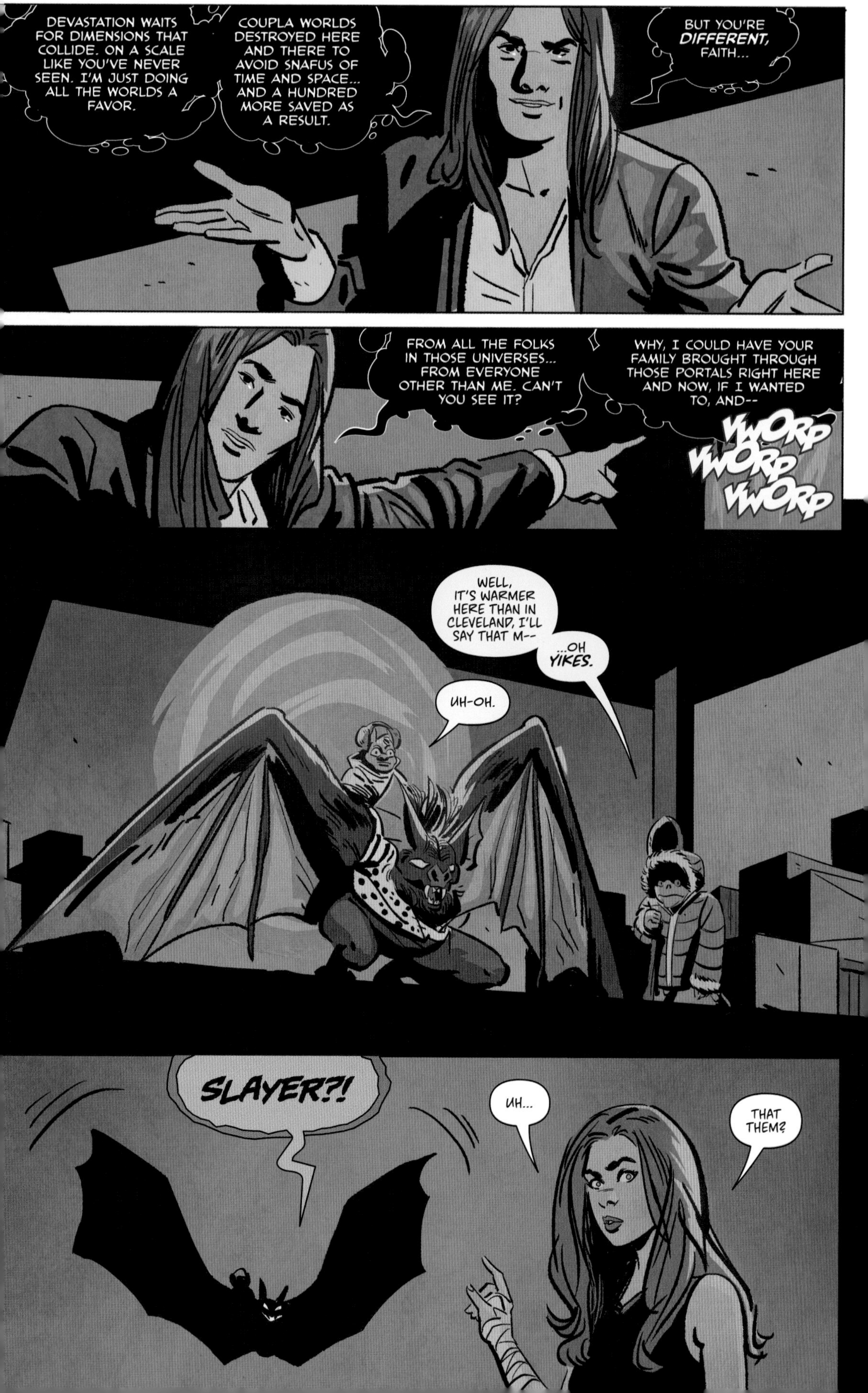
DEVASTATION WAITS FOR DIMENSIONS THAT COLLIDE. ON A SCALE LIKE YOU'VE NEVER SEEN. I'M JUST DOING ALL THE WORLDS A FAVOR.
COUPLA WORLDS DESTROYED HERE AND THERE TO AVOID SNAFUS OF TIME AND SPACE... AND A HUNDRED MORE SAVED AS A RESULT.
BUT YOU'RE DIFFERENT, FAITH...
FROM ALL THE FOLKS IN THOSE UNIVERSES... FROM EVERYONE OTHER THAN ME. CAN'T YOU SEE IT?
WHY, I COULD HAVE YOUR FAMILY BROUGHT THROUGH THOSE PORTALS RIGHT HERE AND NOW, IF I WANTED TO, AND--
VWORP VWORP VWORP
WELL, IT'S WARMER HERE THAN IN CLEVELAND, I'LL SAY THAT M--
...OH YIKES.
UH-OH.
SLAYER?!
UH...
THAT THEM?

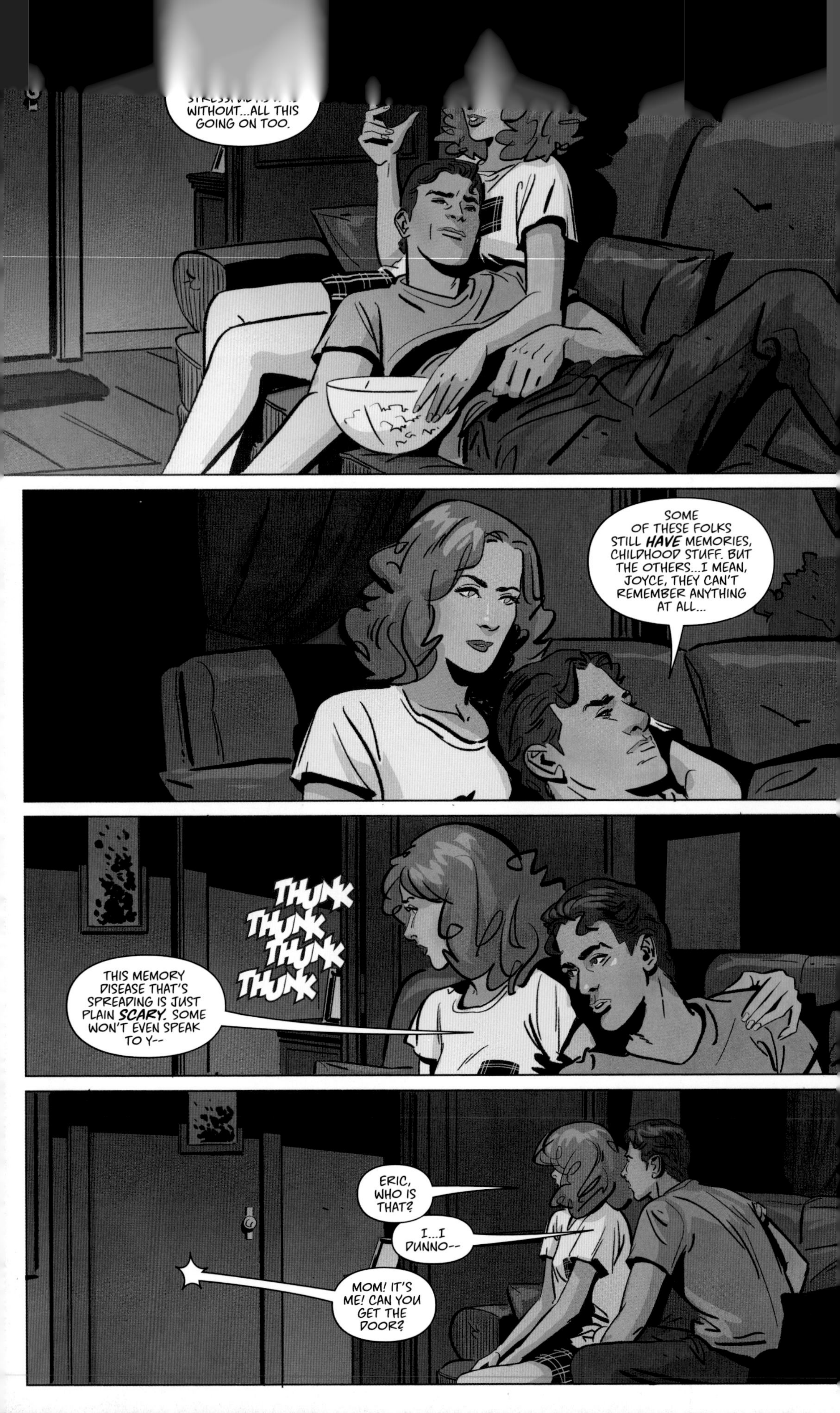
WITHOUT...ALL THIS GOING ON TOO.
SOME OF THESE FOLKS STILL HAVE MEMORIES, CHILDHOOD STUFF. BUT THE OTHERS...I MEAN, JOYCE, THEY CAN'T REMEMBER ANYTHING AT ALL...
THUNK THUNK THUNK THUNK
THIS MEMORY DISEASE THAT'S SPREADING IS JUST PLAIN SCARY. SOME WON'T EVEN SPEAK TO Y--
ERIC, WHO IS THAT?
I...I DUNNO--
MOM! IT'S ME! CAN YOU GET THE DOOR?

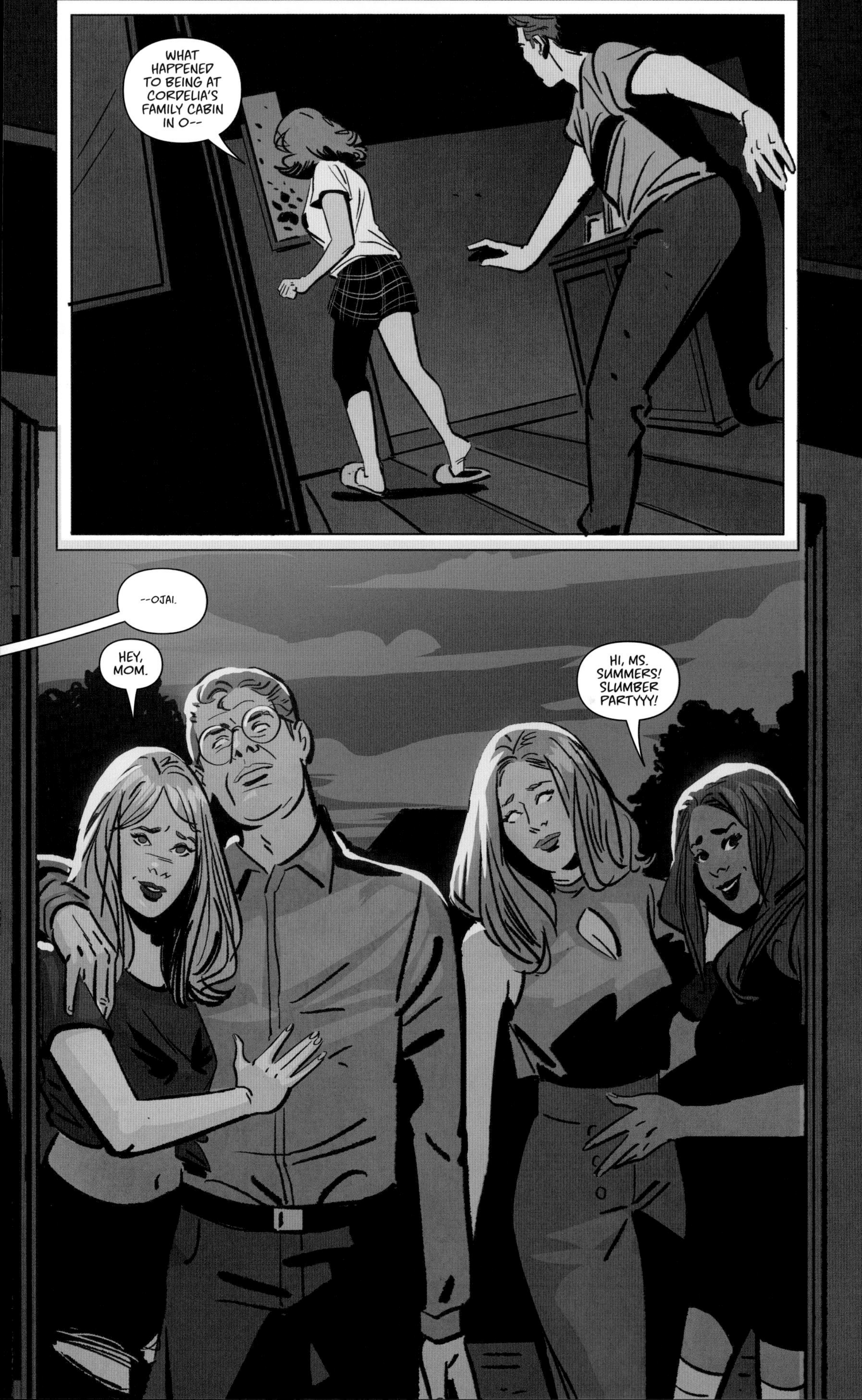
WHAT HAPPENED TO BEING AT CORDELIA'S FAMILY CABIN IN O--
--OJAI.
HEY, MOM.
HI, MS. SUMMERS! SLUMBER PARTYYY!

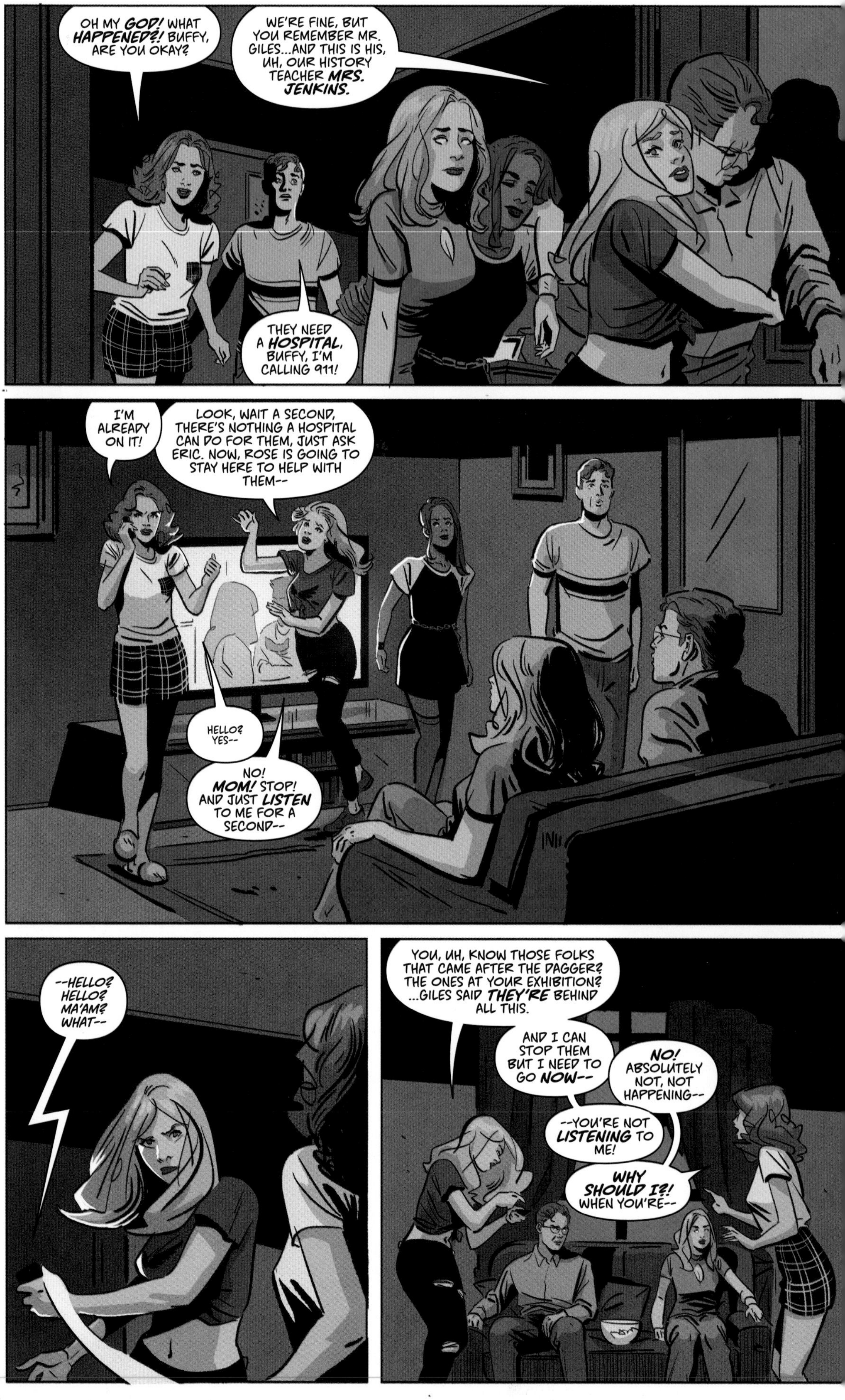
OH MY GOD! WHAT HAPPENED?! BUFFY, ARE YOU OKAY?
WE'RE FINE, BUT YOU REMEMBER MR. GILES...AND THIS IS HIS, UH, OUR HISTORY TEACHER MRS. JENKINS.
THEY NEED A HOSPITAL, BUFFY, I'M CALLING 911!
I'M ALREADY ON IT!
LOOK, WAIT A SECOND, THERE'S NOTHING A HOSPITAL CAN DO FOR THEM, JUST ASK ERIC. NOW, ROSE IS GOING TO STAY HERE TO HELP WITH THEM--
HELLO? YES--
NO! MOM! STOP! AND JUST LISTEN TO ME FOR A SECOND--
--HELLO? HELLO? MA'AM? WHAT--
YOU, UH, KNOW THOSE FOLKS THAT CAME AFTER THE DAGGER? THE ONES AT YOUR EXHIBITION? ...GILES SAID THEY'RE BEHIND ALL THIS.
AND I CAN STOP THEM BUT I NEED TO GO NOW--
NO! ABSOLUTELY NOT, NOT HAPPENING--
--YOU'RE NOT LISTENING TO ME!
WHY SHOULD I?! WHEN YOU'RE--

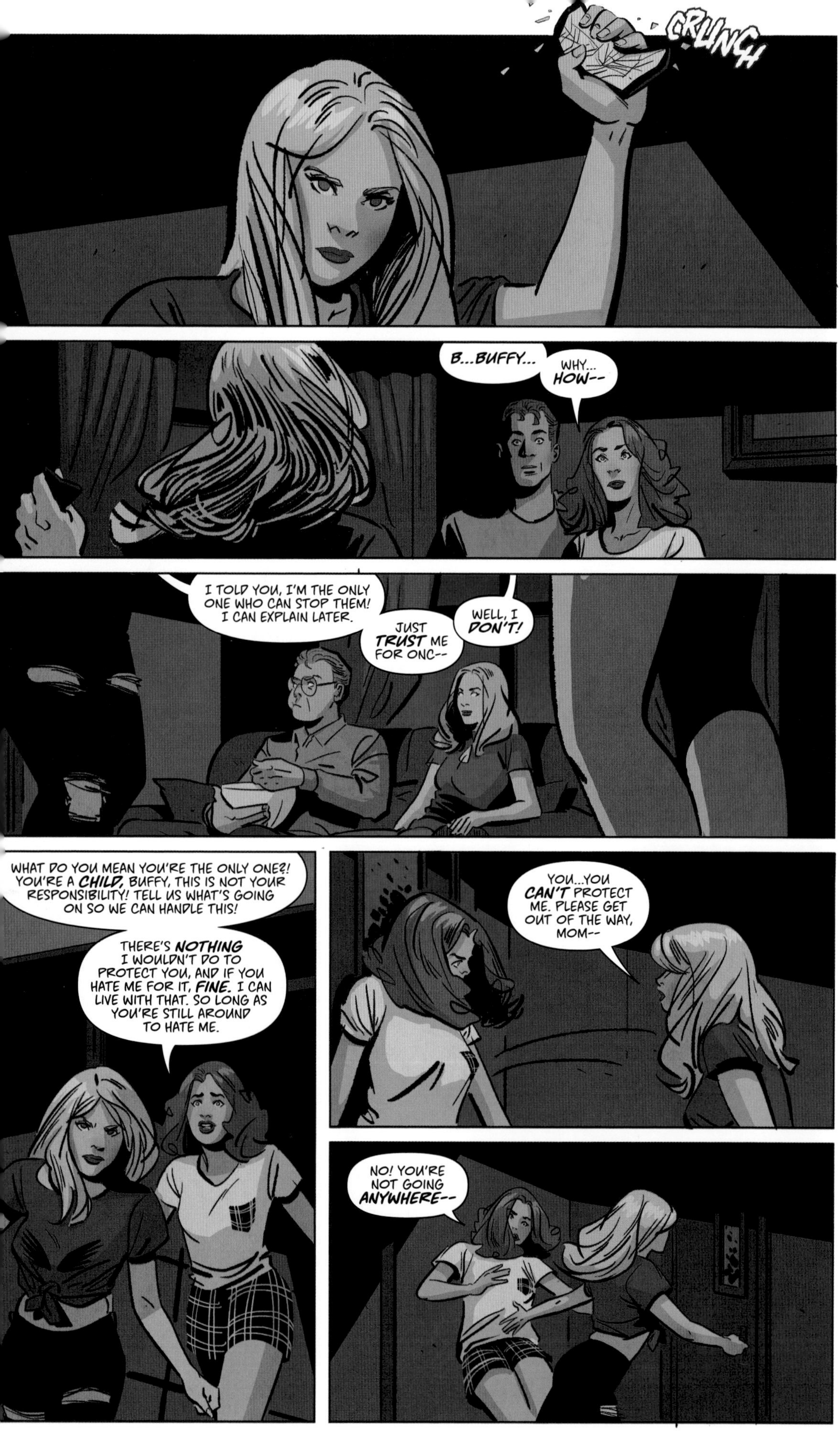
CRUNCH
B...BUFFY...
WHY... HOW--
I TOLD YOU, I'M THE ONLY ONE WHO CAN STOP THEM! I CAN EXPLAIN LATER.
JUST TRUST ME FOR ONC--
WELL, I DON'T!
WHAT DO YOU MEAN YOU'RE THE ONLY ONE?! YOU'RE A CHILD, BUFFY, THIS IS NOT YOUR RESPONSIBILITY! TELL US WHAT'S GOING ON SO WE CAN HANDLE THIS!
THERE'S NOTHING I WOULDN'T DO TO PROTECT YOU, AND IF YOU HATE ME FOR IT, FINE. I CAN LIVE WITH THAT. SO LONG AS YOU'RE STILL AROUND TO HATE ME.
YOU...YOU CAN'T PROTECT ME. PLEASE GET OUT OF THE WAY, MOM--
NO! YOU'RE NOT GOING ANYWHERE--

AGH--

MOM! I'M--

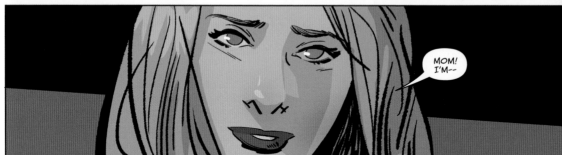

JOYCE!

I'M...I'M OKAY.

YOU KNOW WHAT, BUFFY...FINE. YOU WANT TO DROP ALL THIS ON US AND DISAPPEAR...FINE.

GET THE HELL OUT.

I DIDN'T MEAN TO...

I'M...I'M SORRY.

OH, ERIC, I SHOULDN'T HAVE SAID THAT...I SHOULDN'T HAVE SAID THAT.

C'MON, JOYCE...

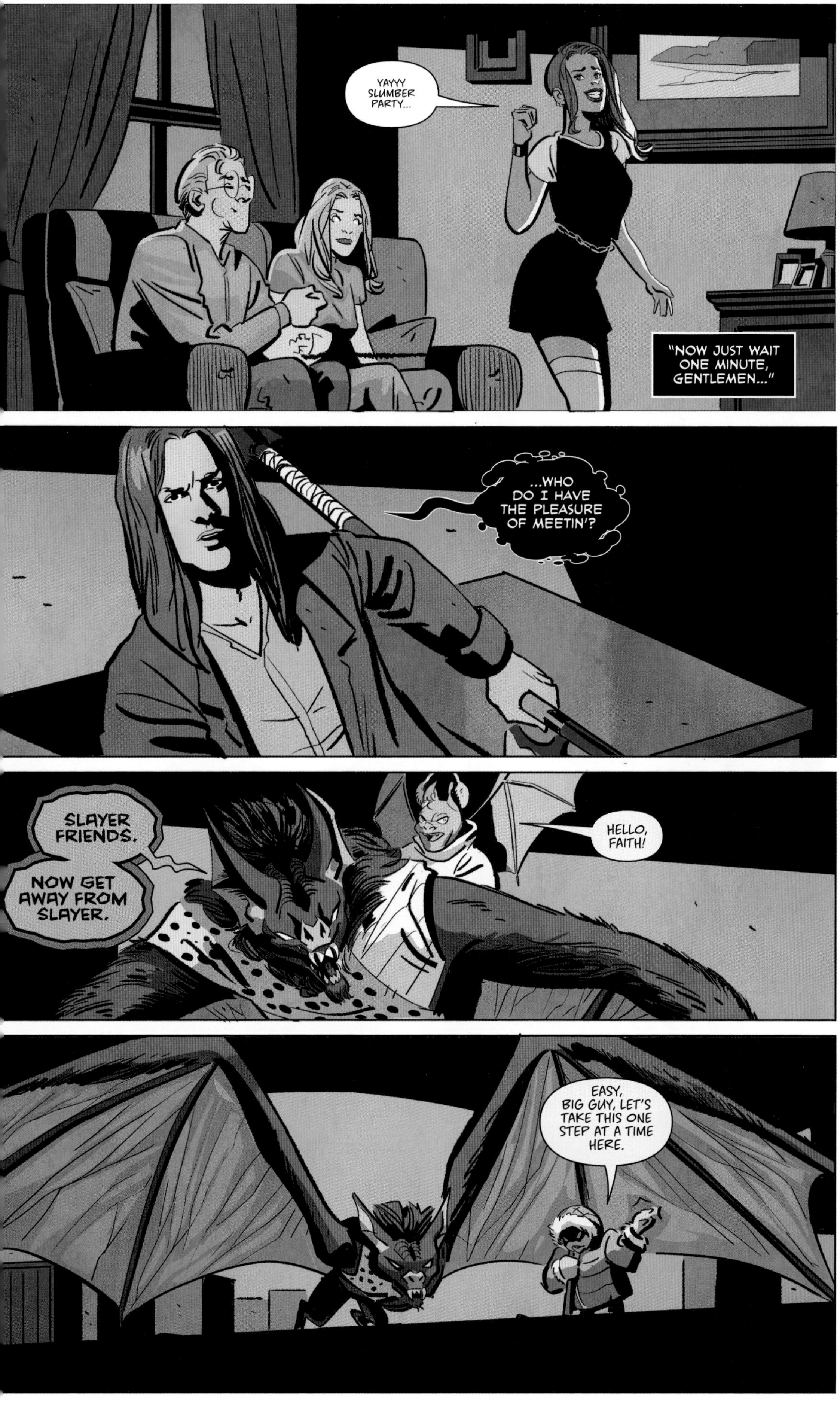
YAYYY SLUMBER PARTY...
"NOW JUST WAIT ONE MINUTE, GENTLEMEN..."
...WHO DO I HAVE THE PLEASURE OF MEETIN'?
SLAYER FRIENDS.
NOW GET AWAY FROM SLAYER.
HELLO, FAITH!
EASY, BIG GUY, LET'S TAKE THIS ONE STEP AT A TIME HERE.

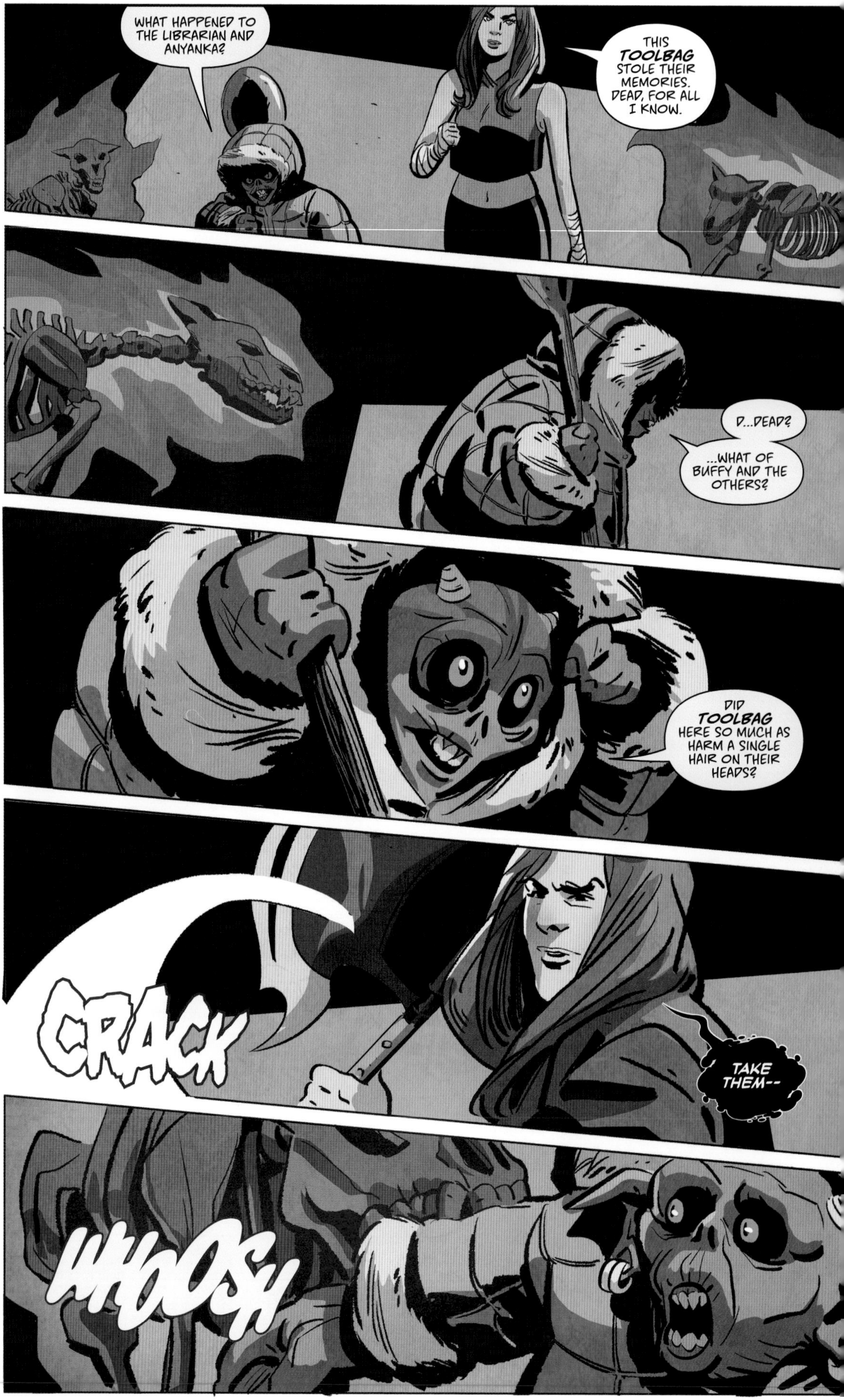
WHAT HAPPENED TO THE LIBRARIAN AND ANYANKA?
THIS TOOLBAG STOLE THEIR MEMORIES. DEAD, FOR ALL I KNOW.
D...DEAD?
...WHAT OF BUFFY AND THE OTHERS?
DID TOOLBAG HERE SO MUCH AS HARM A SINGLE HAIR ON THEIR HEADS?
CRACK
TAKE THEM--
WHOOSH

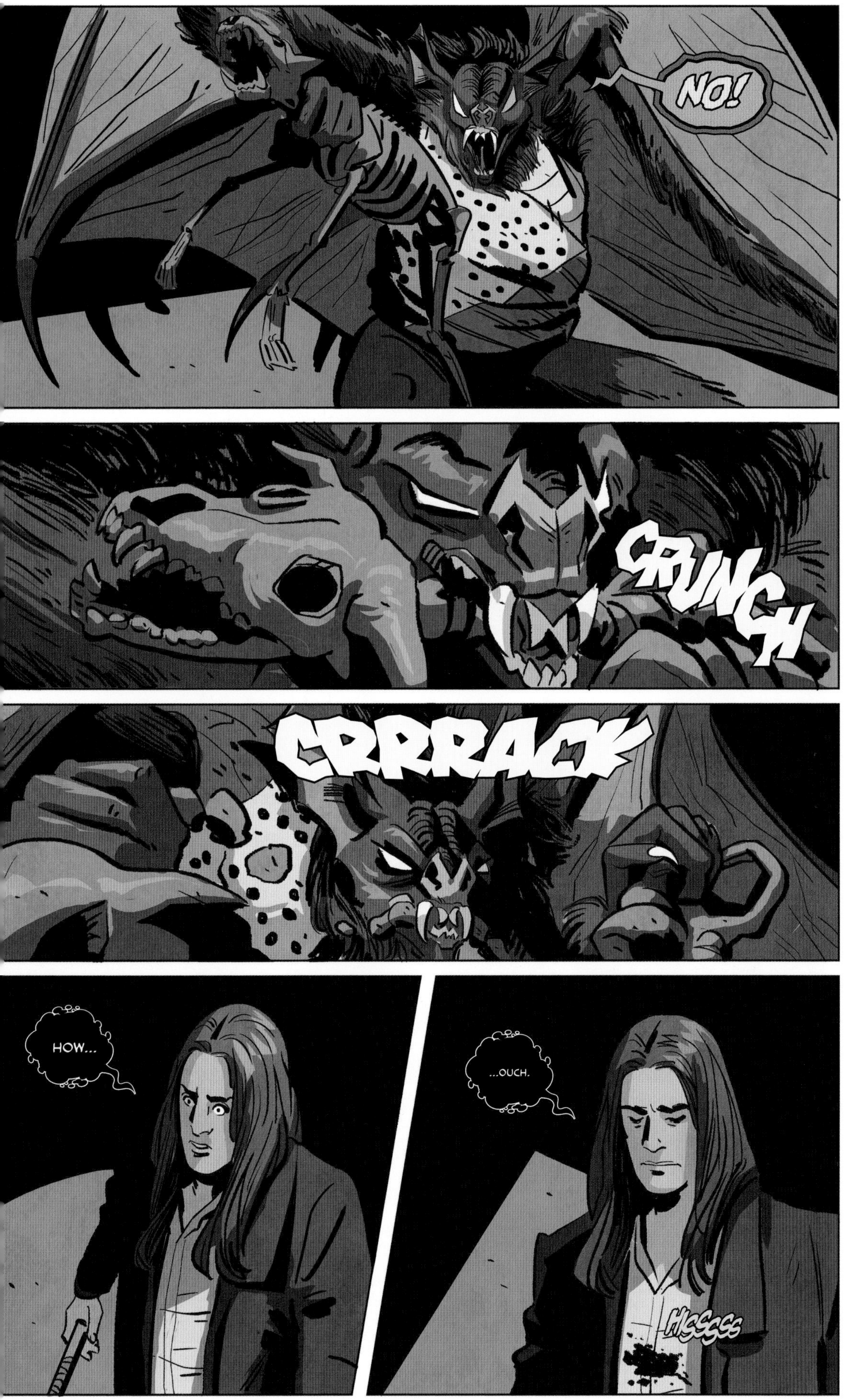
NO!
CRUNCH
CRRRACK
HOW...
...OUCH.
HISSSSS

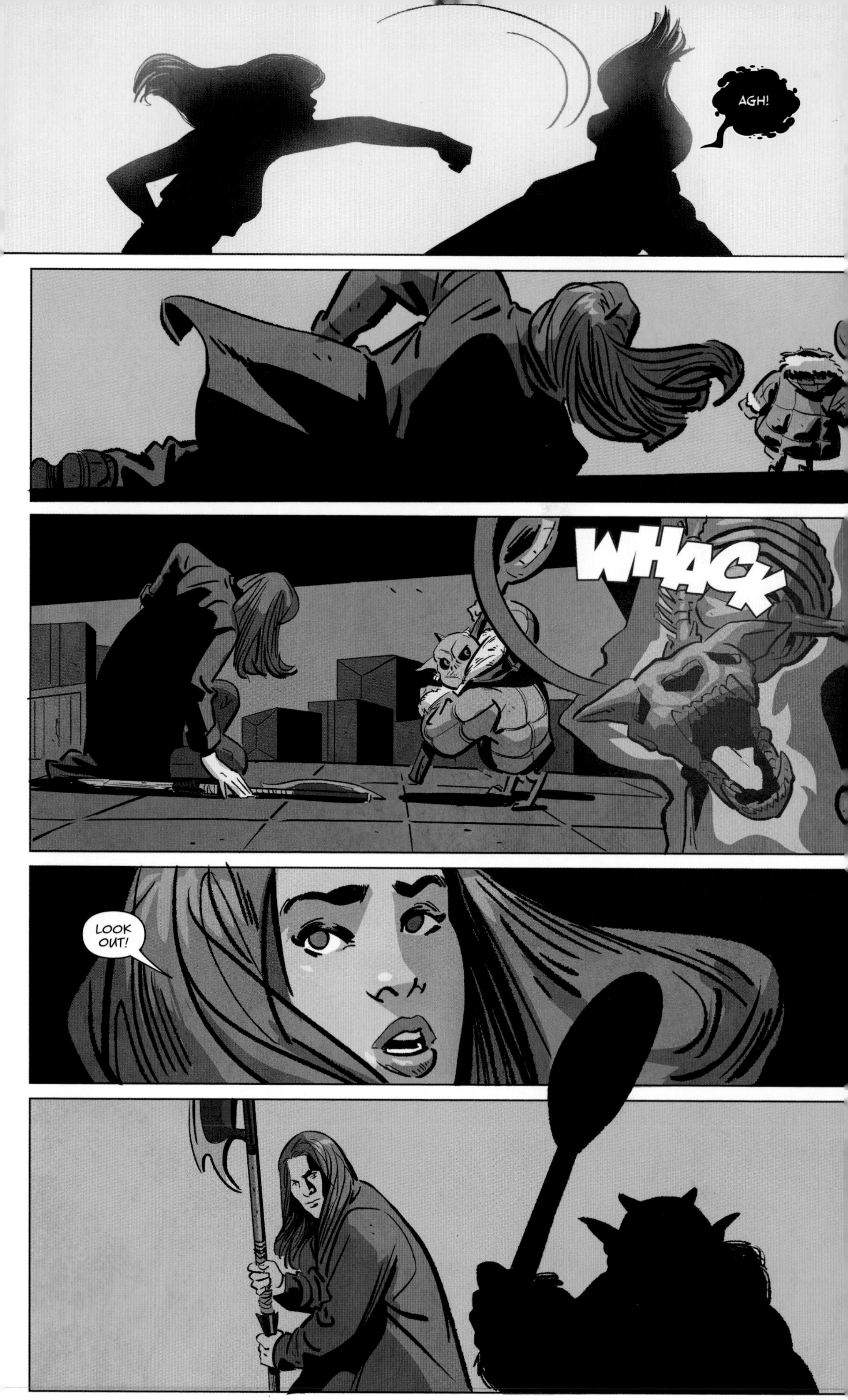
AGH!
WHACK
LOOK OUT!

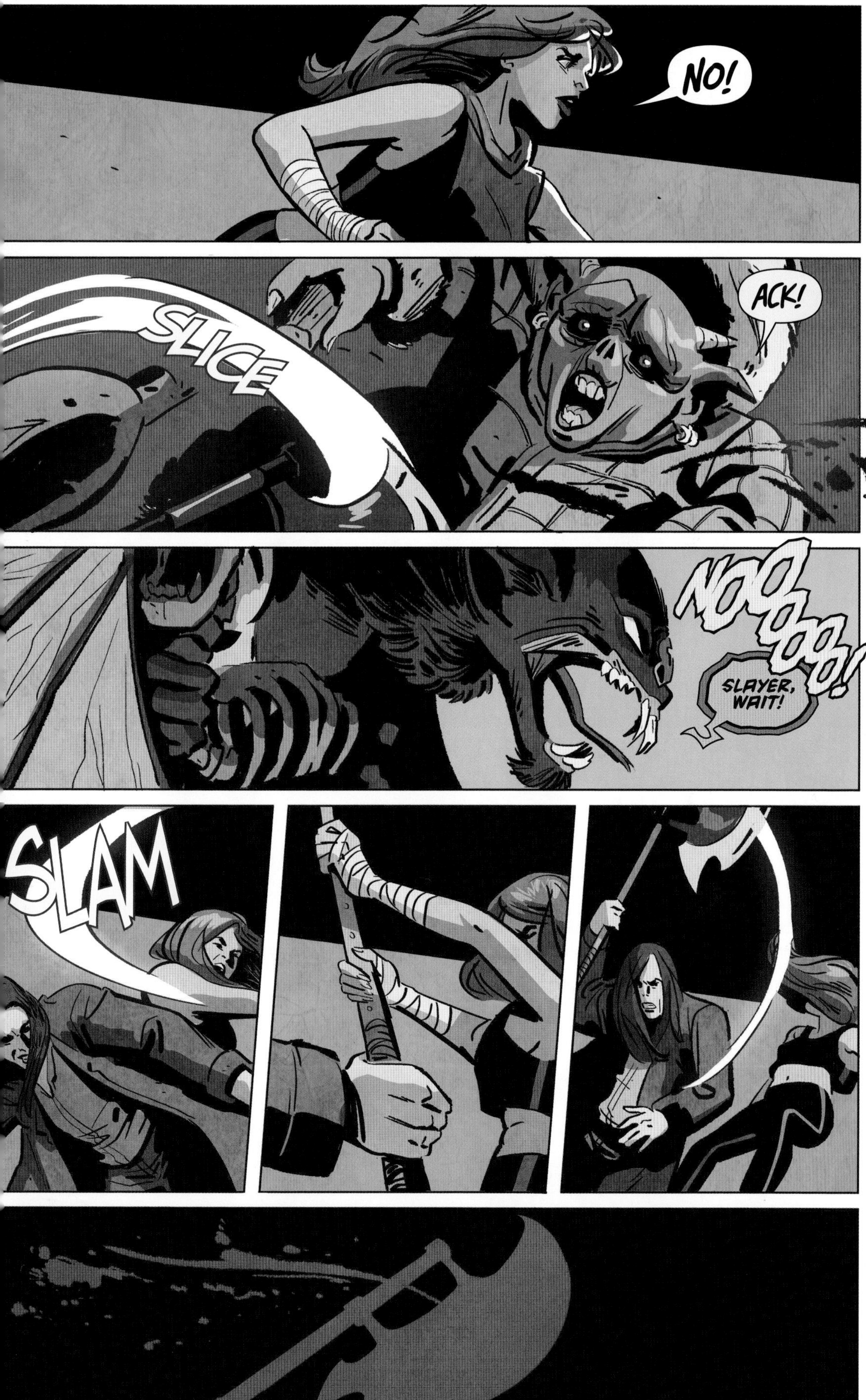
NO!
SLICE
ACK!
NOOOOOO!
SLAYER, WAIT!
SLAM

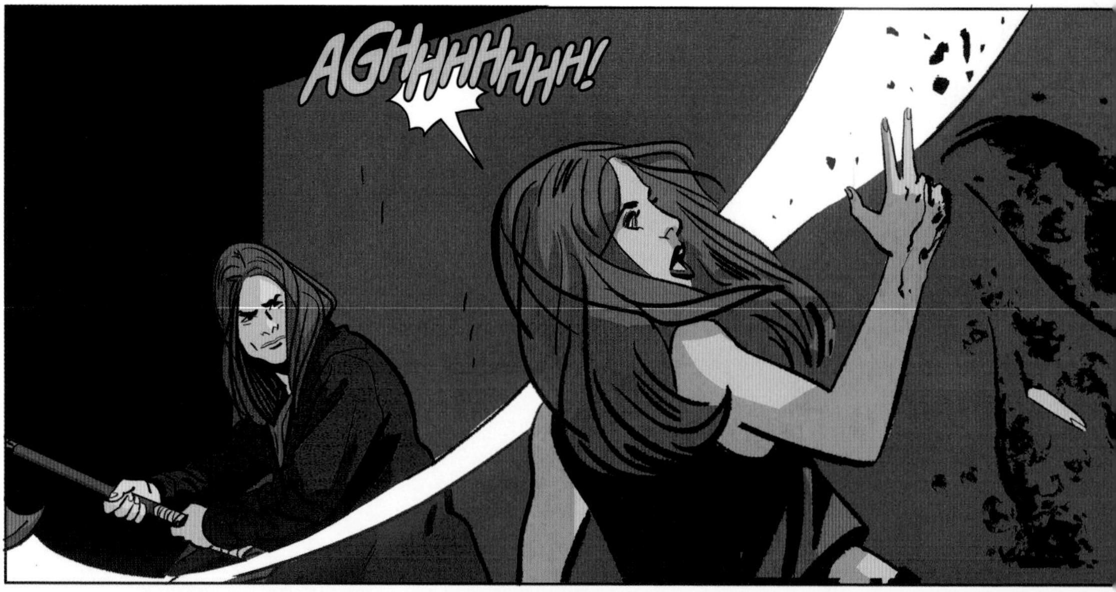
AGHHHHHHH!

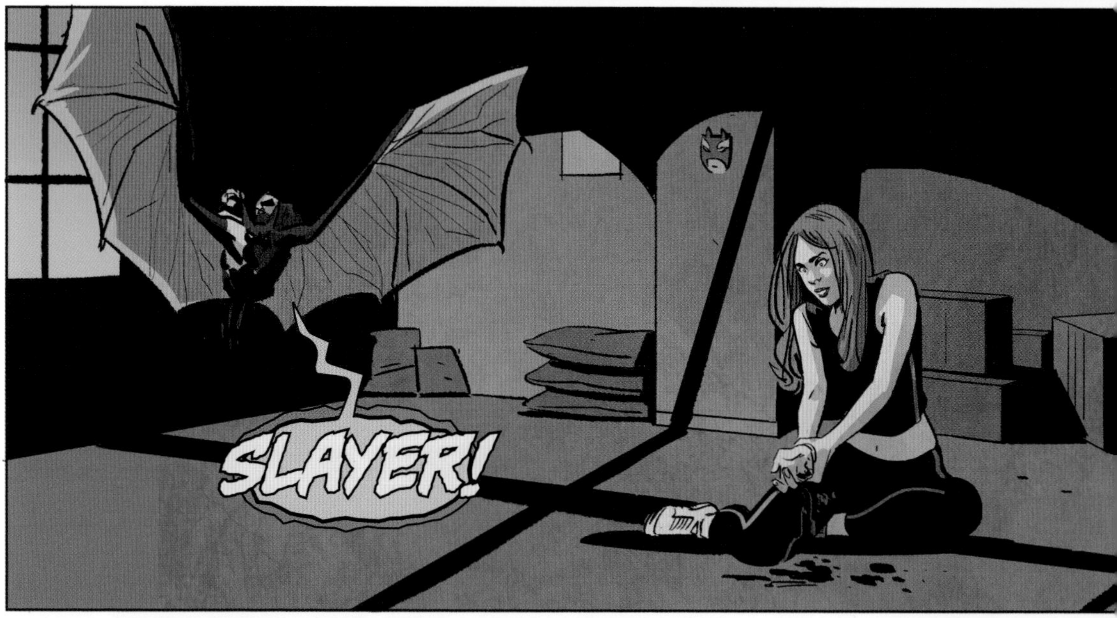
SLAYER!

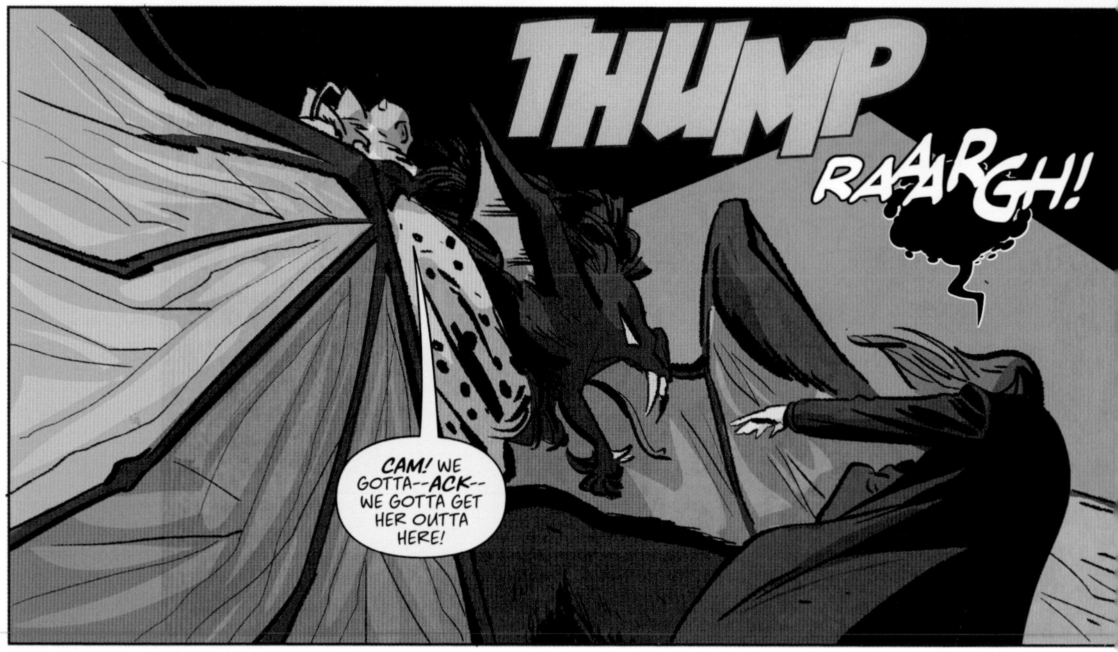
THUMP
RAAARGH!
CAM! WE GOTTA--ACK-- WE GOTTA GET HER OUTTA HERE!

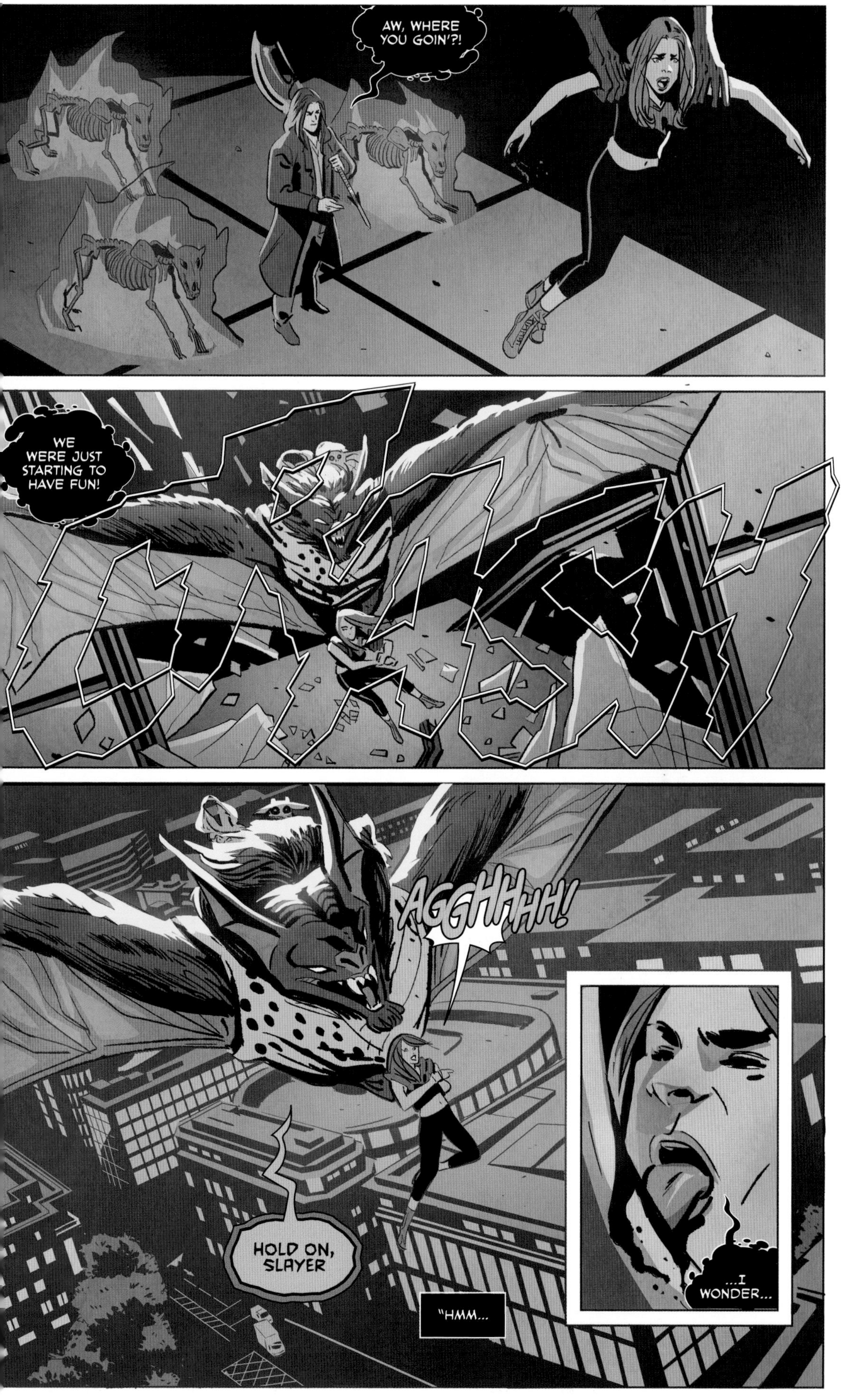
AW, WHERE YOU GOIN'?!
WE WERE JUST STARTING TO HAVE FUN!
AGGHHHH!
HOLD ON, SLAYER
"HMM...
...I WONDER...

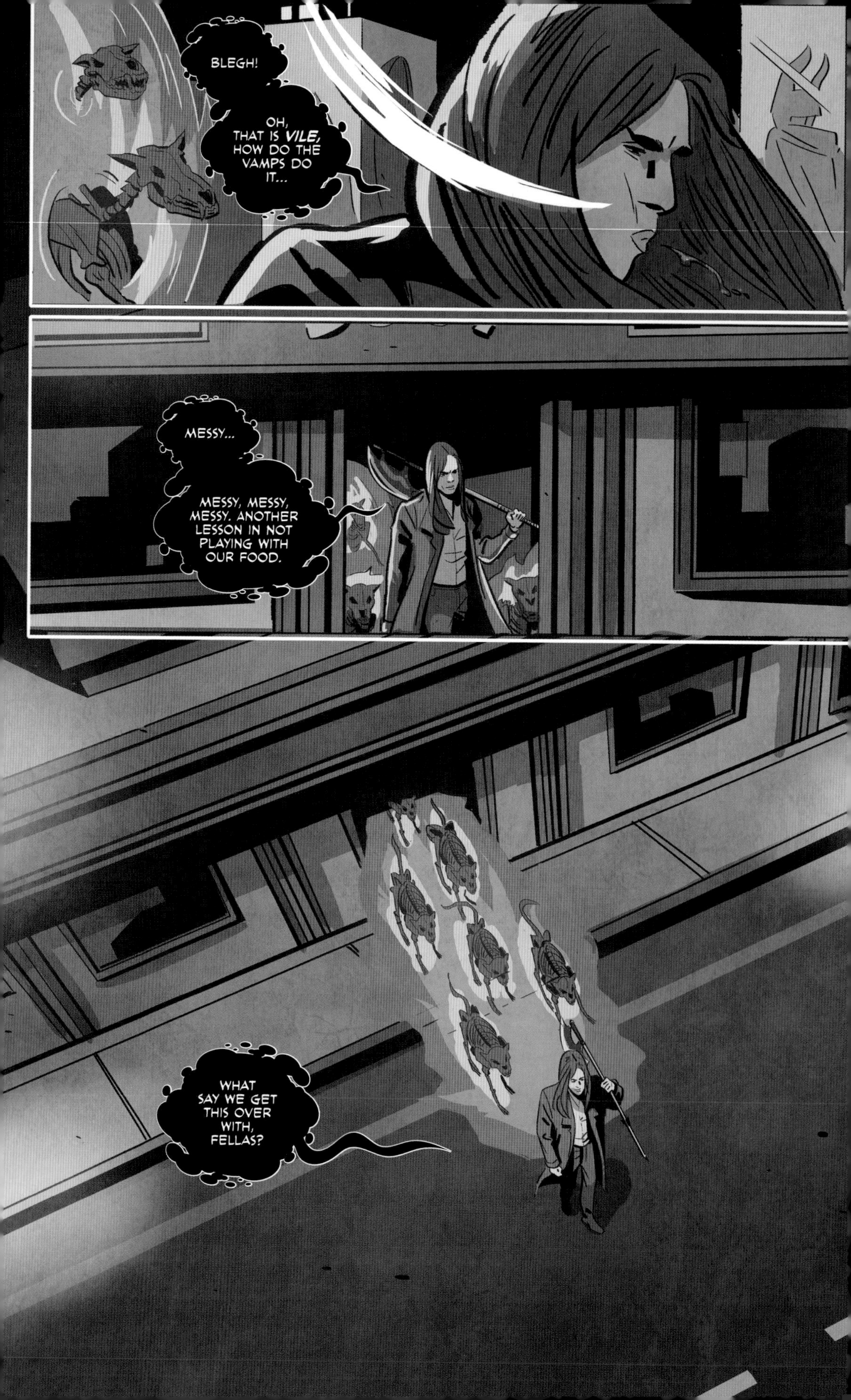
BLEGH!
OH, THAT IS ***VILE,*** HOW DO THE VAMPS DO IT...
MESSY...
MESSY, MESSY, MESSY. ANOTHER LESSON IN NOT PLAYING WITH OUR FOOD.
WHAT SAY WE GET THIS OVER WITH, FELLAS?

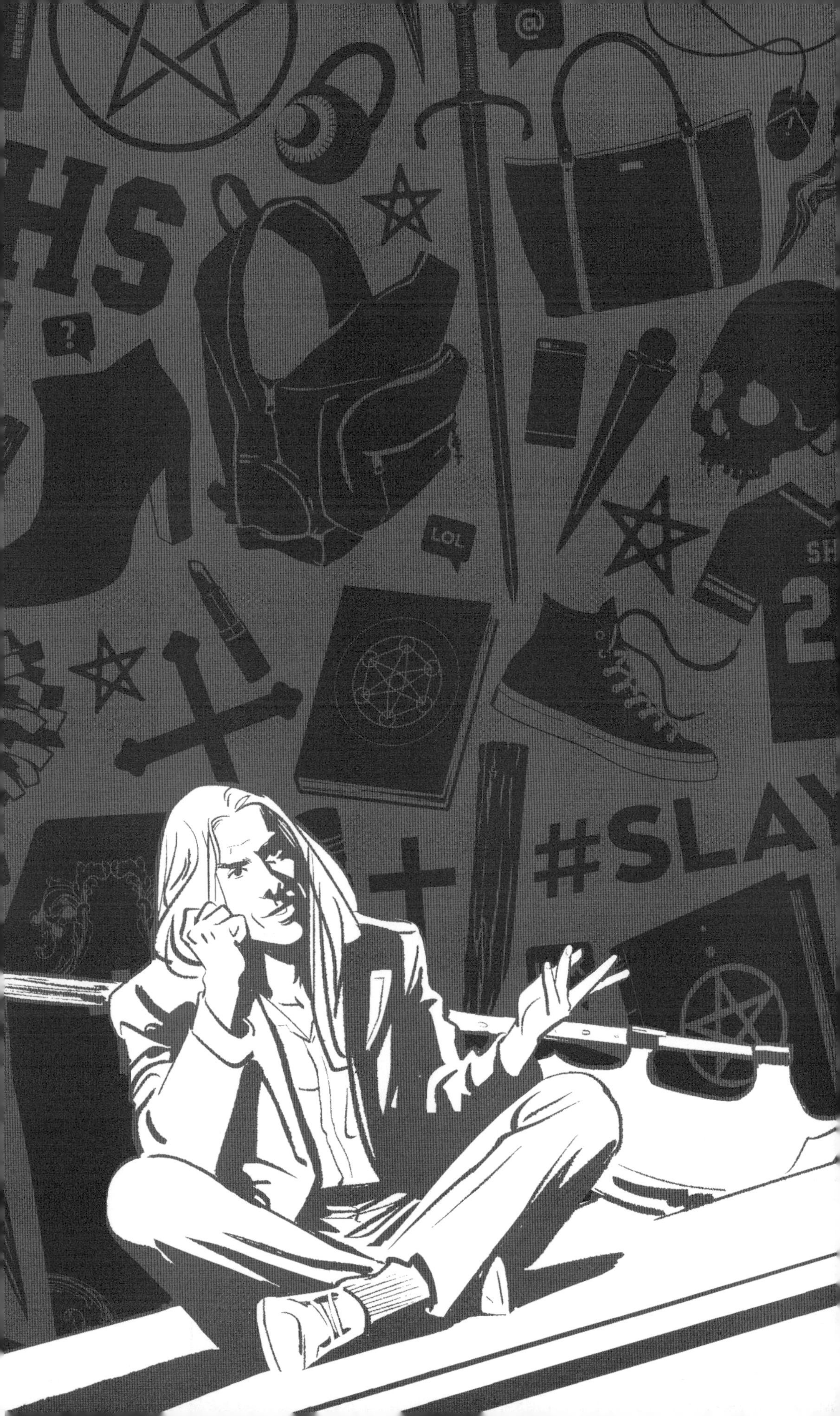

LOL
#SLAY

CHAPTER
THIRTY-TWO

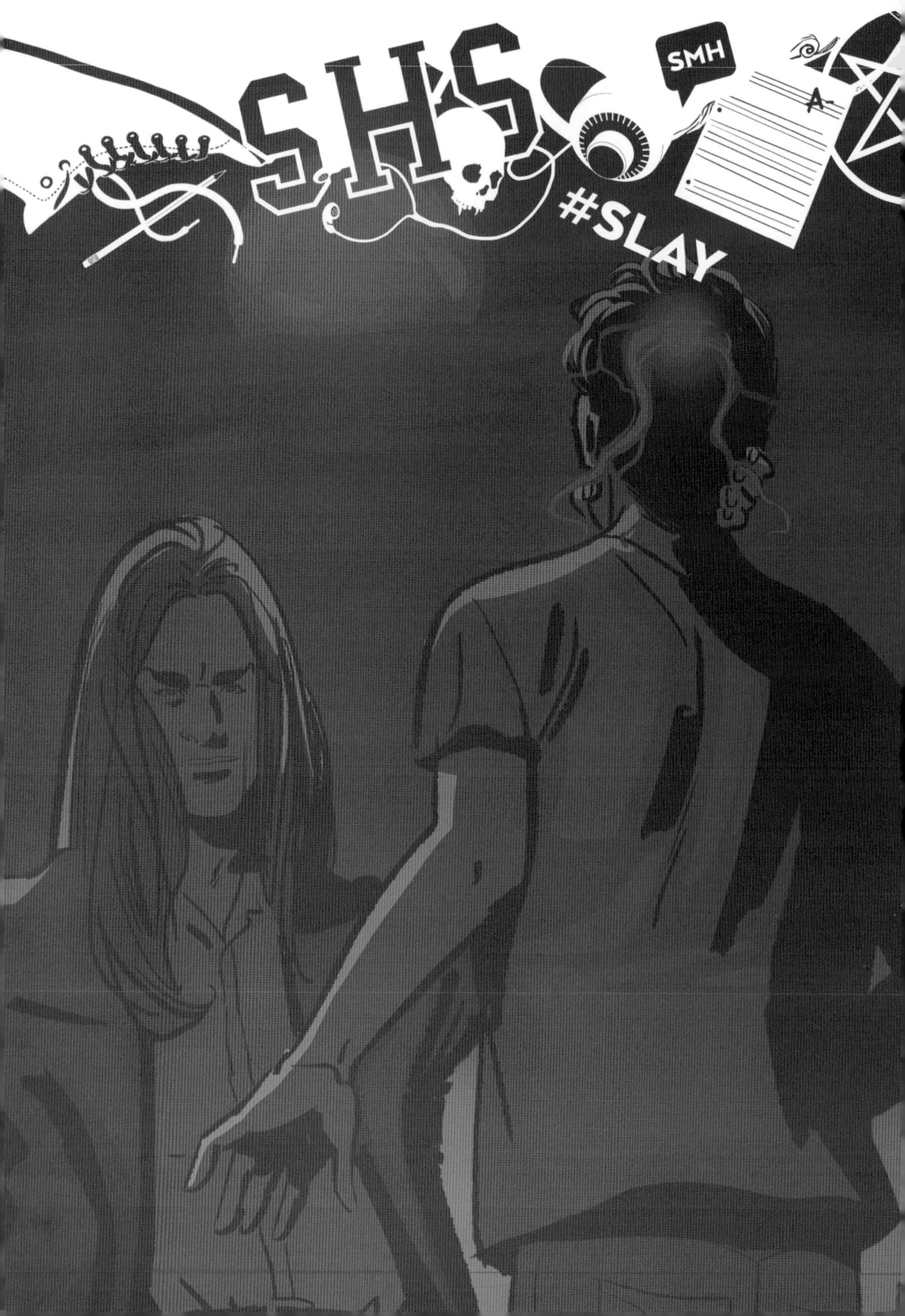
S.H.S.
SMH
#SLAY

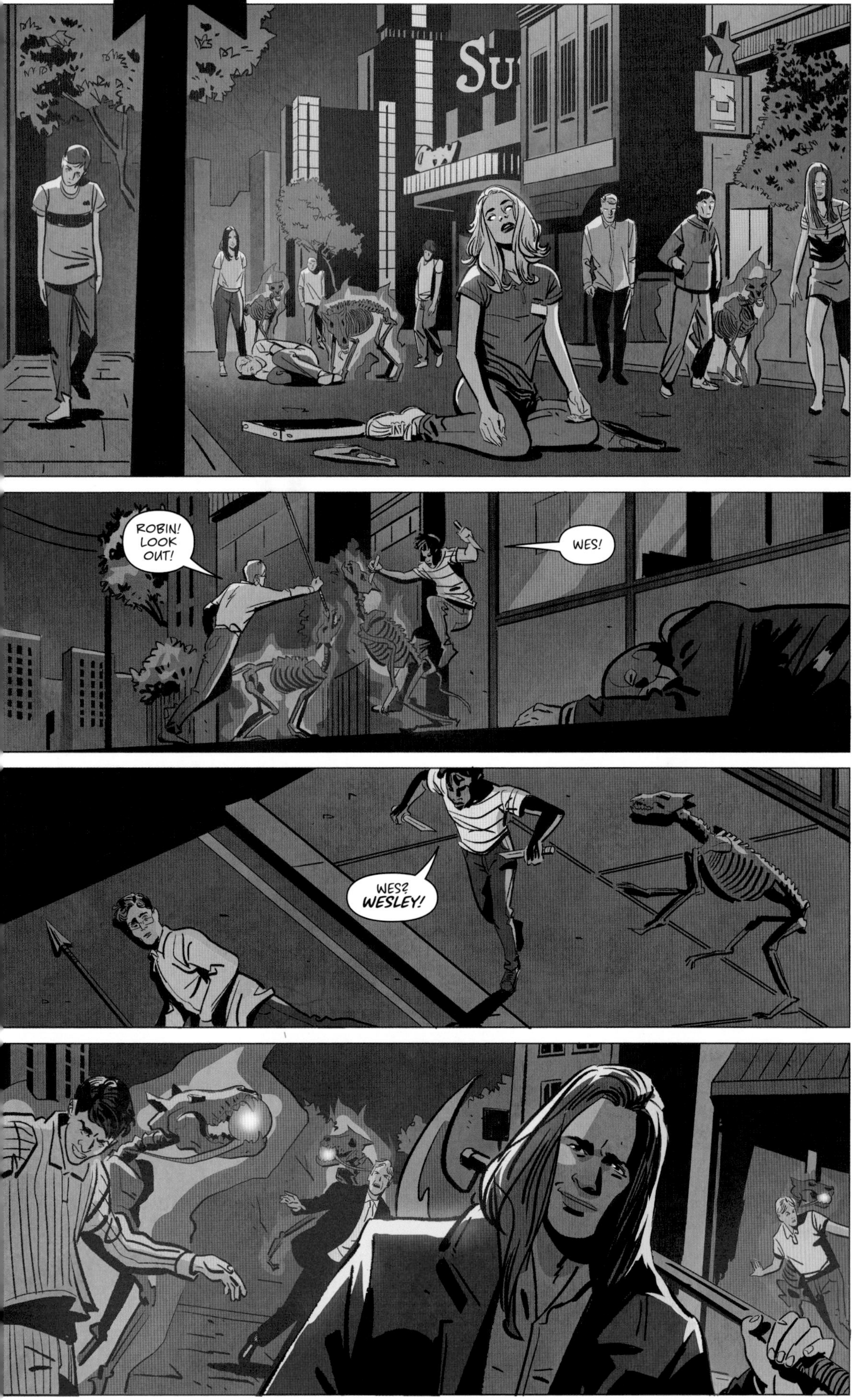
ROBIN! LOOK OUT!
WES!
WES? WESLEY!

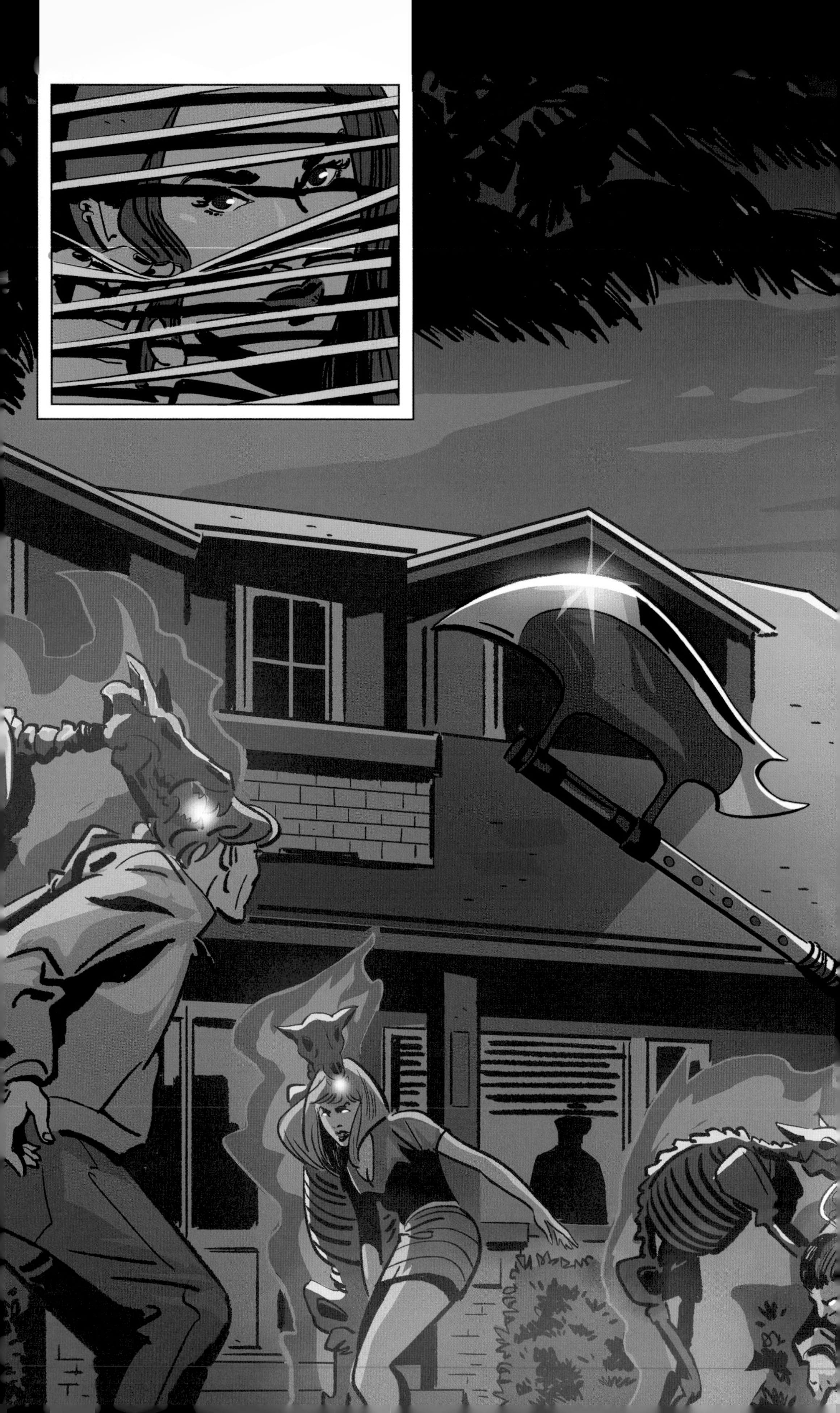

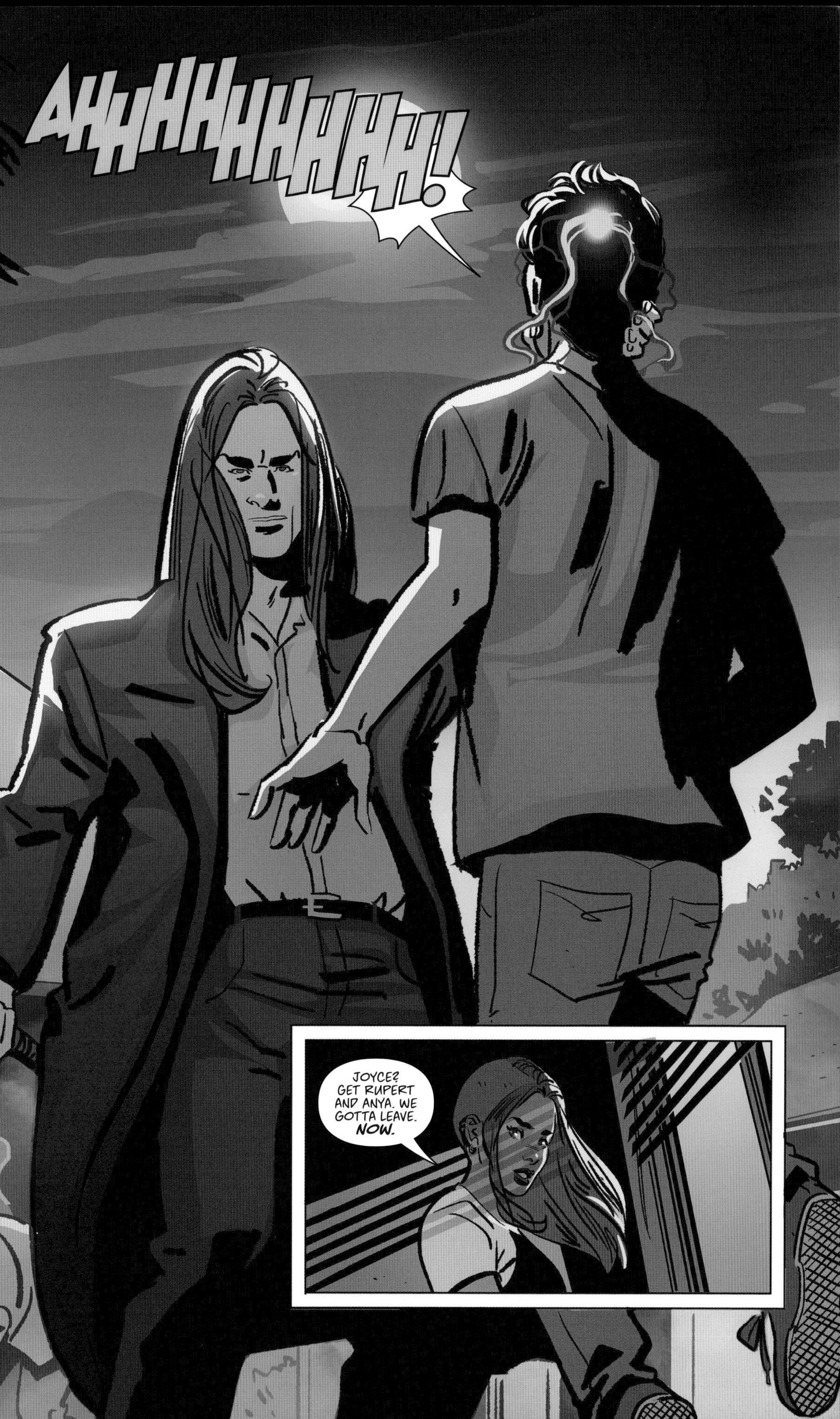
AHHHHHHHHHH!
JOYCE? GET RUPERT AND ANYA. WE GOTTA LEAVE. **NOW.**

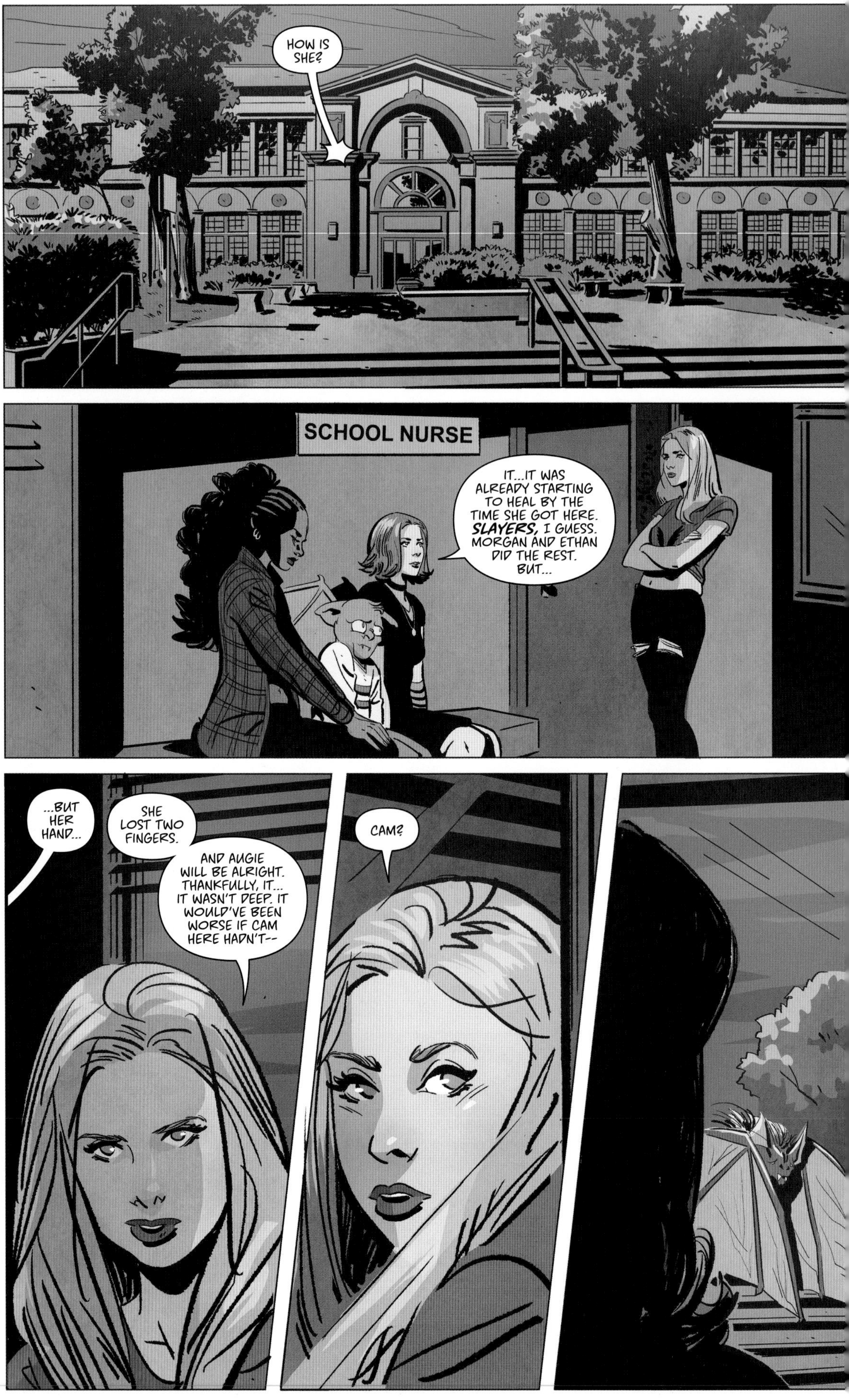
HOW IS SHE?
SCHOOL NURSE
IT...IT WAS ALREADY STARTING TO HEAL BY THE TIME SHE GOT HERE. SLAYERS, I GUESS. MORGAN AND ETHAN DID THE REST. BUT...
...BUT HER HAND...
SHE LOST TWO FINGERS.
AND AUGIE WILL BE ALRIGHT. THANKFULLY, IT... IT WASN'T DEEP. IT WOULD'VE BEEN WORSE IF CAM HERE HADN'T--
CAM?

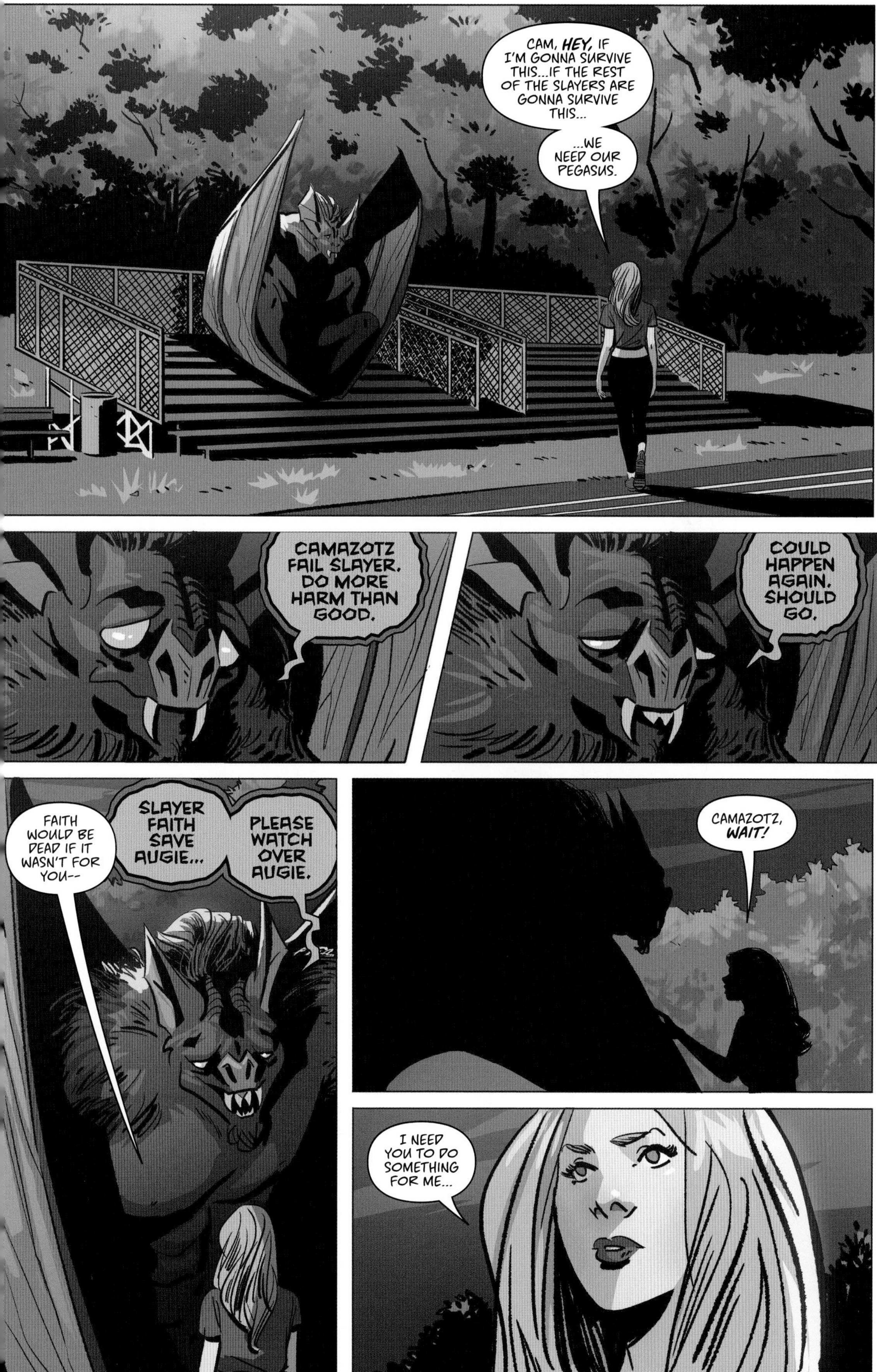
CAM, **HEY,** IF I'M GONNA SURVIVE THIS...IF THE REST OF THE SLAYERS ARE GONNA SURVIVE THIS...
...WE NEED OUR PEGASUS.
CAMAZOTZ FAIL SLAYER. DO MORE HARM THAN GOOD.
COULD HAPPEN AGAIN. SHOULD GO.
FAITH WOULD BE DEAD IF IT WASN'T FOR YOU--
SLAYER FAITH SAVE AUGIE...
PLEASE WATCH OVER AUGIE.
CAMAZOTZ, **WAIT!**
I NEED YOU TO DO SOMETHING FOR ME...

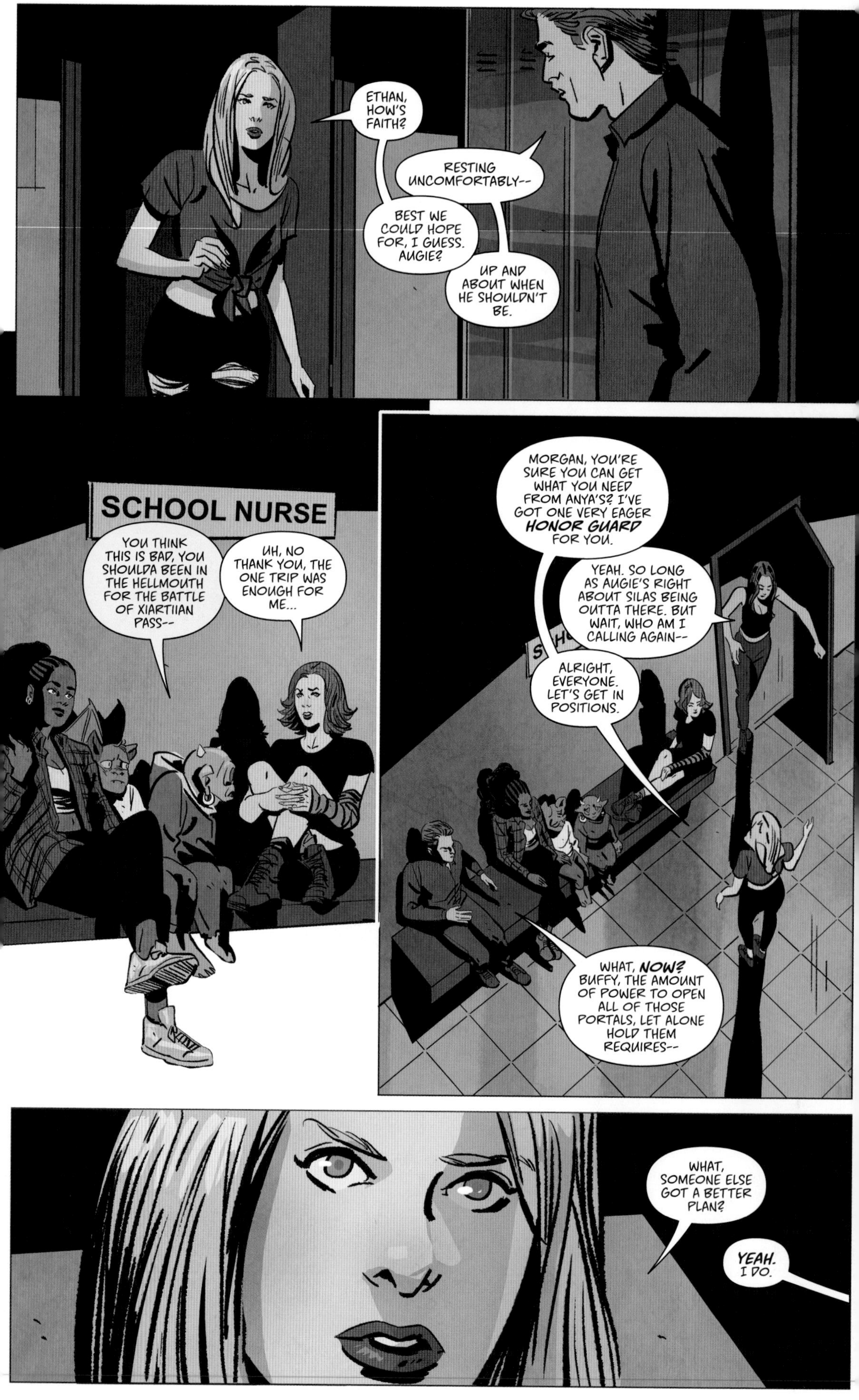
ETHAN, HOW'S FAITH?
RESTING UNCOMFORTABLY--
BEST WE COULD HOPE FOR, I GUESS. AUGIE?
UP AND ABOUT WHEN HE SHOULDN'T BE.
SCHOOL NURSE
YOU THINK THIS IS BAD, YOU SHOULDA BEEN IN THE HELLMOUTH FOR THE BATTLE OF XIARTIIAN PASS--
UH, NO THANK YOU, THE ONE TRIP WAS ENOUGH FOR ME...
MORGAN, YOU'RE SURE YOU CAN GET WHAT YOU NEED FROM ANYA'S? I'VE GOT ONE VERY EAGER **HONOR GUARD** FOR YOU.
YEAH. SO LONG AS AUGIE'S RIGHT ABOUT SILAS BEING OUTTA THERE. BUT WAIT, WHO AM I CALLING AGAIN--
ALRIGHT, EVERYONE. LET'S GET IN POSITIONS.
WHAT, **NOW?** BUFFY, THE AMOUNT OF POWER TO OPEN ALL OF THOSE PORTALS, LET ALONE HOLD THEM REQUIRES--
WHAT, SOMEONE ELSE GOT A BETTER PLAN?
YEAH. I DO.

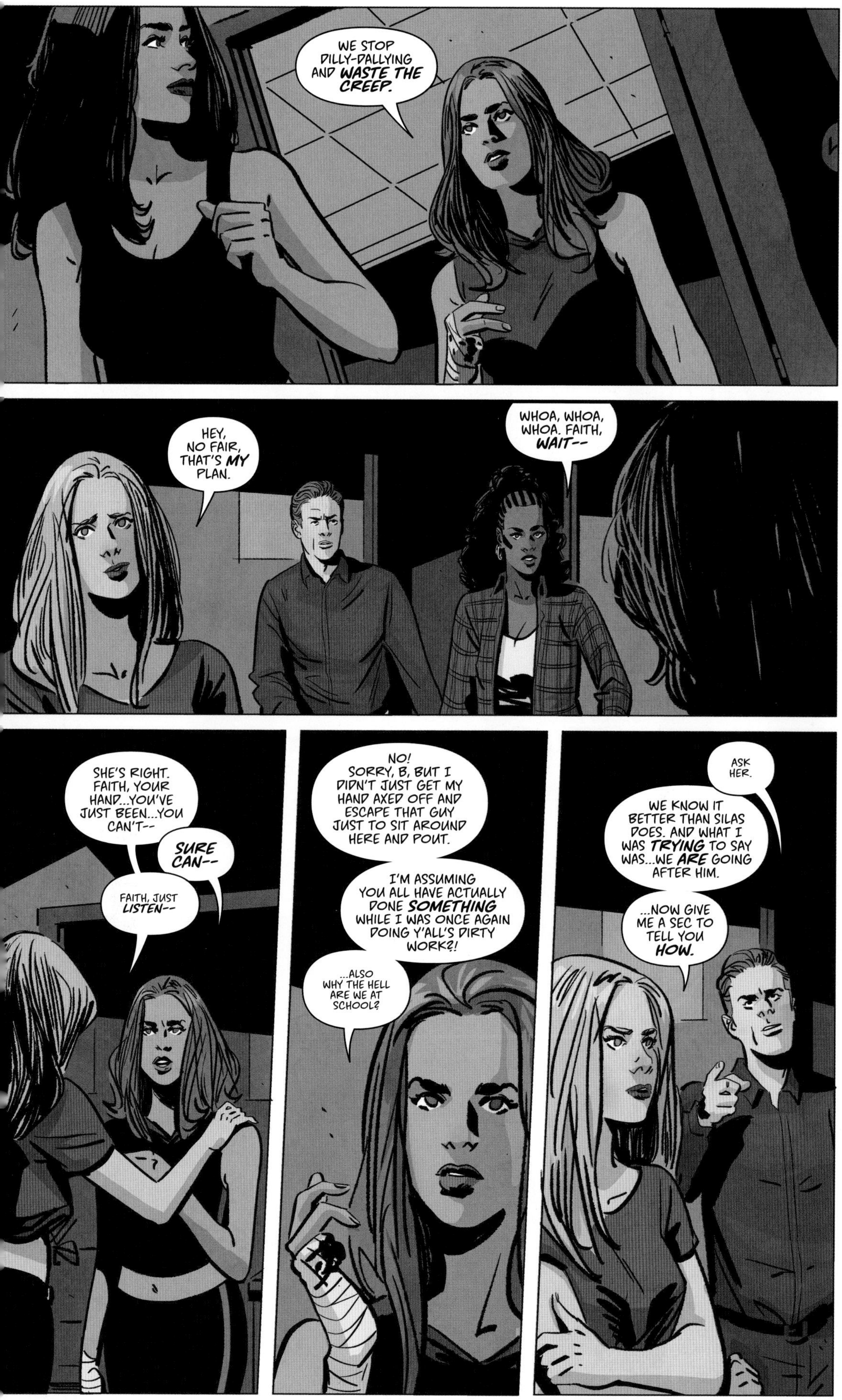
WE STOP DILLY-DALLYING AND WASTE THE CREEP.
HEY, NO FAIR, THAT'S MY PLAN.
WHOA, WHOA, WHOA. FAITH, WAIT--
SHE'S RIGHT. FAITH, YOUR HAND...YOU'VE JUST BEEN...YOU CAN'T--
SURE CAN--
FAITH, JUST LISTEN--
NO! SORRY, B, BUT I DIDN'T JUST GET MY HAND AXED OFF AND ESCAPE THAT GUY JUST TO SIT AROUND HERE AND POUT.
I'M ASSUMING YOU ALL HAVE ACTUALLY DONE SOMETHING WHILE I WAS ONCE AGAIN DOING Y'ALL'S DIRTY WORK?!
...ALSO WHY THE HELL ARE WE AT SCHOOL?
ASK HER.
WE KNOW IT BETTER THAN SILAS DOES. AND WHAT I WAS TRYING TO SAY WAS...WE ARE GOING AFTER HIM.
...NOW GIVE ME A SEC TO TELL YOU HOW.

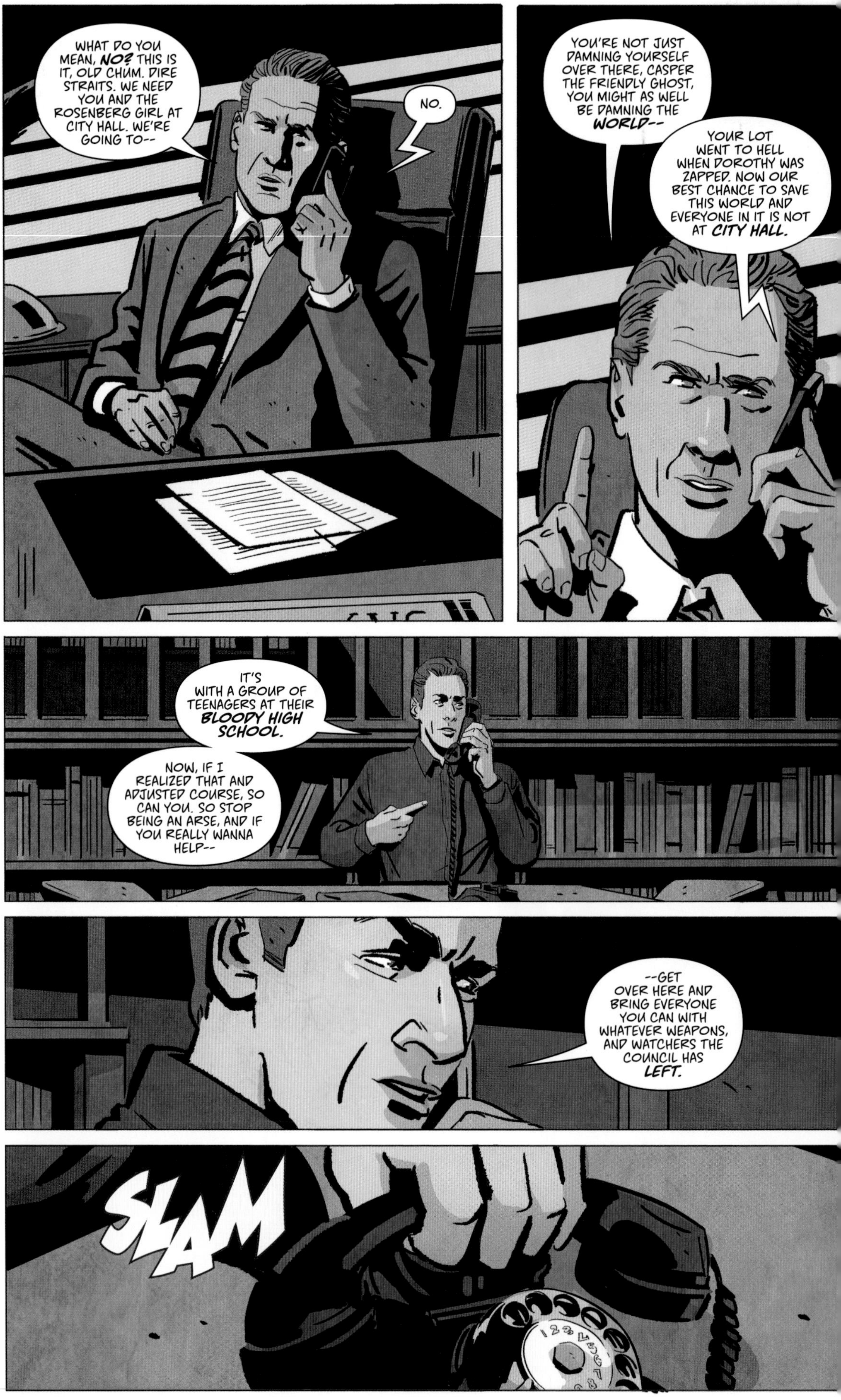
WHAT DO YOU MEAN, NO? THIS IS IT, OLD CHUM. DIRE STRAITS. WE NEED YOU AND THE ROSENBERG GIRL AT CITY HALL. WE'RE GOING TO--
NO.
YOU'RE NOT JUST DAMNING YOURSELF OVER THERE, CASPER THE FRIENDLY GHOST, YOU MIGHT AS WELL BE DAMNING THE WORLD--
YOUR LOT WENT TO HELL WHEN DOROTHY WAS ZAPPED. NOW OUR BEST CHANCE TO SAVE THIS WORLD AND EVERYONE IN IT IS NOT AT CITY HALL.
IT'S WITH A GROUP OF TEENAGERS AT THEIR BLOODY HIGH SCHOOL.
NOW, IF I REALIZED THAT AND ADJUSTED COURSE, SO CAN YOU. SO STOP BEING AN ARSE, AND IF YOU REALLY WANNA HELP--
--GET OVER HERE AND BRING EVERYONE YOU CAN WITH WHATEVER WEAPONS, AND WATCHERS THE COUNCIL HAS LEFT.
SLAM

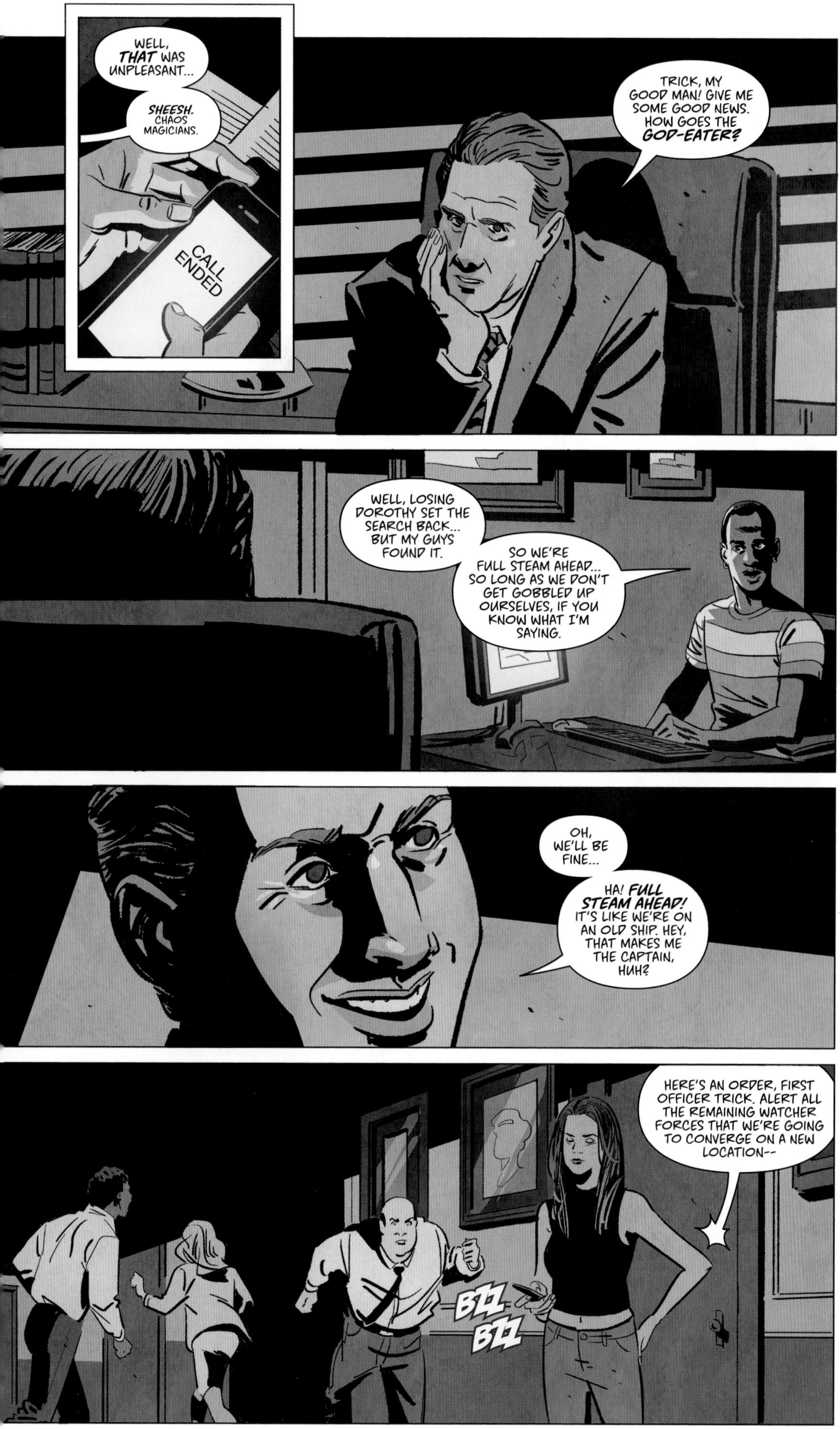
WELL, THAT WAS UNPLEASANT...
SHEESH. CHAOS MAGICIANS.
CALL ENDED
TRICK, MY GOOD MAN! GIVE ME SOME GOOD NEWS. HOW GOES THE GOD-EATER?
WELL, LOSING DOROTHY SET THE SEARCH BACK... BUT MY GUYS FOUND IT.
SO WE'RE FULL STEAM AHEAD... SO LONG AS WE DON'T GET GOBBLED UP OURSELVES, IF YOU KNOW WHAT I'M SAYING.
OH, WE'LL BE FINE...
HA! FULL STEAM AHEAD! IT'S LIKE WE'RE ON AN OLD SHIP. HEY, THAT MAKES ME THE CAPTAIN, HUH?
HERE'S AN ORDER, FIRST OFFICER TRICK. ALERT ALL THE REMAINING WATCHER FORCES THAT WE'RE GOING TO CONVERGE ON A NEW LOCATION--
BZZ
BZZ

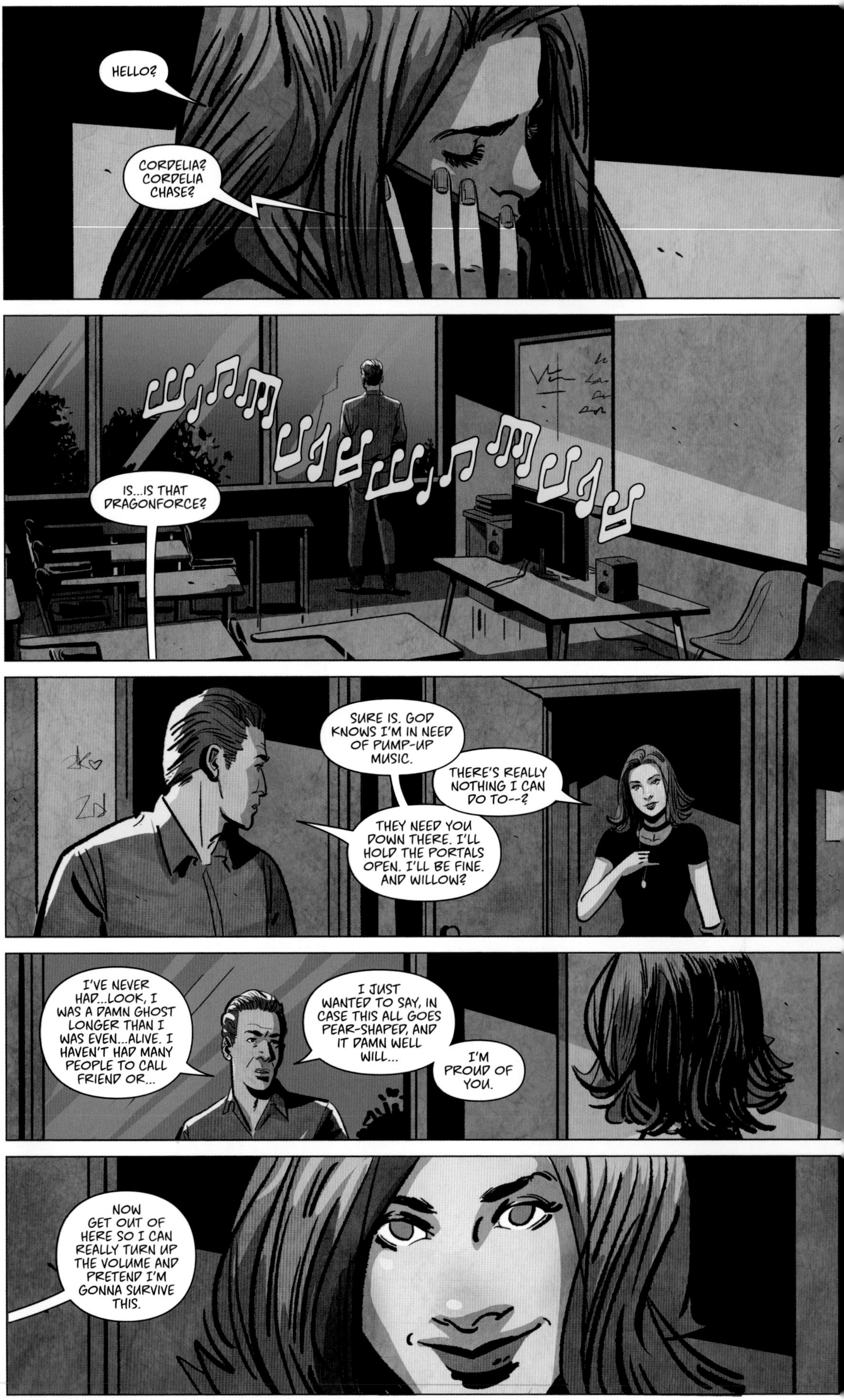
HELLO?
CORDELIA? CORDELIA CHASE?
IS...IS THAT DRAGONFORCE?
SURE IS. GOD KNOWS I'M IN NEED OF PUMP-UP MUSIC.
THERE'S REALLY NOTHING I CAN DO TO--?
THEY NEED YOU DOWN THERE. I'LL HOLD THE PORTALS OPEN. I'LL BE FINE. AND WILLOW?
I'VE NEVER HAD...LOOK, I WAS A DAMN GHOST LONGER THAN I WAS EVEN...ALIVE. I HAVEN'T HAD MANY PEOPLE TO CALL FRIEND OR...
I JUST WANTED TO SAY, IN CASE THIS ALL GOES PEAR-SHAPED, AND IT DAMN WELL WILL...
I'M PROUD OF YOU.
NOW GET OUT OF HERE SO I CAN REALLY TURN UP THE VOLUME AND PRETEND I'M GONNA SURVIVE THIS.

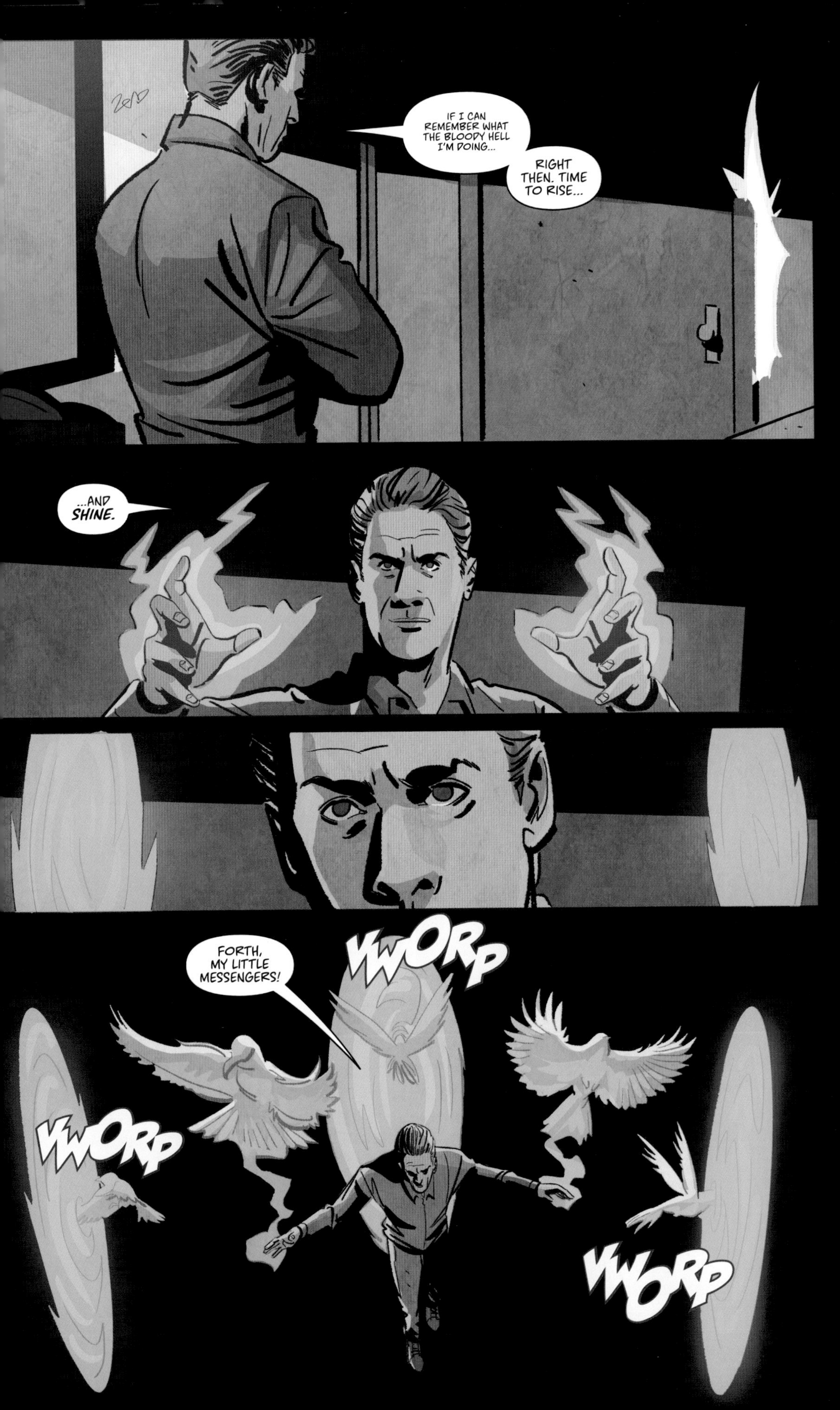
IF I CAN REMEMBER WHAT THE BLOODY HELL I'M DOING...
RIGHT THEN. TIME TO RISE...
...AND SHINE.
FORTH, MY LITTLE MESSENGERS!
VWORP
VWORP
VWORP

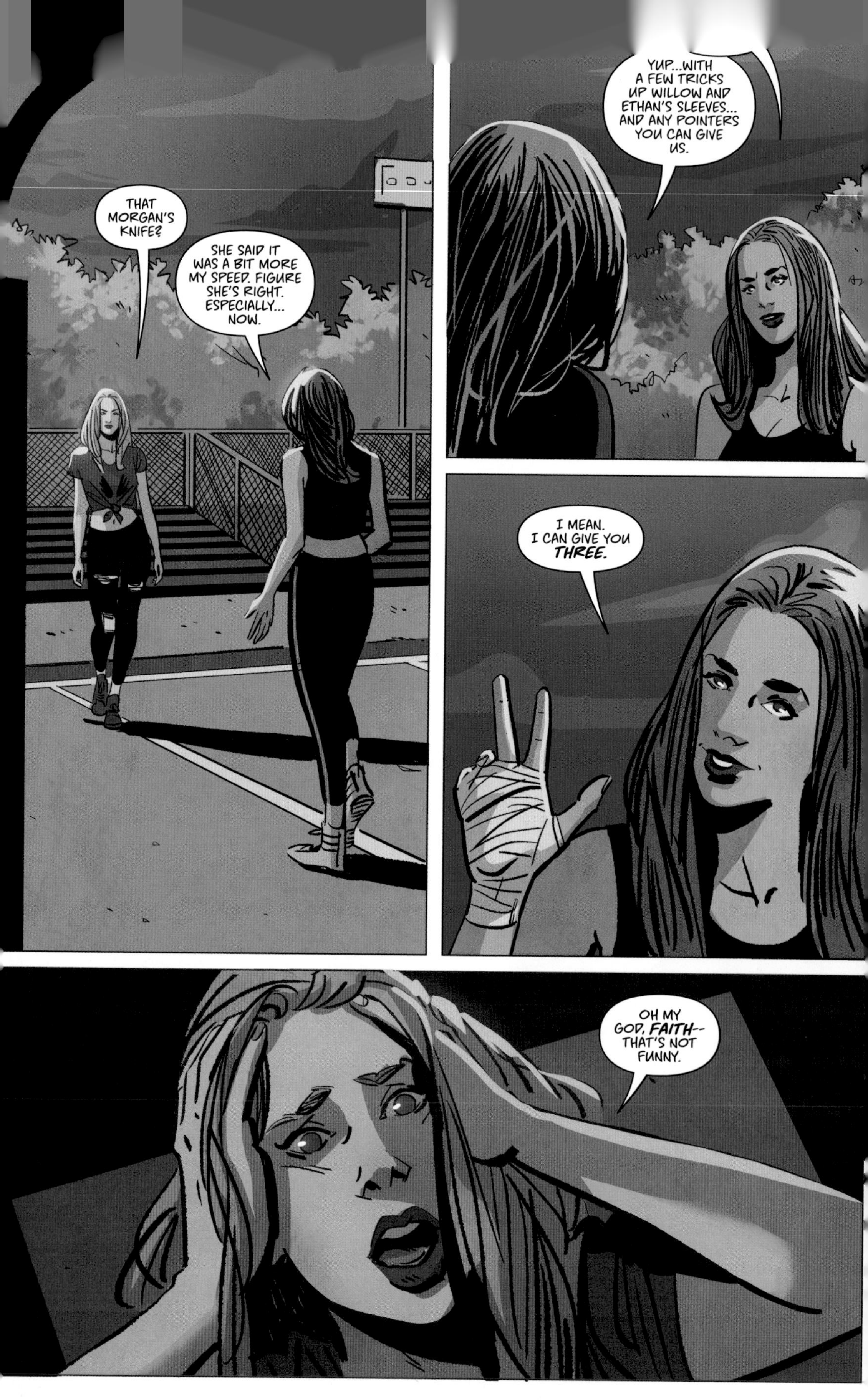
THAT MORGAN'S KNIFE?
SHE SAID IT WAS A BIT MORE MY SPEED. FIGURE SHE'S RIGHT. ESPECIALLY... NOW.
YUP...WITH A FEW TRICKS UP WILLOW AND ETHAN'S SLEEVES... AND ANY POINTERS YOU CAN GIVE US.
I MEAN. I CAN GIVE YOU *THREE.*
OH MY GOD, *FAITH*-- THAT'S NOT FUNNY.

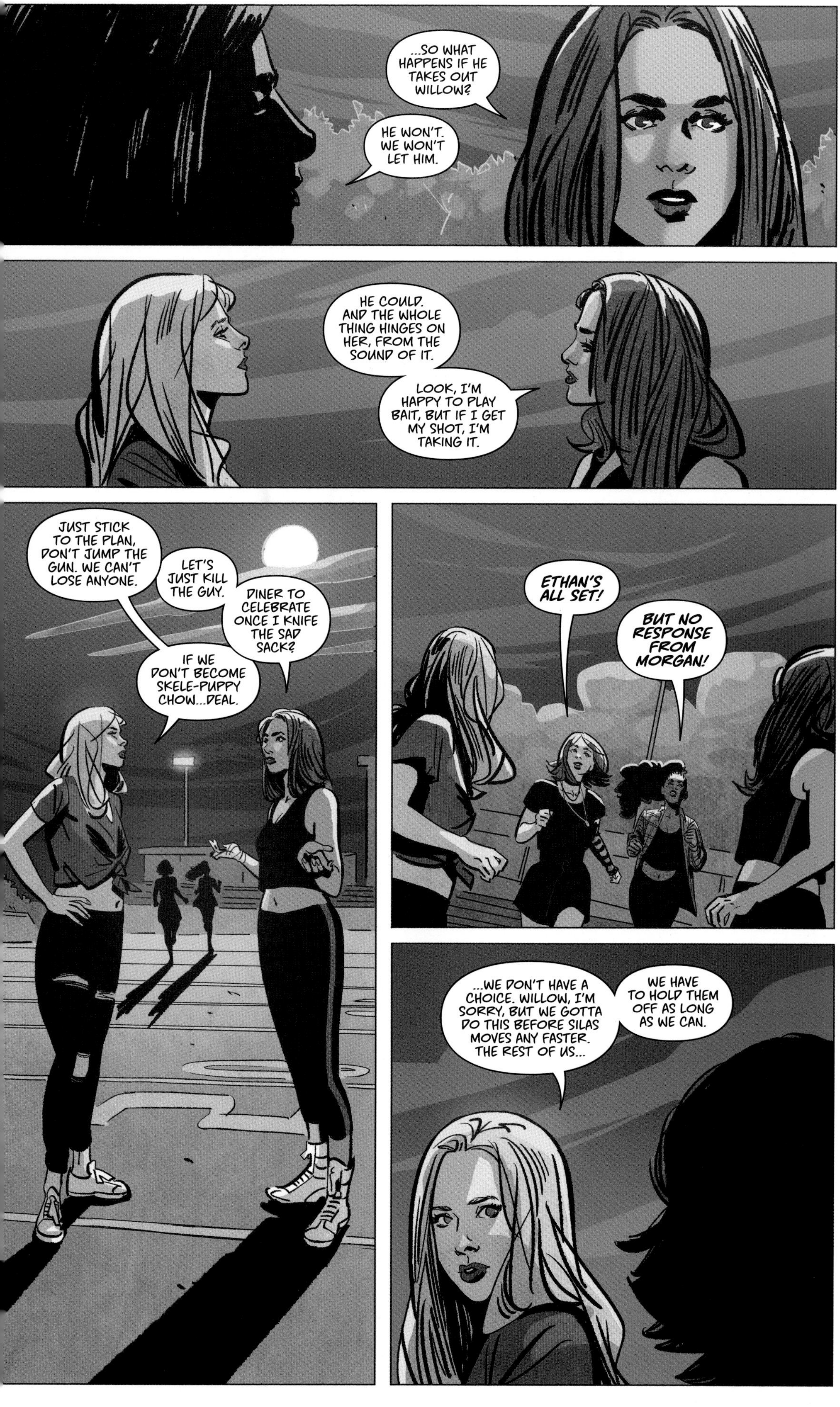

...SO WHAT HAPPENS IF HE TAKES OUT WILLOW?
HE WON'T. WE WON'T LET HIM.
HE COULD. AND THE WHOLE THING HINGES ON HER, FROM THE SOUND OF IT.
LOOK, I'M HAPPY TO PLAY BAIT, BUT IF I GET MY SHOT, I'M TAKING IT.
JUST STICK TO THE PLAN, DON'T JUMP THE GUN. WE CAN'T LOSE ANYONE.
LET'S JUST KILL THE GUY.
DINER TO CELEBRATE ONCE I KNIFE THE SAD SACK?
IF WE DON'T BECOME SKELE-PUPPY CHOW...DEAL.
ETHAN'S ALL SET!
BUT NO RESPONSE FROM MORGAN!
...WE DON'T HAVE A CHOICE. WILLOW, I'M SORRY, BUT WE GOTTA DO THIS BEFORE SILAS MOVES ANY FASTER. THE REST OF US...
WE HAVE TO HOLD THEM OFF AS LONG AS WE CAN.

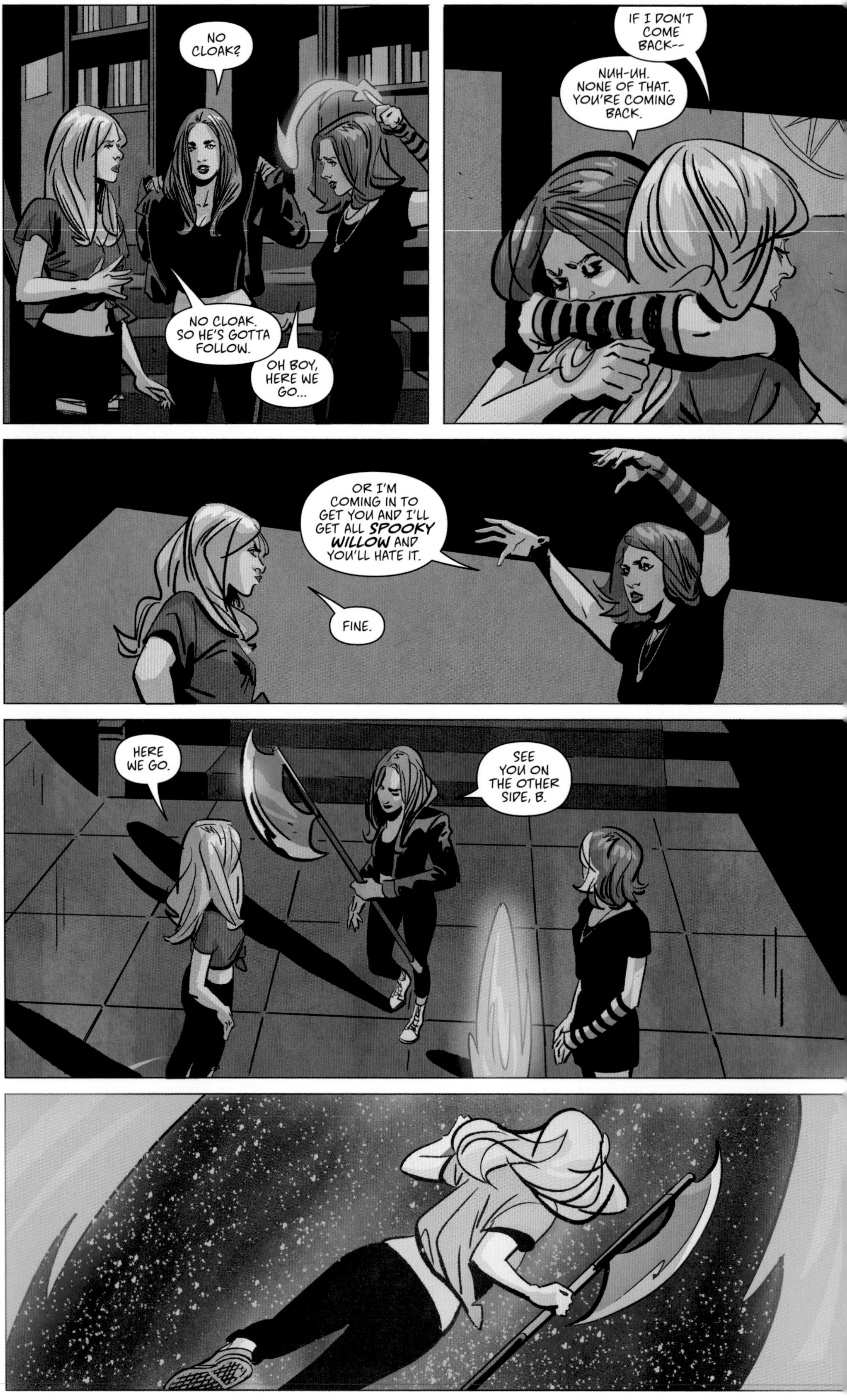
NO CLOAK?
NO CLOAK. SO HE'S GOTTA FOLLOW.
OH BOY, HERE WE GO...
IF I DON'T COME BACK--
NUH-UH. NONE OF THAT. YOU'RE COMING BACK.
OR I'M COMING IN TO GET YOU AND I'LL GET ALL **SPOOKY WILLOW** AND YOU'LL HATE IT.
FINE.
HERE WE GO.
SEE YOU ON THE OTHER SIDE, B.

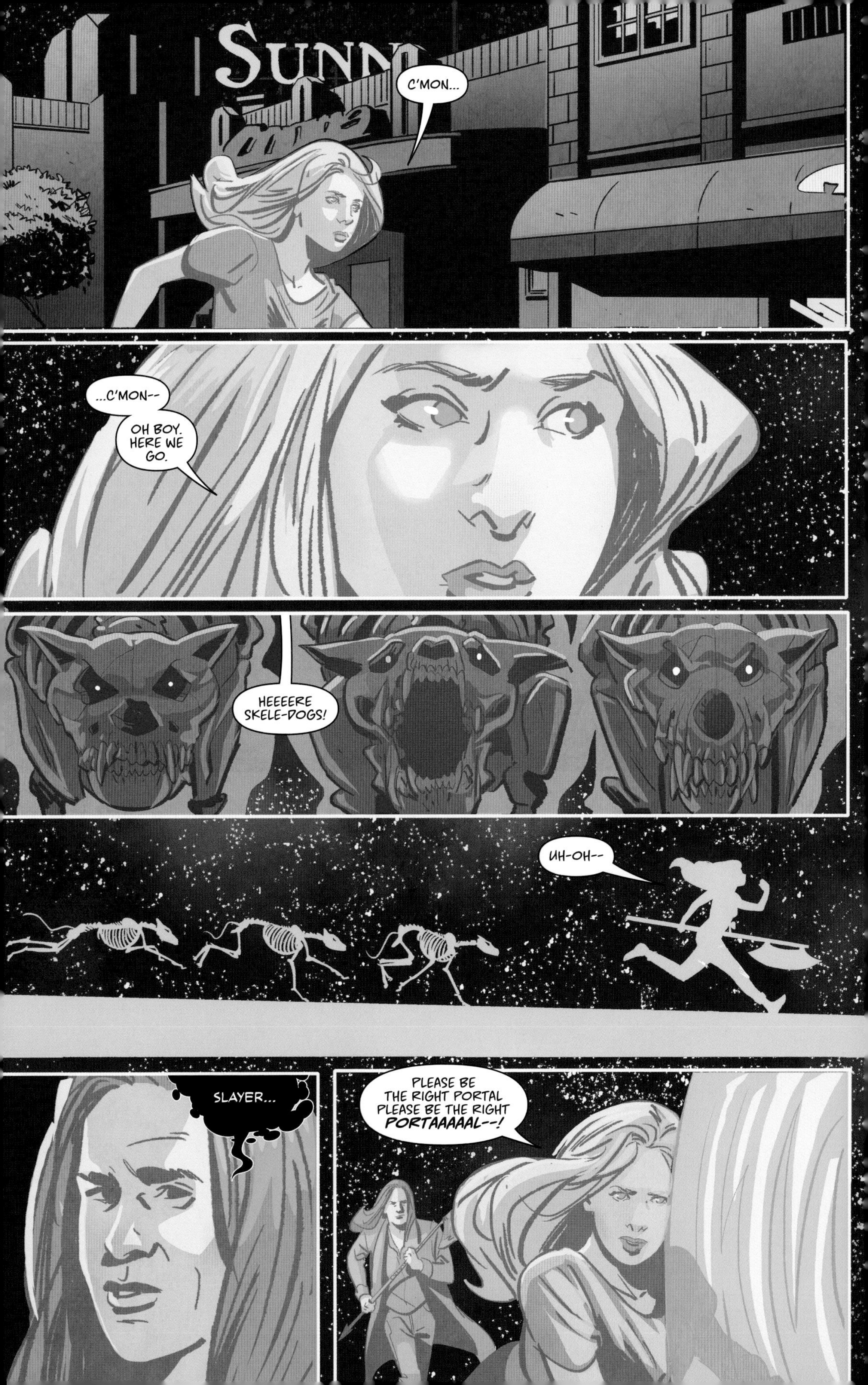
SUNN
C'MON...
...C'MON--
OH BOY. HERE WE GO.
HEEEERE SKELE-DOGS!
UH-OH--
SLAYER...
PLEASE BE THE RIGHT PORTAL PLEASE BE THE RIGHT PORTAAAAAL--!

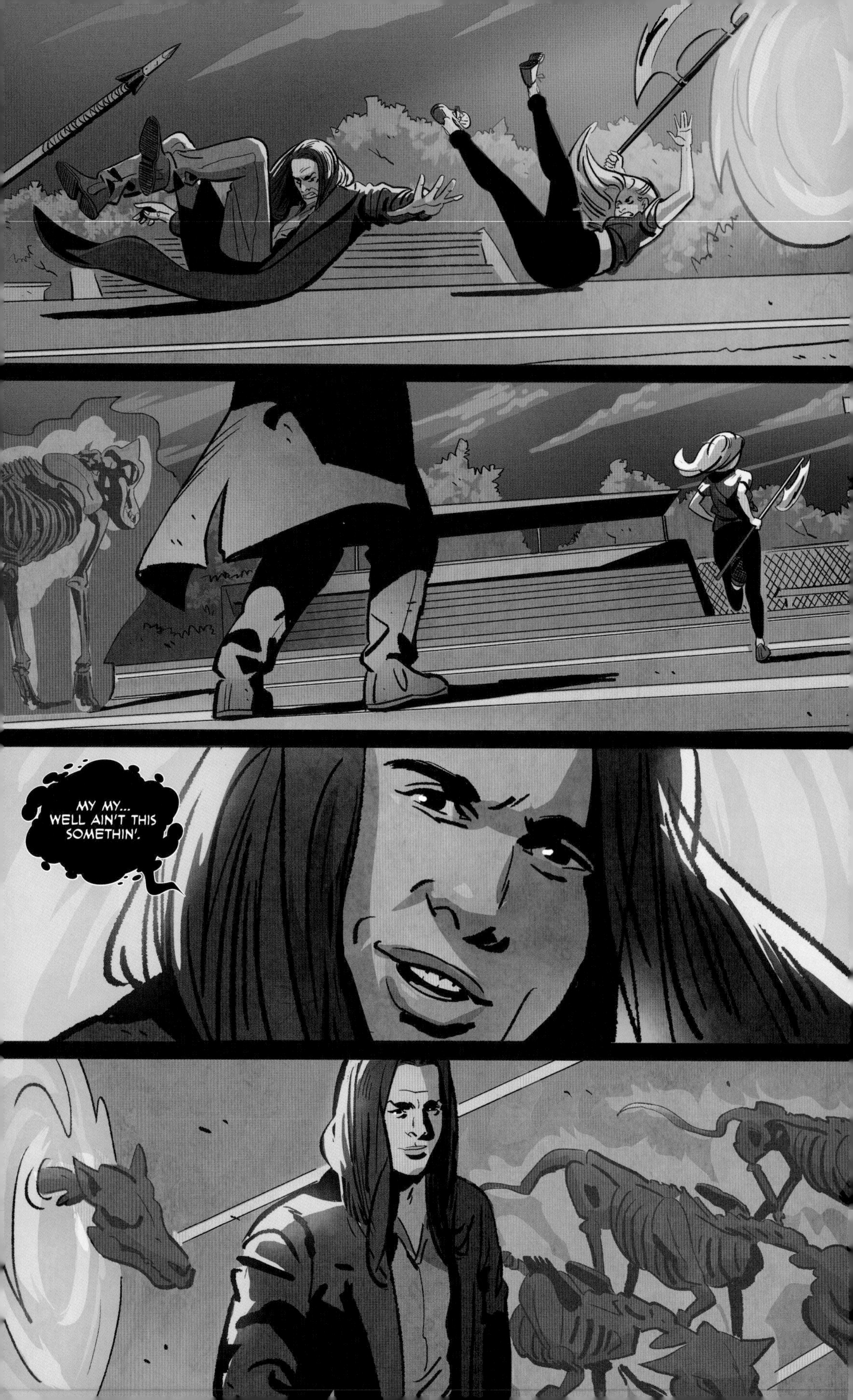
MY MY...
WELL AIN'T THIS
SOMETHIN'.

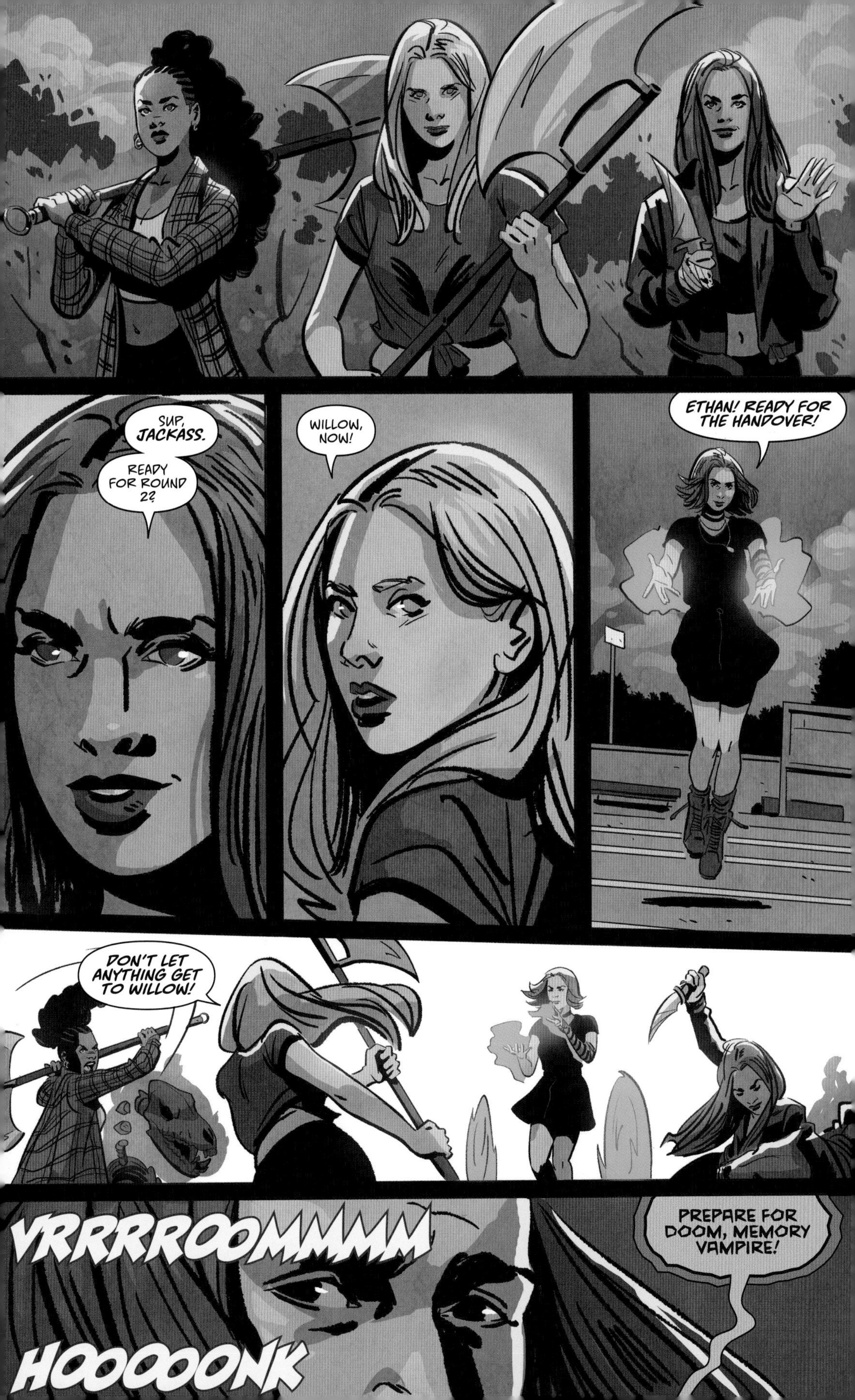
SUP, JACKASS.
READY FOR ROUND 2?
WILLOW, NOW!
ETHAN! READY FOR THE HANDOVER!
DON'T LET ANYTHING GET TO WILLOW!
VRRRROOMMMM
HOOOOONK
PREPARE FOR DOOM, MEMORY VAMPIRE!

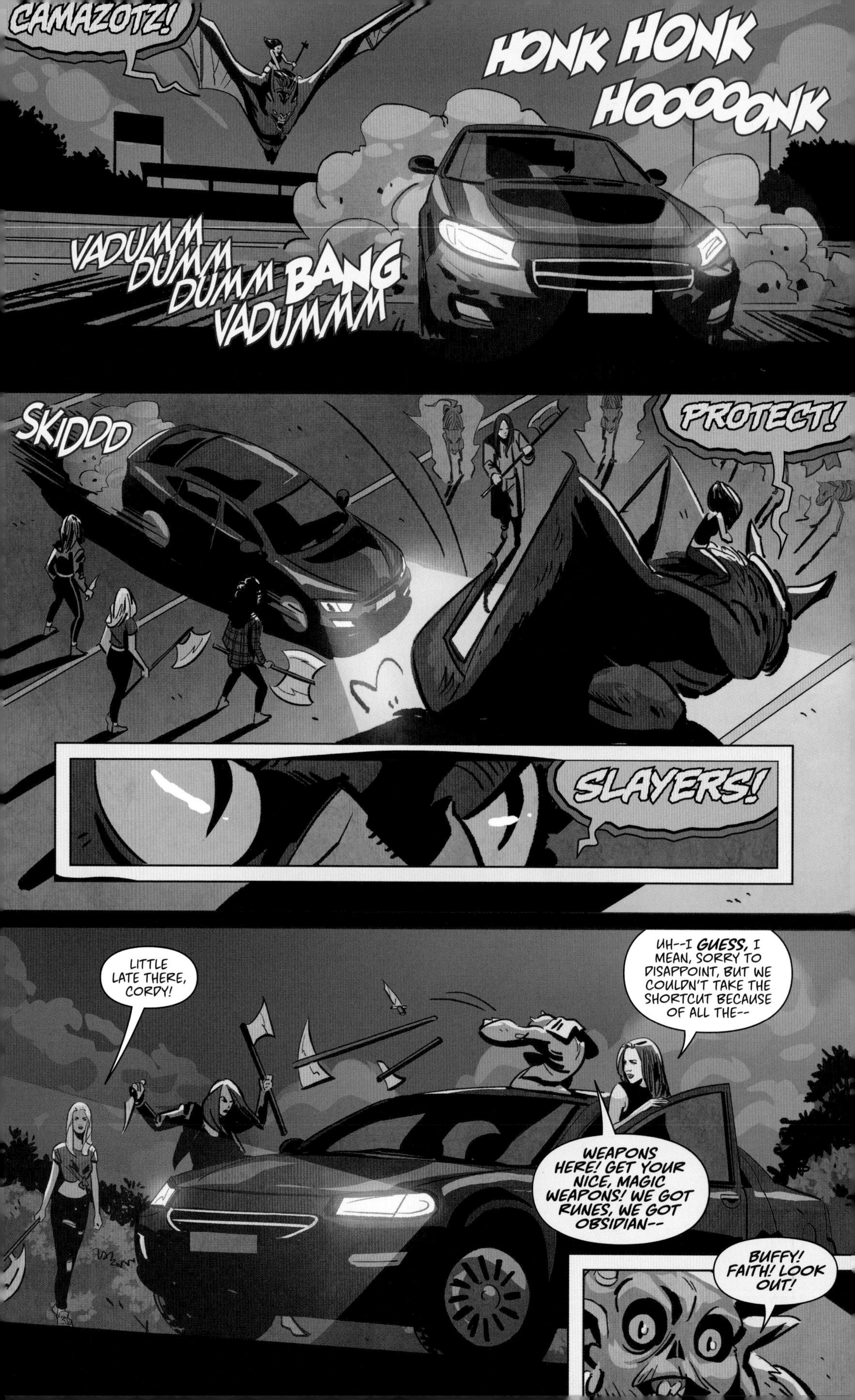
CAMAZOTZ!
HONK HONK
HOOOOOONK
VADUMM
DUMM
DUMM
BANG
VADUMMM
SKIDDD
PROTECT!
SLAYERS!
LITTLE LATE THERE, CORDY!
UH--I GUESS, I MEAN, SORRY TO DISAPPOINT, BUT WE COULDN'T TAKE THE SHORTCUT BECAUSE OF ALL THE--
WEAPONS HERE! GET YOUR NICE, MAGIC WEAPONS! WE GOT RUNES, WE GOT OBSIDIAN--
BUFFY! FAITH! LOOK OUT!

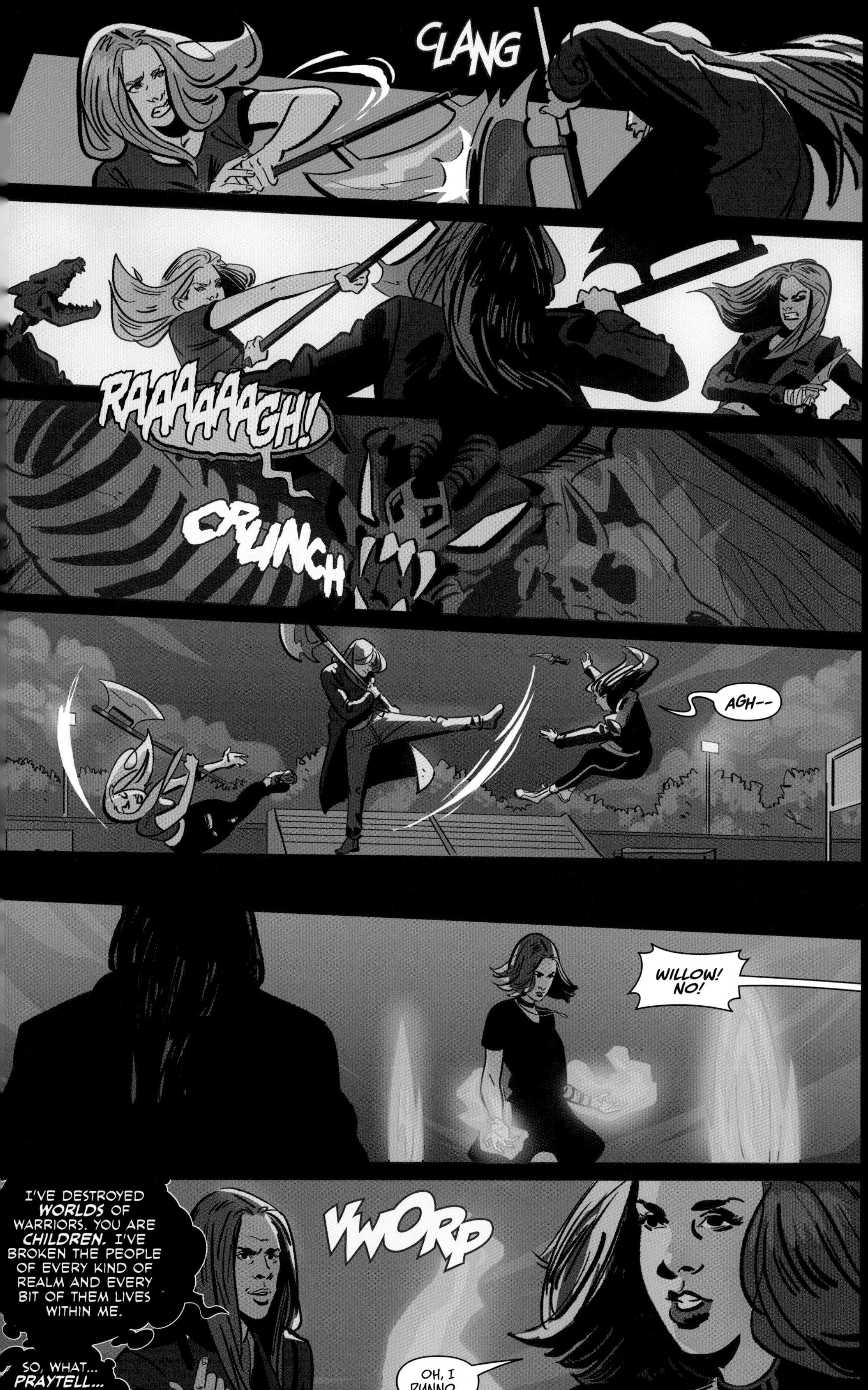

CLANG
RAAAAAAAGH!
CRUNCH
AGH--
WILLOW! NO!
I'VE DESTROYED WORLDS OF WARRIORS. YOU ARE CHILDREN. I'VE BROKEN THE PEOPLE OF EVERY KIND OF REALM AND EVERY BIT OF THEM LIVES WITHIN ME.
SO, WHAT... PRAYTELL... COULD YOU POSSIBLY DO?
VWORP
OH, I DUNNO...

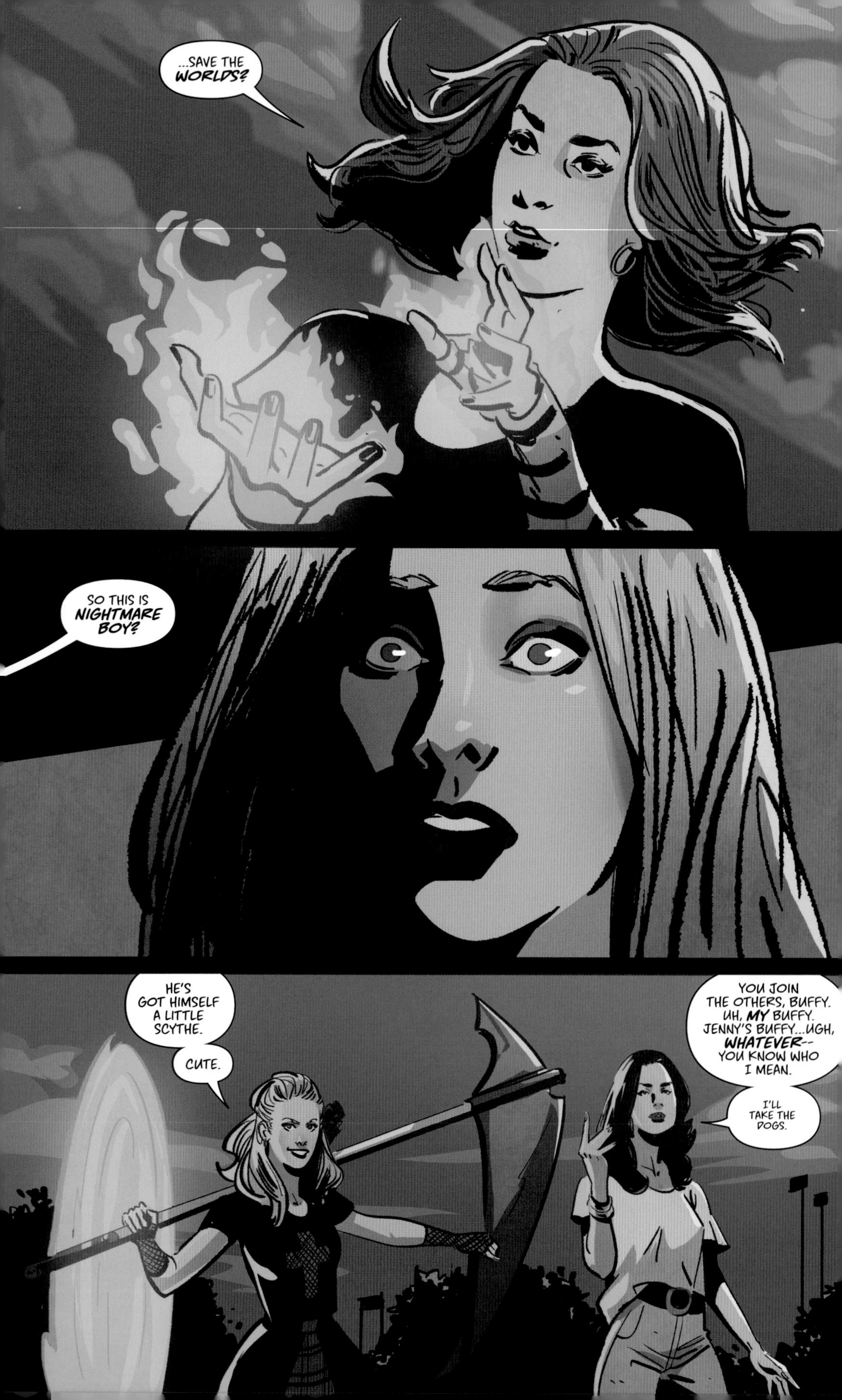
...SAVE THE WORLDS?
SO THIS IS NIGHTMARE BOY?
HE'S GOT HIMSELF A LITTLE SCYTHE.
CUTE.
YOU JOIN THE OTHERS, BUFFY. UH, MY BUFFY. JENNY'S BUFFY...UGH, WHATEVER-- YOU KNOW WHO I MEAN.
I'LL TAKE THE DOGS.

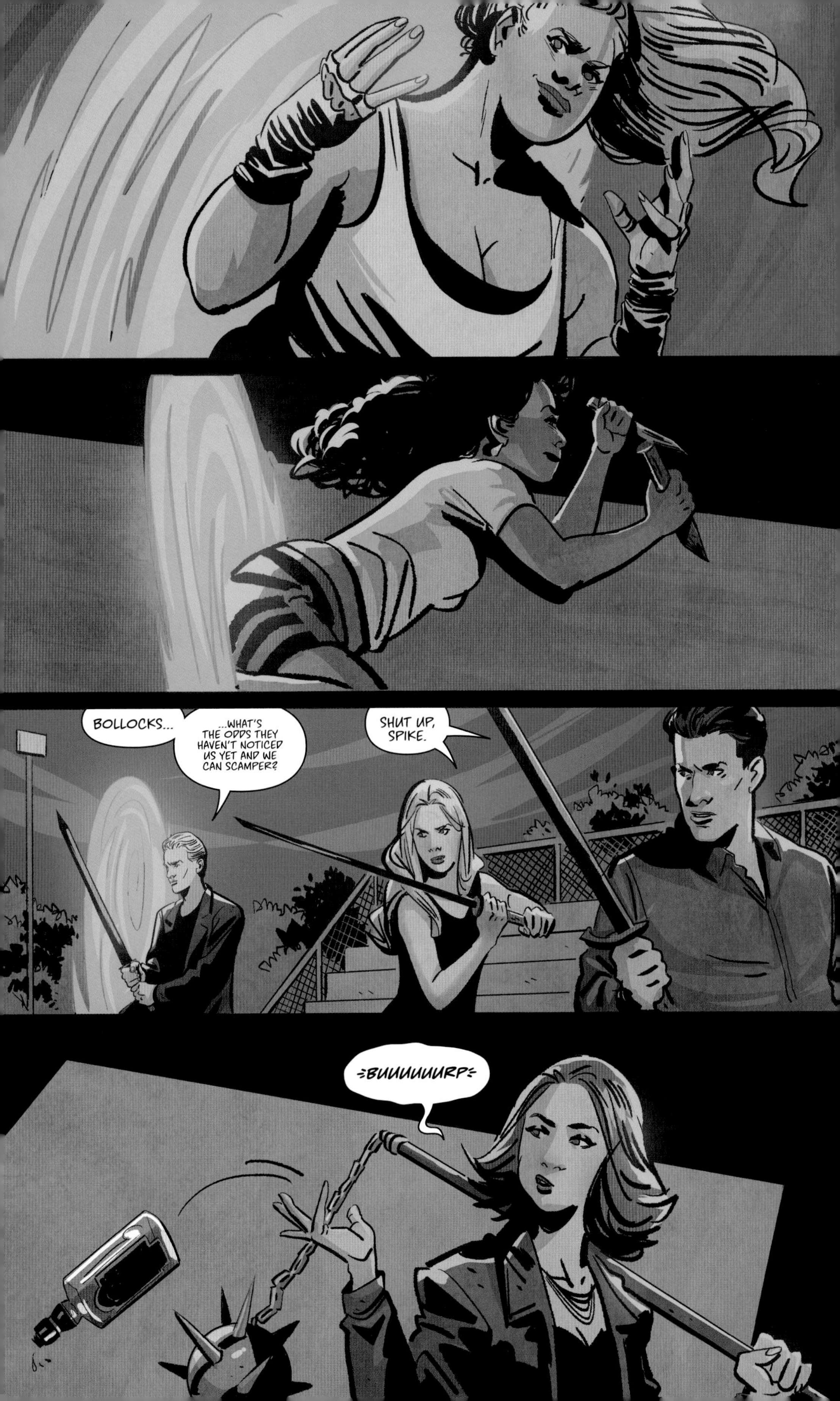
BOLLOCKS...
...WHAT'S THE ODDS THEY HAVEN'T NOTICED US YET AND WE CAN SCAMPER?
SHUT UP, SPIKE.
=BUUUUUURP=

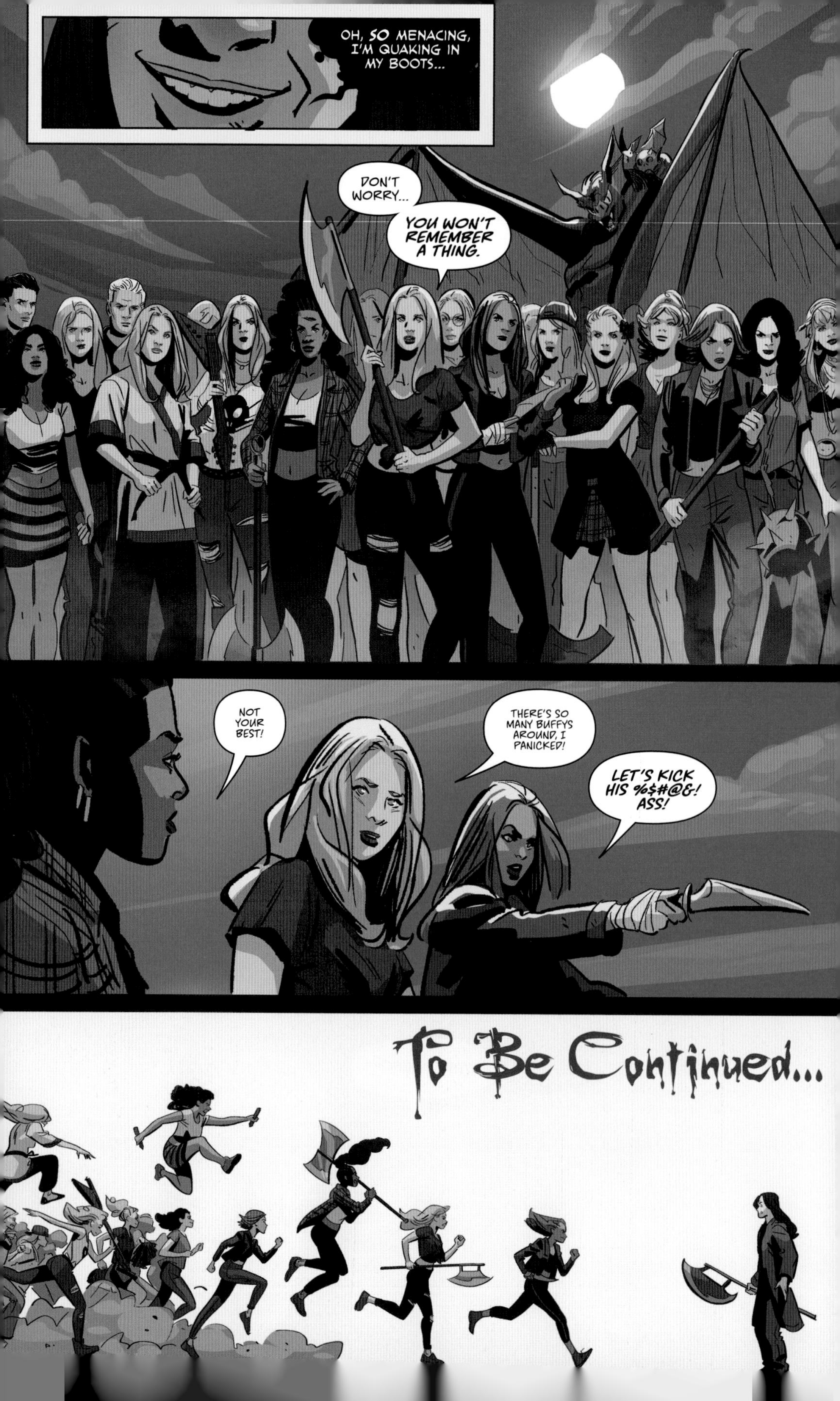
OH, SO MENACING, I'M QUAKING IN MY BOOTS...
DON'T WORRY...
YOU WON'T REMEMBER A THING.
NOT YOUR BEST!
THERE'S SO MANY BUFFYS AROUND, I PANICKED!
LET'S KICK HIS %$#@&! ASS!
To Be Continued...

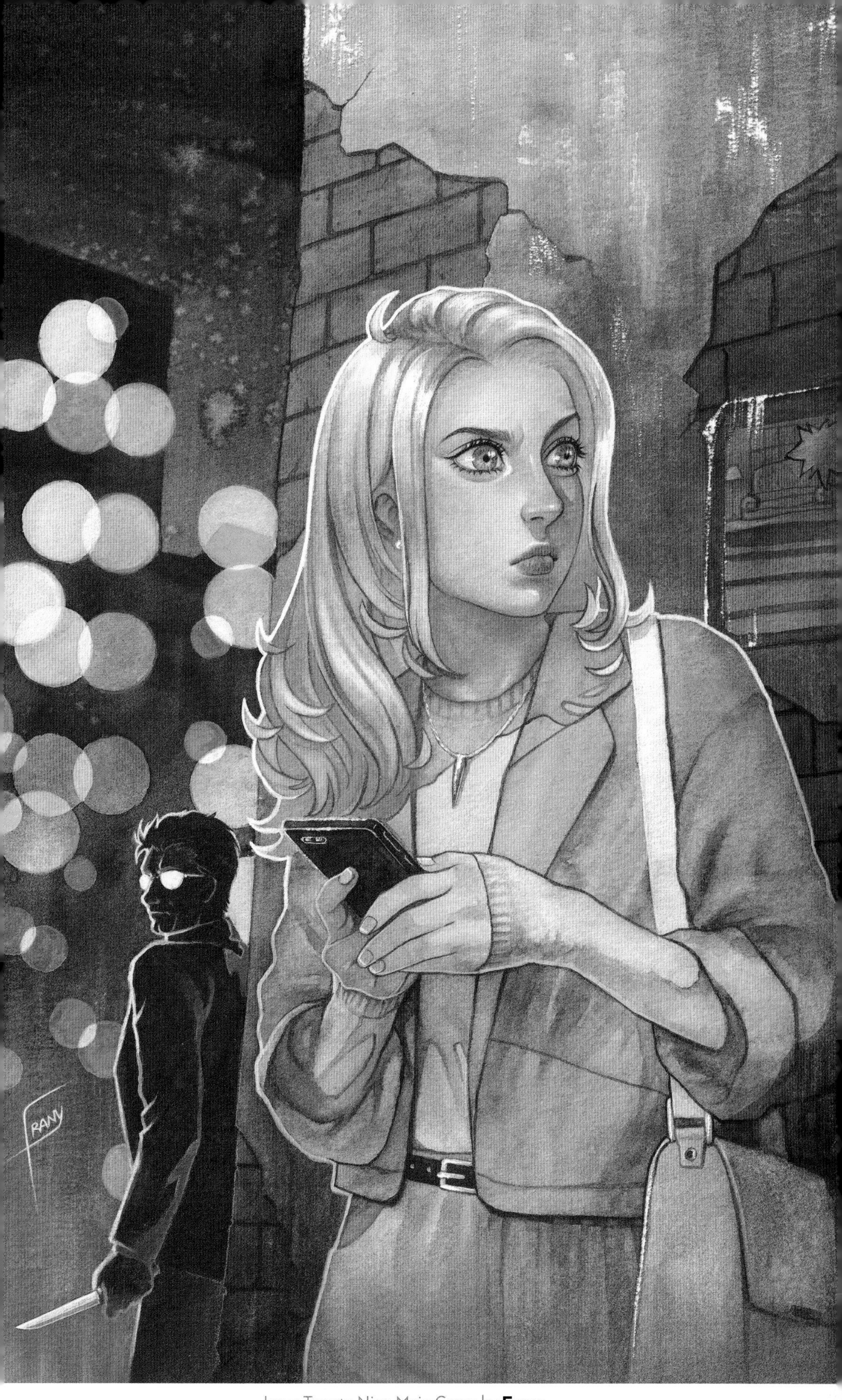
FRANY

Issue Twenty Nine Main Cover by **Frany**

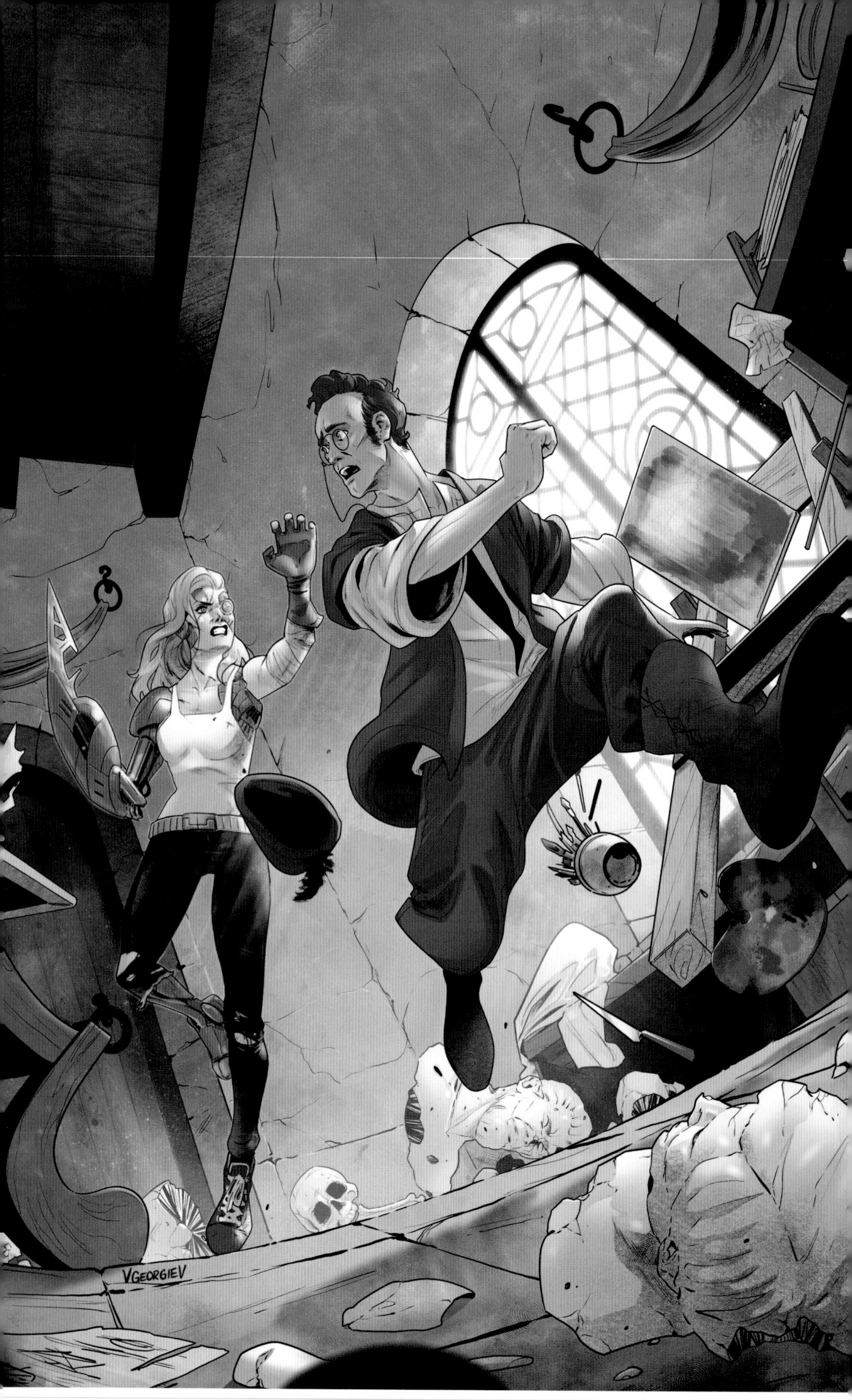
VGEORGIEV
Issue Twenty Nine Multiversus Cover by **Vasco Georgiev**

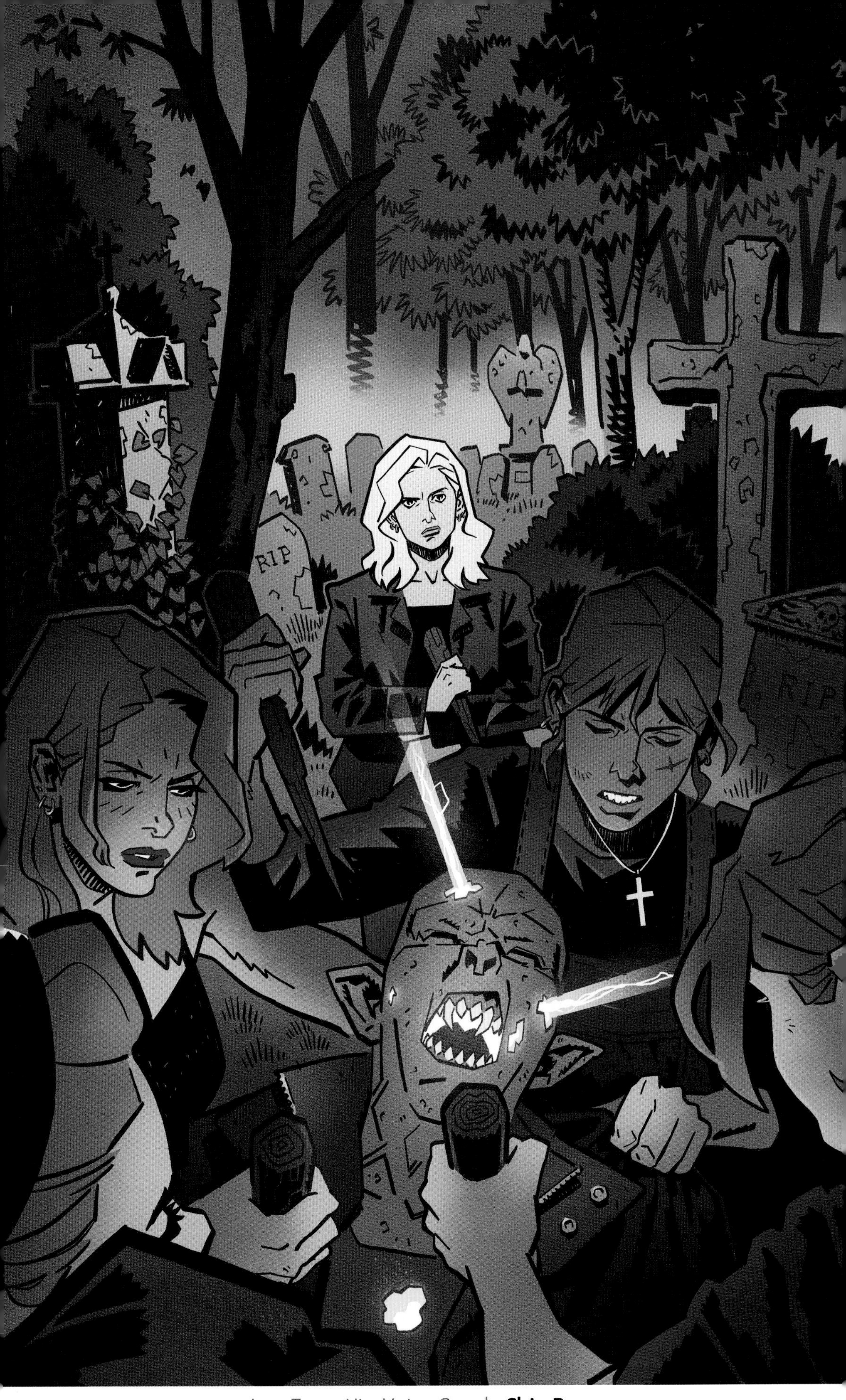
RIP
RIP
Issue Twenty Nine Variant Cover by **Claire Roe**

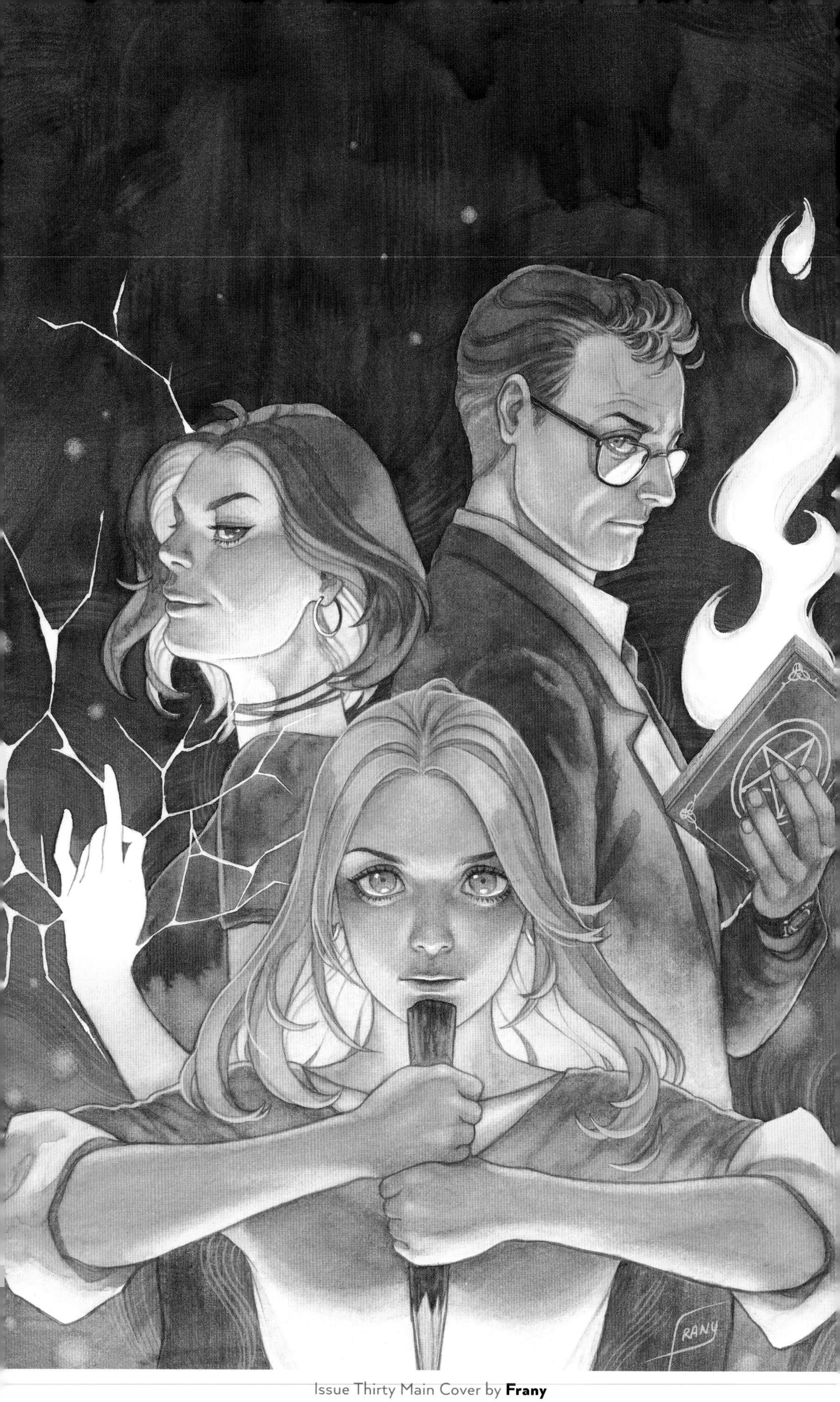
FRANY

Issue Thirty Main Cover by **Frany**

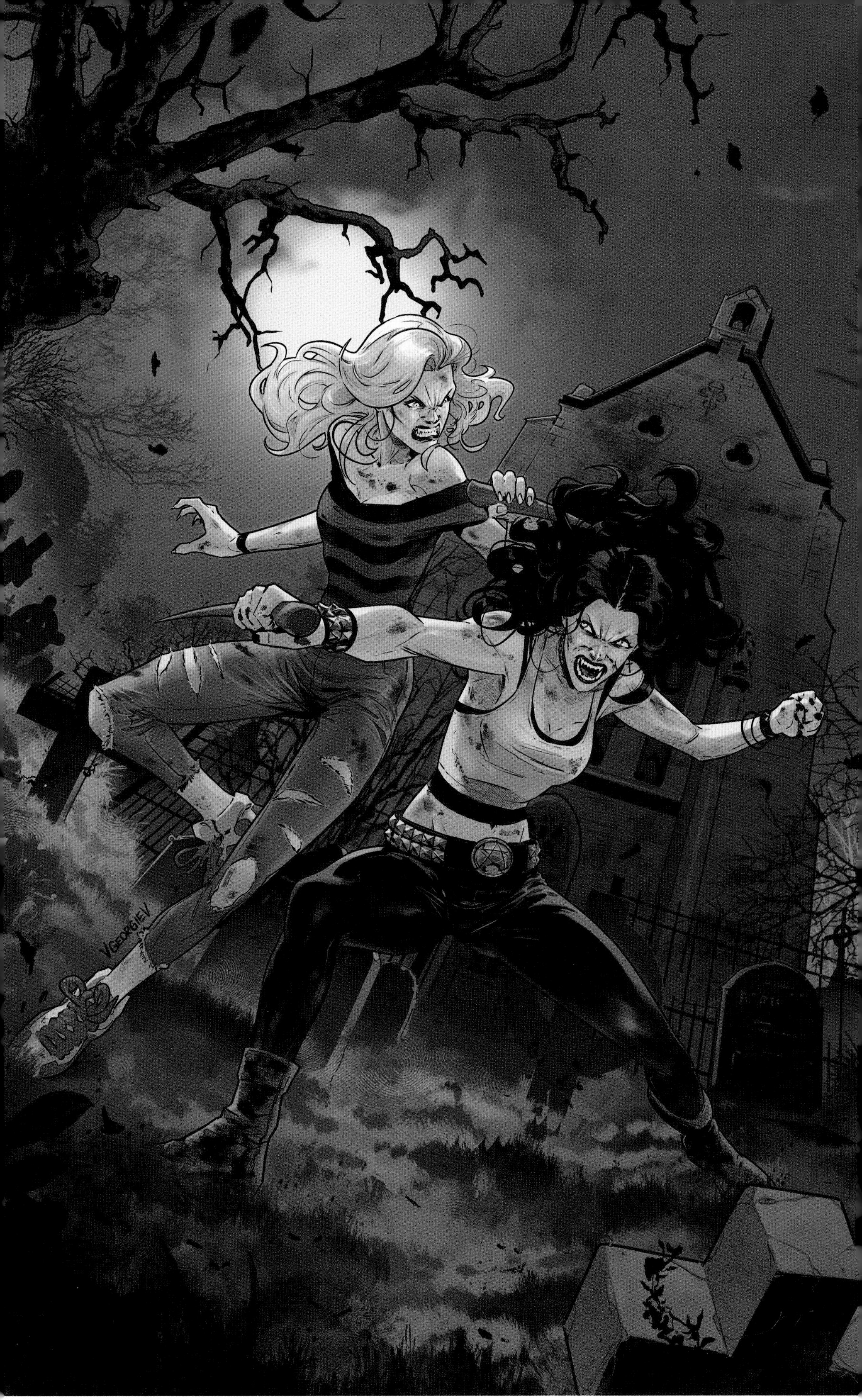
VGEORGIEV

Issue Thirty Multiversus Cover by **Vasco Georgiev**

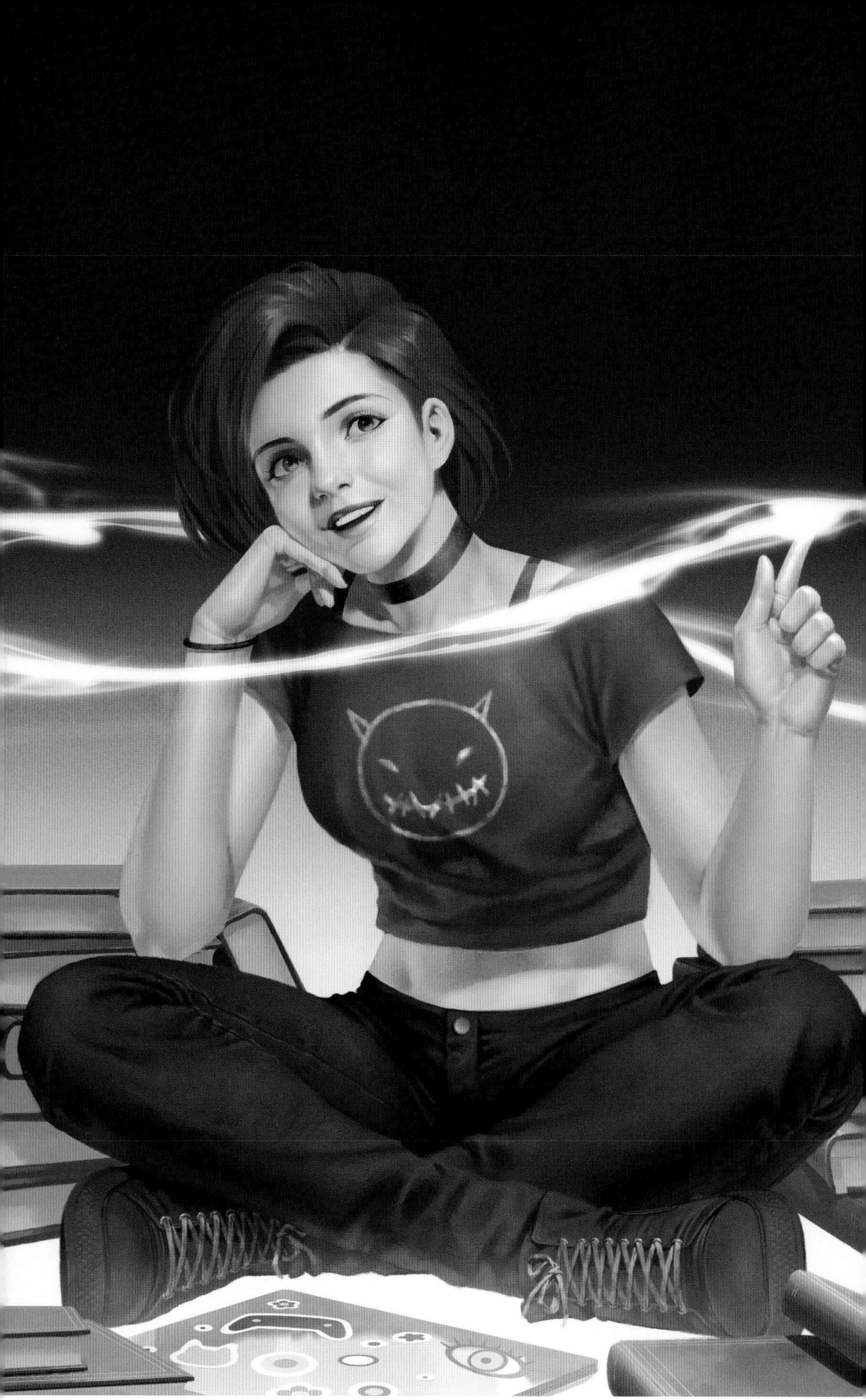

Issue Thirty Variant Cover by **Junggeun Yoon**

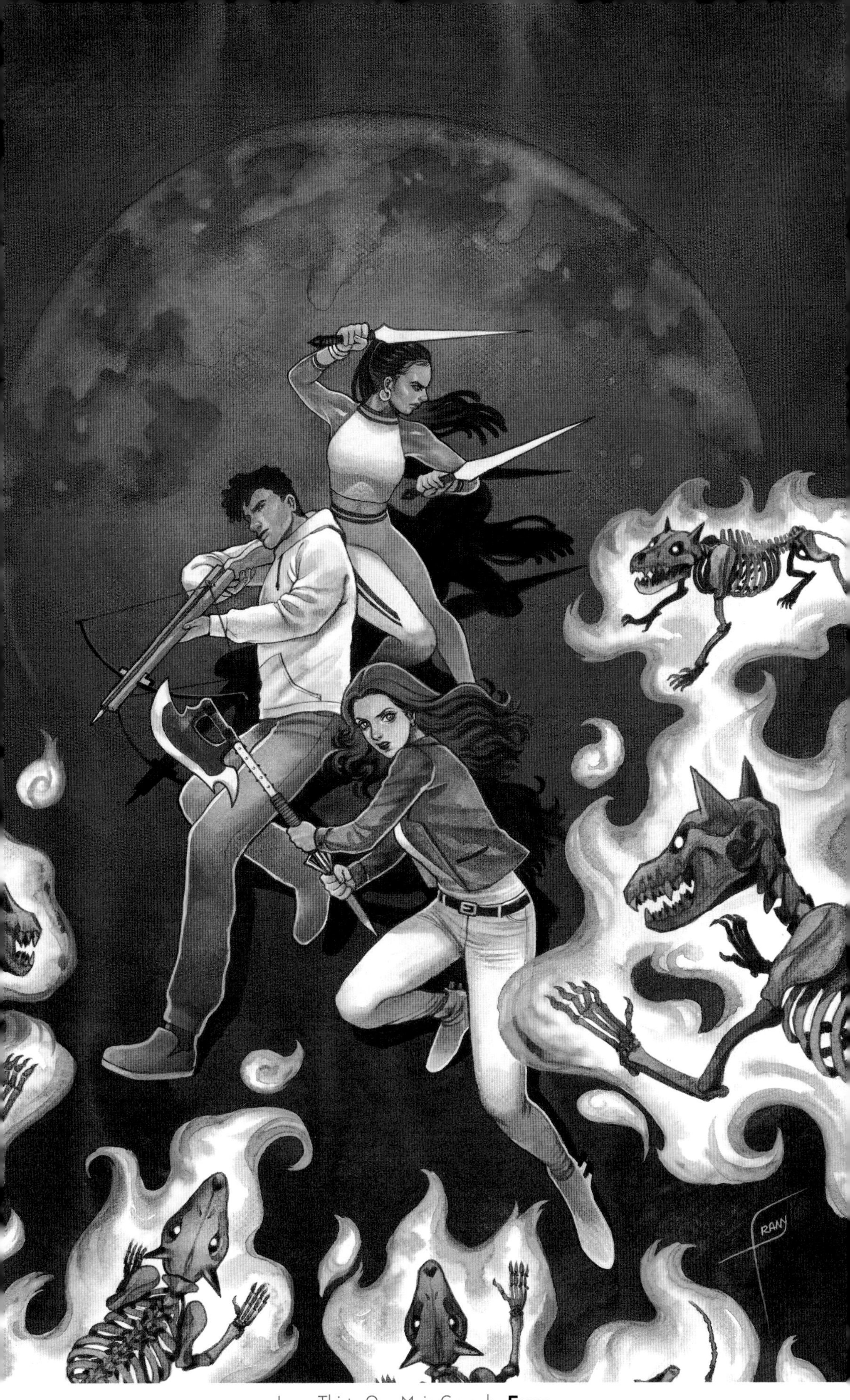
FRANY
Issue Thirty One Main Cover by **Frany**

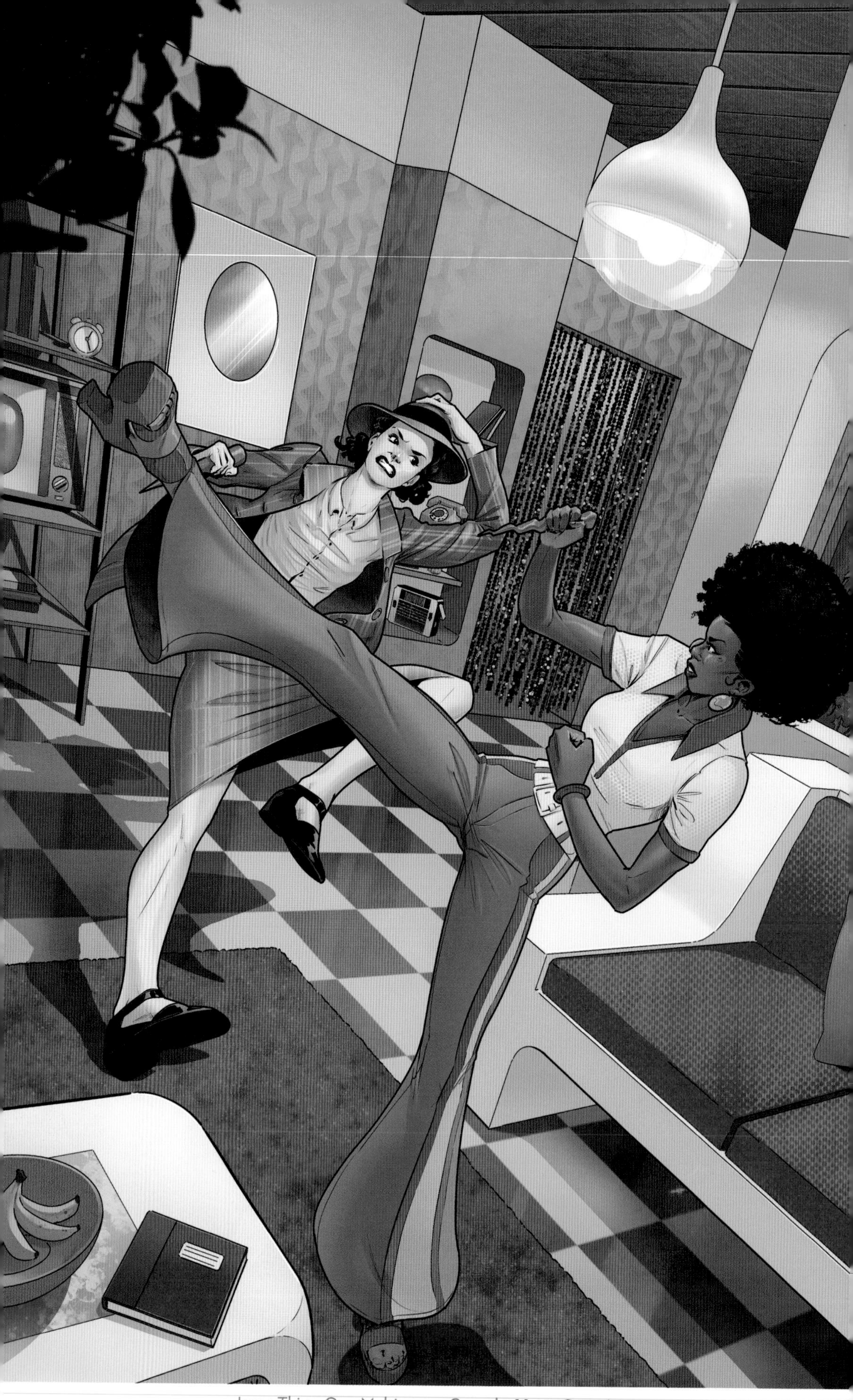

Issue Thirty One Multiversus Cover by **Vasco Georgiev**

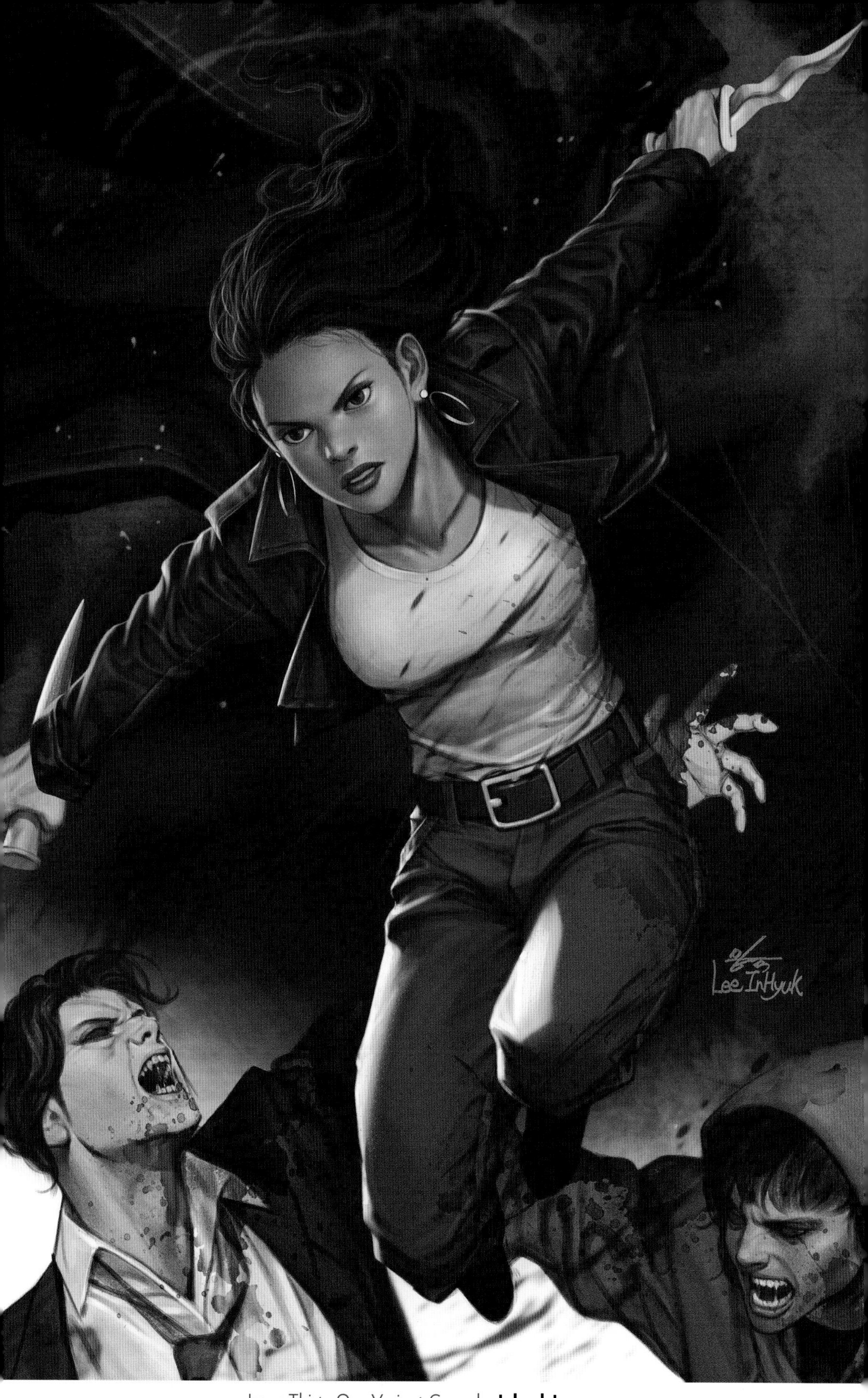
Lee InHyuk

Issue Thirty One Variant Cover by **Inhyuk Lee**

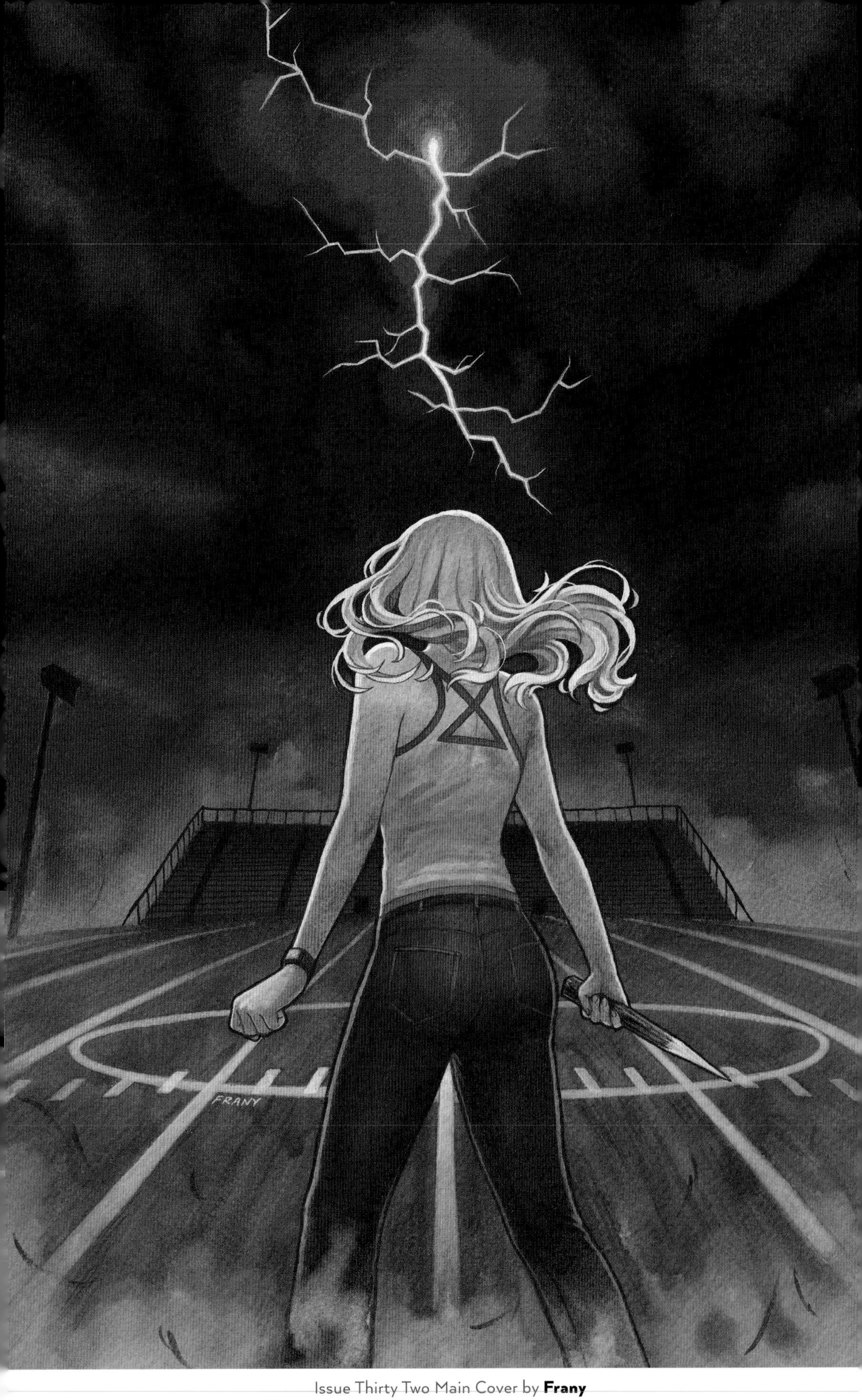
FRANY

Issue Thirty Two Main Cover by **Frany**

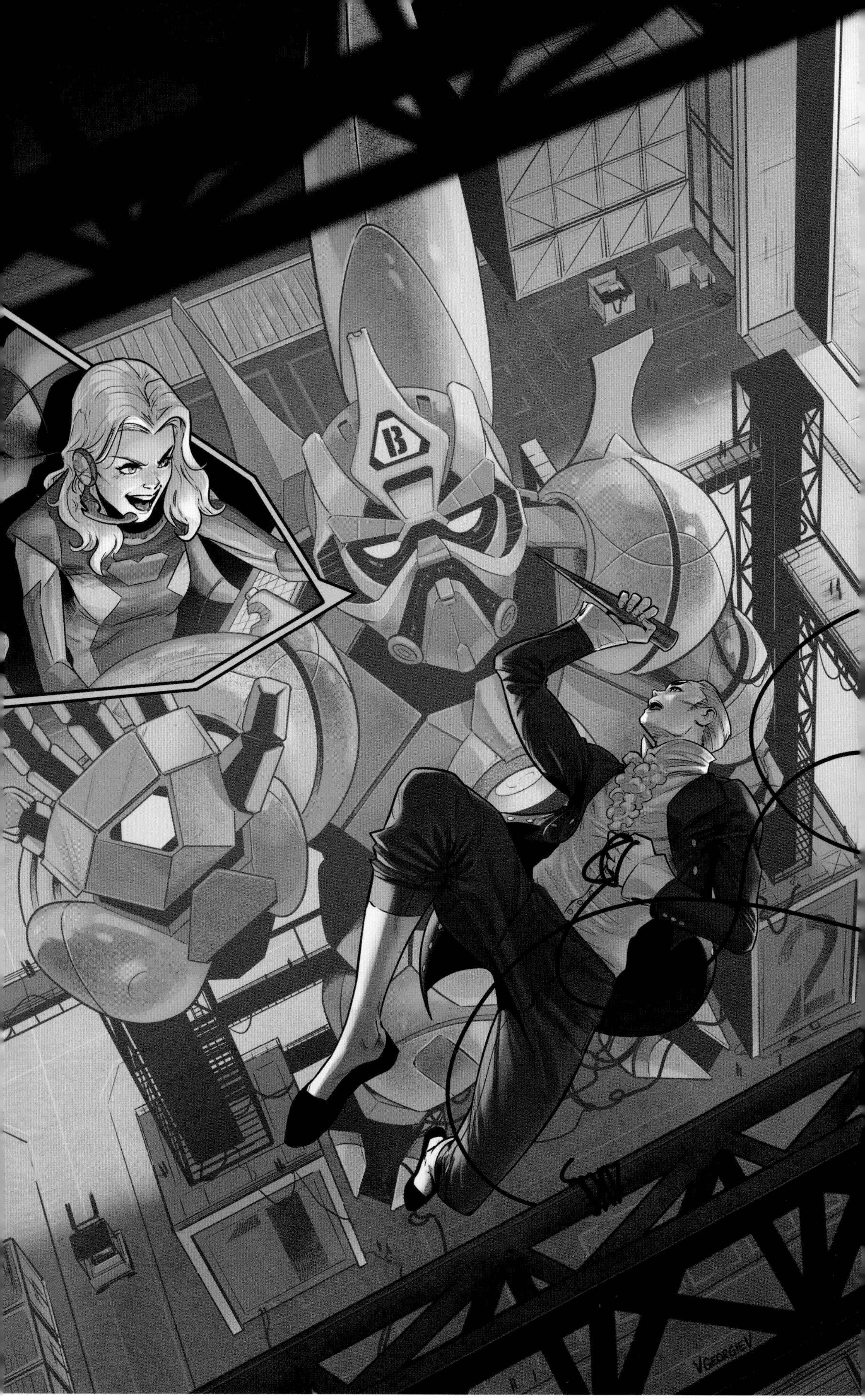
VGEORGIEV

Issue Thirty Two Multiversus Cover by **Vasco Georgiev**

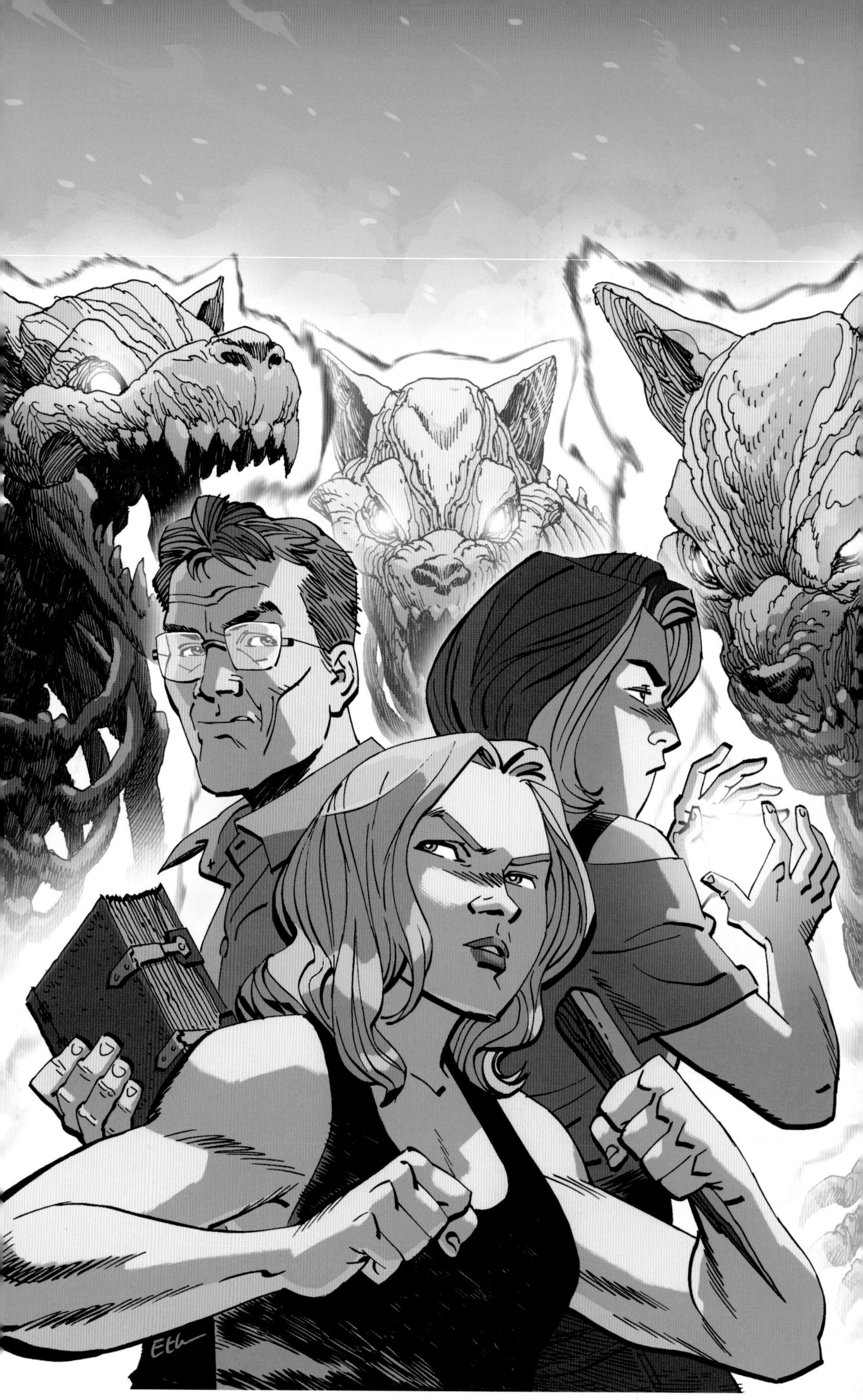

Issue Thirty Two Variant Cover by **Ethan Young**